# Lawyers Crossing Lines

# Lawyers Crossing Lines

## Nine Stories

James L. Kelley

Carolina Academic Press
Durham, North Carolina

ISBN 0-89089-603-8
LCCN 00-109734


Carolina Academic Press
700 Kent Street
Durham, North Carolina
Telephone (919) 489-7486
Fax (919) 493-5668
E-mail: cap-press.com
www.cap-press.com

Printed in the United States of America.

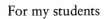
For my students

# Contents

# Preface

This is a collection of true stories about lawyers who crossed lines and ended up being sued for malpractice, disbarred, or prosecuted. Based on the records of litigated cases, the stories are rich in detail, sometimes bizarre, and always sad — sad because they are about self-inflicted wounds and betrayals of trust.

*Lawyers Crossing Lines* is intended as supplemental reading for students in professional responsibility courses at American law schools. I have taught professional responsibility as an adjunct professor at Georgetown University Law Center in Washington, D.C. for the past several years, assigning widely used casebooks. Casebooks include much essential material, but their manner of presentation — whether of appellate decisions, rules, or excerpts from commentary — is necessarily somewhat abstract. The stories in this book go beyond the dry recitations in edited cases to the settings and human elements that emerge from court testimony, revealing more of the realities of law practice and the people behind the parties and their counsel. Each story is followed by comments and questions on the issues it presents.

Why tell stories to students of professional responsibility? Of course, there is nothing wrong with making a law school class interesting for the students. More important, principles of legal ethics are more effectively conveyed, and more likely to be remembered, when narratives of real events supplement traditional casebooks. Oliver Sachs said it well in *The Man Who Mistook His Wife for a Hat*: "To restore the human subject at the centre, we must deepen a case history to a narrative or tale."

A course in professional responsibility should be about more than "learning the rules" well enough to pass the Multistate Professional Responsibility Examination. It should prepare students for the problems and pressures they are likely to face after graduation. For example, a story about a firm fraudulently increasing billable hours (Chapter 5, "Two Scorpions on a Bottle") can be an effective launch for discussion of the minimum billable-hours requirements imposed on associates in many big firms today, and the pressures those requirements exert to inflate billable hours or do unnecessary work. A story about a partner overriding associates' conflict-of-interest concerns (Chapter 3, "Breaking Up Is Hard to Do") poses a not uncommon dilemma and may suggest questions students might raise in job interviews. Will my ethics concerns be respected? Can I take my concerns anonymously to an ethics committee?

— "Liars in Court" relates painful realities in representing a client who turns out to be a liar and subsequently sues the lawyer for malpractice. The lawyer is caught between conflicting duties of loyalty to the client and telling the truth.

— "The Case of the Frozen Broccoli" tells the story of two lawyers who crossed, sometimes leaped over, lines between legitimate representation of a criminal enterprise—the Columbian cocaine cartel—and assisting criminal activity.

— Conflicts of interest are a core concern of professional responsibility. "Breaking Up Is Hard to Do" introduces the subject with a straightforward conflict between current clients. "Of Chinese Walls and Comfort Zones" involves a former-client situation that raises complex theoretical and policy issues.

— "The Gatekeeper" is about an associate who gets in over his head representing an underwriter in a questionable securities offering. The partner ostensibly responsible for supervising the associate leaves him twisting in the wind.

— The setting of "Hot Seat" is Salomon's Brothers, then the dominant government bond trader in New York and the subject of the best-selling memoir, *Liar's Poker*. A trader submitted a false bid in a Treasury auction which senior management failed to report to the government, contrary to the advice of its chief legal officer. The story illustrates pressures on in-house counsel and the "whistleblower" problem

— "Ambulance Chasing Redux" describes aggressive and tacky solicitation of victims of an airplane crash by the firm of John O'Quinn, a nationally-known tort lawyer. Nevertheless, it calls phrophylactic solicitation rules into question, considering the quality of representation provided by lawyers like O'Quinn and the need to level the playing field against insurance adjusters.

— "Spectator Sport" describes a particularly egregious failure to provide effective representation to a defendant in a capital case in a system—including prosecutors and judges, as well as defense lawyers—which condones, even supports, incompetence.

The selection of a case for chapter treatment was based on three criteria: whether it raises significant issues of legal ethics; whether it lends itself to classroom discussion; and whether a good story could be extracted from its voluminous record. Several prominent experts appear in the stories as witnesses or counsel, including Sherman Cohn, David Epstein, Marvin Frankel, Stephen Gillers, Geoffrey Hazard, Thomas Morgan, and Charles Wolfram. The cases I selected are relatively recent. All were decided, initially or on appeal, between 1992 and 2001.

It's a myth that public records, like trial transcripts, are readily available to the private citizen, whether for research or other purposes. Some courts or court reporters charge $1 or more per page, making source material from the courts for a book like this prohibitively expensive. Fortunately, in most cases I was granted free access to the full trial record by the prevailing party's lawyer. I had the bulk of the records—ranging from 2,000 to 7,000 pages per case, some 30,000 pages in all—duplicated at commercial copy shops at reasonable cost. All of the stories are based on transcripts and other court records, with one exception. The record of the SEC investigation related to the Salomon false-bid scandal from which the "Hot Seat" story is drawn fills seven hundred storage boxes. In response to my Freedom of Information Act request, the SEC advised that the cost of its pre-release review would be "several hundreds of thousands of dollars." That story had to be based on the SEC's published decision and media accounts.

Over half of the stories involve misconduct, or alleged misconduct, in law firms of one hundred or more lawyers. Three of those firms— Gibson, Dunn & Crutcher, Pillsbury, Madison & Sutro, and, until it dissolved in the wake of malpractice and fraud judgments, Keck, Mahin & Cate—are (or were) among the biggest firms in the country. Two stories involve lawyers in specialized criminal defense and personal injury practices, and a third concerns an in-house counsel for a large company. The book includes only one story about a sole general practitioner, the type of lawyer who (complaints to disciplinary authorities suggest) commits most of the malpractice. In the main, however, those complaints charge neglect, conversion of funds, and other common defaults that, while important to the client, are not good candidates for law school discussion. Because the stories are based entirely on matters of public record, I was free to, and did, use real names of people, law firms, and places, with one exception in which access to the record was conditioned on my not using the real names of the plaintiffs.

The stories collectively involve the diverse sources of law governing ethical responsibilities of lawyers: State ethics codes, common-law fiduciary obligations, and criminal and civil statutes and rules—such as obstruction of justice and securities fraud—having counterparts in codes of ethics. Of those sources, the American Bar Association's Model Rules of Professional Conduct, in force in some form in over forty States and the District of Columbia, are most frequently involved, either in the story itself or in the comments and questions following it. In the four stories of civil malpractice, the court and parties relied substantially on the Model Rules as evidence of the standard of care, despite the disclaimer in the Rules that a violation "should not give rise to a cause of action, nor should it create any presumption that a legal duty has been breached." The most relevant rules are cited—and quoted, if short—as they arise in the stories. Students can refer to their selected standards books for the longer rules and official comments.

Several chapters describe gross misconduct—billing fraud, falsifying evidence, harassing accident victims—the kinds of things that give lawyers a bad name. It should go without saying that the book is not intended as a portrait of how the profession as a whole behaves. These are cautionary tales. There is, of course, no objective way to measure levels of ethical conduct among lawyers. Informed judgments about the seriousness and scope of misconduct come from practitioners, disciplinary authorities, malpractice insurers, and students of the problem. Based on thirty years as a lawyer in private practice and government and as a law school teacher of ethics, I believe that the great majority of lawyers play by the rules—most of them scrupulously, others in their fashion. Not many flout them.

The stories show how the rules apply to lawyer misconduct in some typical settings. Why lawyers break the rules raises difficult questions to which there are no complete answers. It is sometimes possible, however, to identify recurring patterns which may contribute to misconduct, and which may point the way to corrective regulation. A few such patterns are sketched in the afterword.

J.L.K.
Takoma Park, Maryland
October 2000

# Acknowledgments

I am grateful to Professors Peter Byrne, Sherman Cohn, David Luban, and Julie O'Sullivan of Georgetown University Law Center and Lisa Lerman of Catholic University School of Law for reading drafts of chapters. Their comments greatly improved the product. Special thanks to Professor Milton Regan of Georgetown who commented on much of the text and made many helpful suggestions. Thanks also to legal ethics expert Robert O'Malley for helping me understand the *Maritrans* case, and to criminal defense lawyer John Villa for his perspectives on Chapter 2.

I was given access to court records and transcripts by Stephen Bright, Director, Southern Center for Human Rights, by Assistant United States Attorney Edward Ryan, Southern District of Florida, and by practicing attorneys Plato Cacheris, John Dowd and Jonathan Tycko in Washington, D.C.; Denise Pallante in Philadelphia; Kathy Patrick in Houston; and Broadas Spivey in Austin, Texas. Thanks to my neighbor, Bryan Sayer, for debugging my computer, and to my niece, Cathy Harbour, for copy editing.

The idea for this book came from my friend Peter Byrne and was refined with him over numerous lunches at *The Irish Times*. I appreciate the freedom that Keith Sipe, publisher of Carolina Academic Press, allowed me in developing the original proposal, based on things I learned along the way. Finally, my thanks to the Virginia Center for the Creative Arts for giving me a friendly and stimulating place to finish this book.

# Lawyers Crossing Lines

# Chapter 1

# A Liar for a Client

"If I had a dollar for every time a client asked me to lie, I wouldn't be sitting here. I would be in the south of France, living it up."
—Walter Stratton, partner in Gibson, Dunn & Crutcher,
testifying in *Breezevale, Ltd. v. Dickinson, et al.*

John Millian, a senior associate with Gibson, Dunn & Crutcher, was in London for the firm's client, Breezevale, Ltd. Breezevale, an agent for volume tire sales in the Middle East, had sued Bridgestone-Firestone, Inc. for breach of contract. The suit, pending in federal court in Cleveland, Ohio, was based on Firestone's alleged breach of Breezevale's exclusive agency for the sale of tires to Iraq during the late 1980s, and for backing out of a project to build a tire manufacturing plant in Nigeria. On Sunday evening, October 13, 1991, Millian was in the suburban London home of Rebecca Paul, a Breezevale employee, preparing her for a deposition to begin in the morning. Paul was facing days of questioning by a lawyer from Jones, Day, Reavis & Pogue, a Cleveland-based firm with a hardball reputation, and she was noticeably apprehensive. "Can't I just be sick or something?" she asked. Millian replied that they couldn't lie about her health and the two proceeded to review a stack of sales documents that Paul had been responsible for generating. Late in the evening, Millian recalled that Paul "started hinting that there were forged documents." He asked: "Is there something you're trying to tell me?" Paul began to pour out a story of how the documents had been forged. She described the impact of her disclosure: "I was in tears and I called my husband. John Millian was, I have to say, poleaxed. He was just white, shell-shocked. He said to me: "This isn't bloody Nigeria.""

Millian took a cab back to his Central London hotel, arriving around midnight. Appreciating the gravity of the situation, he telephoned the firm's New York office, attempting to reach Wesley Howell, a senior partner and lead lawyer in the *Breezevale* case; he tried to call Walter Stratton, a Gibson, Dunn partner also working on the case who was staying at another London hotel. Unable to reach either, Millian went to bed. He succeeded in reaching Stratton around 7 the next morning and summarized Paul's forgery story. Stratton instructed him to bring her to the Gibson, Dunn office before proceeding to the deposition. The three met there about 8:30 a.m. and Millian and Stratton debriefed Paul about her allegations. During the debriefing, Charles Awit, a senior Breezevale official, telephoned the office and spoke with Stratton who said nothing about Paul's unfolding story.

Paul's deposition was scheduled for 10 a.m. at the London office of Jones, Day. Stratton, the senior lawyer present, had to make a decision: whether to go forward with Paul's deposition; whether to request Jones, Day's consent to a postponement, without giving a reason; or, if consent were refused, whether to postpone the deposition unilaterally. Stratton and Millian had not investigated Paul's allegations. Nor had they informed Breezevale, whose chairman, Habib Habib, was in its London office and who was deeply implicated in Paul's allegations. Stratton decided to go forward with Paul's deposition, hoping (but not realistically expecting) that the Jones, Day lawyer would not inquire into the genuineness of the documents. Stratton's heat-of-battle decision would be second-guessed, and not only by opposing counsel in the malpractice suit it would precipitate. Wesley Howell, the senior Gibson, Dunn partner on the case, told the partner who had brought Breezevale in as a client that he would have postponed Paul's deposition. As it happened, however, Howell had been unreachable —fishing for steelheads in British Columbia—when Paul dropped her bombshell.

The subject of forgery didn't come up during the Monday morning session of the deposition. During the lunch break, Stratton and Millian went to the Breezevale office and informed Habib of Paul's allegations, without indicating whether they believed her—an issue which (it seemed to Stratton) Habib did not wish to address. Millian already had doubts about the Breezevale Chairman's integrity. Habib had told him that Breezevale had bribed officials in Nigeria to get business there. Paul had told Millian about a "pep talk" Habib had given her the preceding Friday about her upcoming deposition, telling her that "he was confident in me, that I could outsmart them." Subsequent testimony of Habib and Stratton about that lunchtime discussion would conflict. According to Habib, he had instructed Stratton to postpone the deposition and undertake an immediate investigation. As Stratton recalled, Habib had given no such instructions; rather, they had discussed the implications of seeking a postponement and that Stratton had advised against, calling it a "very bad idea."

Early in the afternoon session, Jones, Day's lawyer focused her questions on offer letters that included price quotations for various types of tires and which purportedly had been sent to Iraq during 1987. Copies of the letters and other documents had been turned over to Jones, Day in response to discovery requests. Displaying them to Paul, the Jones, Day lawyer asked: "Do you have any reason to believe that these were created at a time after they are dated?" Ms. Paul replied: "I think so." With that, the cat was out of the bag. In response to further questions that afternoon and the next day, Paul testified in detail about how she and senior officials of Breezevale had gone about creating offer letters and supporting documentation to bolster their case against Firestone.

The forged documents had been created in February 1991 after Paul reviewed the files and informed Habib that Breezevale hadn't made offers to Iraq in 1987, a critical time period in the pending suit against Firestone. Habib had responded: "Well, you had better make sure we did." Whereupon, Paul and Joseph Abou Jouade, a senior Breezevale official in charge of the Beirut office then working in London, worked together at the same desk creating back-dated offer letters. They consulted a 1987 calendar to make sure their fictitious dates corresponded to business days four years earlier. When Abou Jouade had to return to Beirut before the fake letters were completed, he signed a single sheet of paper eight times so that Paul could cut and paste the signatures to letters she would complete and photocopy later.

Paul testified that she and Abou Jouade had also created back-dated "spread sheets"—file documentation of manufacturer prices, transportation costs, and Breezevale's overhead and mark-ups—as back-up for the fake offering documents. Breezevale had not owned computers in 1987; at that time, Paul had prepared spread sheets by hand. By 1991, the company had acquired computers that Paul used to prepare drafts of the fake spread sheets. The computer-generated drafts were then edited by Abou Jouade and copied by hand to make them appear genuine. Abou Jouade was concerned that their spread-sheet paper looked too new. Paul recalled: "There was a bit of a joke about [Abou Jouade] scrunching it up and sitting on it to make it look old."

On Wednesday morning, Paul arrived at the Jones, Day office, bringing from her home a green, plastic bag full of documents corroborating her allegations, including computer-generated drafts of spread sheets with Abou Jouade's handwritten edits and the sheet of paper with his eight signatures. These documents were made a part of the deposition record, and Paul's deposition was terminated without further questioning.

Within days, Jones, Day began to prepare a motion for sanctions, alleging fraud and misconduct and seeking costs, attorneys' fees and dismissal of Breezevale's suit against Firestone. Before the forgery came to light, Firestone had made a settlement offer of $3.5 million, plus a lucrative new sales agreement, which Breezevale had rejected. Under threat of the sanctions motion, Firestone made a take-it-or-leave settlement offer of $100,000. Gibson, Dunn advised Breezevale that the judge in Cleveland would probably impose sanctions, possibly including outright dismissal of their case, and that if they went to trial, they might later be indicted for perjury. Habib thought he might be able to cut a better deal with a Firestone official he knew, but that door turned out to be closed. On Gibson, Dunn's recommendation, Breezevale reluctantly accepted the settlement.

In October 1994, Breezevale sued Gibson, Dunn & Crutcher in the Superior Court of the District of Columbia, charging its former lawyers with "negligent, reckless, and intentional malpractice and breach of fiduciary and ethical obligations" focusing on their handling of the Paul deposition. Gibson, Dunn undertook further investigation of Paul's allegations and, in October 1995, filed a counterclaim alleging that Breezevale, by relying on fake documents, was litigating in bad faith. The case was assigned to Judge Steffen Graae who bifurcated the two claims, ruling that Breezevale's malpractice claim would be tried first to a jury, after which Gibson, Dunn's equitable counterclaim would be decided by the court.

The jury phase was tried in the fall of 1996. Breezevale's theory was that Gibson, Dunn should have postponed Paul's deposition, that had they done so, her allegations of forgery could have been disproved, and that Breezevale could have prevailed at trial and recovered some $20 million from Firestone. Under that theory, Stratton's decision to allow Paul's deposition to go forward, rather than first conducting an investigation, became the linchpin of the malpractice case.

Walter Stratton, a veteran trial lawyer, had been an associate and partner with the New York firm of Donovan, Leisure, Newton & Irvine for twenty-eight years. For seven years preceding the Paul deposition in 1991, he had been a partner with Gibson, Dunn. He testified at length concerning his handling of the Paul deposition. When Millian first related Paul's allegations to him by phone on Monday morning, he had been "very shocked"; they represented an "earth-shaking event," even "an atomic explosion." After listening to Paul's story at the Gibson, Dunn office, Stratton had no firm opinion whether she was telling the truth, but she appeared to be sincere and her story seemed plausible. On the other hand, he had reservations at that point because "she was not a person who was totally averse to manufacturing a story." In any event, Stratton realized that they "had a witness who was going to present a huge problem."

Stratton hadn't considered canceling the deposition a realistic option. Although the time and place had been set by agreement of counsel, not by court order, he thought that Gibson, Dunn had been legally obligated to present Paul for questioning that morning in London. Legality aside, Stratton believed that, from a tactical standpoint, "no matter what we did, the story was coming out," and a suspension request "might look like we were trying to cover up something." He also thought the damage would be greater if Gibson, Dunn were to suspend the deposition unilaterally, causing Jones, Day to seek an enforcement order from the presiding judge in Cleveland—in the home state of Firestone and the home city of Jones, Day—who might impose severe sanctions for forgery.

In the days following, Stratton and Millian investigated Paul's claims in an effort to prove them false (a perspective dictated by Breezevale's client status). Habib and Abou Jouade called Paul a liar, charging, without proof, that she had been bribed by Firestone to sabotage Breezevale's case. They disavowed any involvement in forgery and maintained that the offer letters and spread sheets were genuine, but other evidence cast doubt on their denials. In interviews with Stratton, Abou Jouade was asked about the sheet of signatures he had left with Paul. Abou Jouade thought he might have "made it in order to illustrate to her the difference" between English and Arabic script, an explanation Stratton found "absurd." Stratton repeatedly suggested that "a questioned documents expert might be able to examine the paper and ink on the allegedly-backdated documents to see whether they have been created in 1987 or 1991," but Habib "threw cold water" on that idea. Habib's negative attitude toward expert testing had been, in Stratton's mind, "one of the principal bases upon which I concluded that it would not be possible to prove Rebecca's story false, because it was true."

Breezevale called Sherman Cohn, a Professor at Georgetown University Law Center, for expert testimony in support of its position that Gibson, Dunn had committed malpractice in allowing the Paul deposition to go forward, and on related issues. Cohn had impressive qualifications. He had been a teacher of professional responsibility and civil procedure at Georgetown for some twenty-five years, and had written extensively on those subjects. He had testified as an expert in numerous legal malpractice cases, for both plaintiffs and defendants. Cohn is a member of the American Law Institute and a consultant to its project-in progress, a Restatement of the Law Governing Lawyers.

Cohn began by stressing the concept of the lawyer as fiduciary, with attendant duties of utmost care and loyalty to the client. He cited metaphors for the relationship suggested by Harvard Professor Charles Fried ("a best friend"), and by Georgetown Professor Robert Drinan ("parent and child"). According to Cohn's view of the record, Stratton had crossed a Rubicon and violated the standard of care when he decided to go forward with Paul's deposition without investigating her allegations or consulting Breezevale. "Going forward under those circumstances colored and controlled the rest of the case," and was tantamount to "selling their own client down the river."

Among the jurisdictions adopting the Model Rules of Professional Conduct, the effect of the rules in determining standards of care in legal malpractice cases ranges from none to near conclusive. Cohn's opinions rested substantially on the Model Rules, as they have been modified and adopted in the District of Columbia, and where the courts have recognized them as evidence of standards of care. Cohn testified that Stratton had violated Rule 1.4(a), "Communications," in his initial meeting with Paul on Monday morning. The rule provides: "A lawyer shall keep a client reasonably informed about the status of a matter and promptly comply with reasonable requests for information." When Breezevale's Awit had phoned the Gibson, Dunn office while Paul was telling her story, Stratton "had a duty [under Rule 1.4] to [tell him] that something very significant had happened" and that he needed to talk to Awit and Habib as soon as possible. Cohn went on to fault Stratton at virtually every step of his involvement in Paul's deposition.

Cohn testified that when Stratton had heard Paul's story, he should have realized that her deposition had to be postponed. Postponement wasn't a judgment call; under the circumstances, it was the only reasonable thing to do. Specifically, Stratton should have called the Jones, Day lawyer and told her: "I must postpone this deposition. I ask your indulgence and permission to do so. But if you do not [agree], I still must do so." If pressed for a reason, he could say: "I cannot tell you at this time." He could offer to pay Jones, Day's costs associated with the post-ponement. In failing to postpone, Cohn opined that Stratton had violated Rule 1.1 which requires lawyers to provide "competent representation" to their clients. He further opined that he had violated Rule 1.3, which requires "zealous and diligent" representation of the client. Implicit in Cohn's argument was a cost-benefit analysis: unilateral postponement of the deposition, while representing a minor breach of legal obligation by Gibson, Dunn, had been necessary in order to avoid serious, and possibly irreparable, damage to their client's interest. In Cohn's view, Gibson, Dunn "in effect abandoned their client that Monday morning.... They were more concerned about themselves."

Had they postponed the deposition, Cohn continued, Stratton and Millian should have immediately begun a thorough investigation of Paul's allegations, including "calling paper and ink experts in London"—as Stratton had suggested, but not insisted on—and "checking the files in Iraq as to whether [the offer letters] had actually arrived in 1987." (Abou Jouade testified that he had drafted the offer letters in Beirut and had them hand-carried to Baghdad.) Cohn contended that had they been able to discredit Paul's allegations, the Paul deposition could have gone forward later with greatly reduced injury to Breezevale's interests. In Cohn's opinion, their investigation had been incomplete and amounted to belated damage control, more for the benefit of Gibson, Dunn than for Breezevale.

Stratton and Millian testified that their client at the deposition had been Breezevale, not Paul, that they were not representing her personally, but only in a limited sense as Breezevale's employee, and that they had explained that relationship to Paul. Stratton had taken the view that the interests of Paul and Breezevale had not become "adverse" in the conflict-of-interest sense until Tuesday evening when Habib had decided to fire Paul and was considering suing her to recover records. On Wednesday morning Stratton had advised Paul not to return to the Breezevale office, and to consult her own solicitor. Paul never did return to the Breezevale office.

Cohn acknowledged that a lawyer representing a corporation may ordinarily appear in the deposition of an employee, including one who gives testimony damaging to the employer, without becoming involved in a conflict of interest—for example, the Safeway employee who admits seeing, but not picking up, a banana peel. But "where you have an employee about to testify that the corporation may have committed a crime, their interests have diverged." At that point, an employee in Paul's position, who may also be guilty of a crime, has an interest in being believed that conflicts directly with her employer's interest in her being disbelieved. Stratton and Millian had represented Breezevale and Paul in just those circumstances. Cohn expressed the view that, if Paul were considered a "client," Gibson, Dunn had violated Rule 1.7, the rule generally prohibiting representation of clients with conflicting interests. On the other hand, if the situation were analyzed under Rule 1.13 governing representation of entities, the practical result was the same. Official commentary to that rule states that: "The lawyer should advise any [employee] whose interest the lawyer finds adverse to the organization of the conflict of interest, that the lawyer cannot represent the [employee], and that [the employee] may wish to obtain independent representation."

Close questions arose whether Gibson, Dunn was either obligated, or permitted, to reveal the forgeries to Jones, Day, either before the deposition or before any settlement could be reached. If Paul's story were true, the Gibson, Dunn lawyers had unknowingly made misstatements of fact when they provided Jones, Day with forged documents and false interrogatory answers based on those documents during discovery. The District of Columbia's modification of Rule 1.6, "Confidentiality of Information," provides that "a lawyer shall not *knowingly*" reveal a "secret" the disclosure of which would be "embarrassing" or "detrimental" to the client—standards plainly applicable to the Breezevale documents and statements of its officers, if, indeed, they were false. Cohn stressed the importance of *knowing* that documents are false before any duty arises to tell the other side, pointing to the Rule definition of knowing as "actual knowledge" of the matter in question, implying the person's mental state and its accurate perception of reality. (The Rule goes on the state, however, that "knowledge may be inferred from circumstances.") Putting himself in Stratton's position before the deposition and in the days immediately following, Cohn stated: "I don't know whether those documents are false or whether the interrogatories are untruthful." Lacking that knowledge, loyalty to the client precludes the lawyer from disclosing damaging information.

The rules concerning false evidence and access to evidence are ambiguous as applied to this situation. Rule 3.3, "Candor Towards the Tribunal," prohibits offering false evidence, but, again, only if the lawyer knows it is false. Moreover, Cohn pointed out that under case law the rule only applies when false evidence is offered in court, not when it is turned over to the opposing lawyer in discovery. Even assuming the rule applies in discovery, as it can be read to do, when the lawyer discovers that he has turned over forged documents, his duty is to "call upon the client to rectify the fraud," not to rectify it himself.

Rule 3.4, "Fairness to Opposing Counsel," governs access to evidence. It does apply to both pretrial and trial interactions between opposing lawyers. Among other things, the rule prohibits "obstructing access to" or "concealing" evidence, language which arguably requires a lawyer who learns he has been a conduit of fake documents and false answers to tell the other side. One can argue, however, that keeping quiet about discovered forgery does not amount to obstruction or concealment.

Going into the Paul deposition, Stratton had been aware of these considerations and the need for some delicate balancing. "I hoped that the story would not come out. I had no reason to believe that Jones, Day knew about it. We still have an adversary system. It was up to them to dig it out, not up to me to give it to them. I wasn't going to make it any easier, but I wasn't going to mess them up either." He took the position, however, that "Jones, Day had been misled by fraud and we couldn't settle as long as the record is in that shape." For Stratton, then, disclosure became a matter of timing.

On cross-examination, Gibson, Dunn's lawyer probed Cohn's position with a hypothetical case, asking him to assume that:

> While food shopping, your client slips on a banana peel, injuring her neck. She complains of pain and inability to do household chores. You sue Safeway for damages. Your client's orthopedist sends you x-rays showing serious damage to vertebrae in her neck, which you turn over to Safeway's lawyer. Safeway offers $10,000 in settlement. While that offer is on the table, your client's orthopedist phones to tell you that they sent you the wrong x-ray by mistake, and that your client's x-ray shows no damage. You call your client, who insists you have her x-ray.

Cohn was then asked whether he could ethically phone Safeway's lawyer and say: "Hey, I'll take the $10,000" without telling them about a possible mix-up with the x-ray. Cohn replied: "Yes, sir. If you have evidence from one witness and others are denying it, it's not your job to be judge and jury and decide who is telling the truth. At that point, your case is weaker and you can certainly go ahead and settle it before the other side finds out about it. You're not God. You're a lawyer, an advocate, and you owe loyalty to your client."

Gibson, Dunn's lawyer asked Cohn what the hypothetical woman's lawyer should do if she has a change of heart and tells the lawyer: "I can't live with myself any longer. I've got to tell the truth. It's not my x-ray." Cohn replied that the lawyer now has actual knowledge, not merely conflicting evidence, about the x-ray, and that he cannot ethically accept the $10,000 settlement, at least not at that point. Assuming that Rule 3.3 applies in discovery, the lawyer's obligation is to tell the client to take back the x-ray; the lawyer may not take it back on his own. In any event, under Rule 26(c) of the federal discovery rules, it is the "party," not the lawyer, who is required to amend discovery responses when she learns they are incorrect. If the client refuses to do so, the lawyer may then withdraw from the case, leaving the client free to look for a less scrupulous lawyer. Withdrawal by the lawyer is optional, however, a "may," not a "shall," under Rule 1. 16(b). The lawyer may continue to represent such a client and go on to settle or try the case, knowing that the other side is ignorant of the fraud. Cohn appeared to reach that conclusion with some reluctance, observing that: "That's what the rules seem to say," and adding: "That's called the adversary system."

Gibson, Dunn called Thomas Morgan, a professor at George Washington University Law School, as an expert witness in support of its position that the law firm had met applicable standards of care in the *Firestone* litigation. Like Cohn, Morgan had impressive qualifications. He had taught law for twenty-five years, specializing in professional responsibility and antitrust law. Morgan is co-author of a widely used textbook on professional responsibility and is one of three reporters for the American Law Institute's proposed Restatement of the Law Governing Lawyers. Like Cohn, Morgan had testified as an expert witness in numerous legal malpractice cases.

Morgan and Cohn tended to agree on general principles, while disagreeing at virtually every point in their application to the facts. On the overarching issue, Morgan testified that Stratton's decision to go forward with Paul's deposition, without first investigating her story and without consulting Breezevale, had complied with the same rules of ethics Cohn had cited for the opposite conclusion. As he viewed the situation, Gibson, Dunn had been legally obligated to produce Paul that Monday morning.

Morgan also defended Stratton's decision on tactical grounds. After hearing her story, Stratton had believed that Paul might well be telling the truth, that she would have to testify sometime, and that Gibson,

Dunn should avoid the appearance of a cover-up. Moreover, if Paul were lying, it would be prudent to pin her down by getting her story on the record. (Morgan did not explain why it was preferable to pin her down in the presence of Jones, Day.) Furthermore, Morgan thought that "putting it over would have made matters worse, whichever way you conclude about the truthfulness of her accusations. If the accusations were true, [postponement] would have established a history of delay and, while not literally lying, of being less than candid with respect to the evidence. And if what she is saying is a lie, you haven't lost the ability to demonstrate that"—implying that Paul's fabrications could have been explained away. Wesley Howell, the senior Gibson, Dunn lawyer on the case, disagreed with his own expert on Morgan's last point. Howell believed that Paul's allegations had destroyed the settlement value of the case, whether true or false.

Morgan defended Stratton's decision to allow the deposition to begin before informing Breezevale's Habib. He stressed that Rule 1.4 requires that the client be kept "reasonably" informed. As he saw it, as a lawyer one should "try to get the picture before you discuss it with the client."

Morgan testified that Gibson, Dunn had not had a conflict of interest in representing Paul and Breezevale at the deposition. Paul could not be considered a "client" because clients within the meaning of Rule 1.7 are people or entities whose "interests" are adverse. Morgan read the "interest" concept narrowly to mean those having an interest in winning or losing the case—a type of interest Breezevale had, but Paul lacked. He rejected the suggestion that Paul's interest in not committing perjury, versus her employer's interest in her doing so, fell within the rule.

Morgan further testified that Gibson, Dunn had complied with Rule 1.13 governing representation of a corporation and appearing for its employees in depositions incident to representation. Under that rule, Breezevale, not Paul, was Gibson, Dunn's client. As an employee under oath, Paul was obliged to tell the truth but, as Morgan put it, "if the truth was inconsistent, or embarrassing, or troublesome to Breezevale, that doesn't constitute a conflict of interest" in the technical sense. Morgan disagreed with Cohn that Paul's dilemma—commit perjury or lose your job—rose to the level of an adverse interest such that the firm was disqualified from representing her from the time they first heard her story. Morgan agreed, however, that by Tuesday evening when Paul had been fired and Breezevale was considering suing her, "you clearly had a conflict" and it was "appropriate to advise her to seek a solicitor of her own."

Morgan was asked whether Gibson, Dunn could have postponed Paul's deposition and, without investigating her allegations and with Breezevale's officers denying them, proceeded to settlement without disclosing those allegations to Jones, Day. Disagreeing with Cohn, Morgan responded: "The answer is no." Gibson, Dunn may not have actual knowledge of fraud at that point. "But you never know something one hundred percent." More importantly, Morgan continued: "If there is a consistent understanding in this area, it is that a lawyer may not intentionally prevent himself from becoming knowledgeable." Where there is reason to inquire further, the lawyer must do so. And if he settles the case without further inquiry, and without disclosing what he knows, according to Morgan the settlement "wouldn't be worth the paper it is written on. If Firestone ever found out what happened, they could set aside the settlement for fraud." Furthermore, the lawyer would be vulnerable to a charge of misconduct and possible disbarment under Rules 1.2 and 8.4 for assisting a client to commit a fraud.

The questions whether Firestone *would* find out what happened, and therefore whether the lawyer would face disciplinary action were left hanging. Morgan agreed with Cohn that the duty under Rule 3.3 to reveal fraud would be the client's, not the lawyer's, and that under the District of Columbia's version of Rule 1.6, the lawyer would be barred from revealing the client's fraud. Morgan pointed out, however, that some States—including Ohio, where the Firestone case had been filed—have adopted an exception to the general prohibition of revealing client information in situations where the client has used the lawyer's services to commit a fraud causing injury to the financial interest of another—an exception seemingly applicable to this case.

The conflicting testimony of Cohn and Morgan, of document and handwriting experts, and of a parade of fact witnesses went to the jury on Breezevale's malpractice claim in October 1996, following seven weeks of testimony. The jury was given a verdict form and instructed to decide a series of questions. They returned a mixed verdict, but the bottom line favored Breezevale:

- Breezevale established the applicable standard of care which Gibson, Dunn breached;
- Gibson, Dunn's breach proximately caused damage to Breezevale's case;
- Forgeries occurred in which Breezevale executives had participated, but;

- The forgeries had not played a substantial part in damaging Breezevale's case;
- Breezevale would have won its suit against Firestone; and
- Breezevale is entitled to a total of $4,930,000 in damages from Gibson, Dunn.

The jury was not asked to find whether Jones, Day would have discovered that the documents in question were false if the deposition had been postponed, an issue which Judge Graae would consider critical.

Gibson, Dunn filed motions to set aside two of the jury's findings: that it had breached the standard of care in going forward with Paul's deposition, and that the breach was the proximate cause of damages. Judge Graae acknowledged the tactical considerations Stratton had cited to justify his decision to allow the deposition to go forward. He went on to note, however, that "there can be little doubt [that decision] implicated a lawyer's duties to disclose information and follow a client's instructions." Citing the conflicting testimony of Cohn and Morgan, the judge concluded: "These polar-opposite views by noted experts do not lend themselves to judgment as a matter of law." The jury's finding that Gibson, Dunn had breached the standard of care was allowed to stand.

The jury's finding of proximate cause was a different matter. The jury found that the disputed documents were forged, yet it went on to find that Breezevale would have prevailed over Firestone. As Judge Graae viewed them, those findings were inconsistent. The finding of forgery was fully supported in the evidentiary record. As the judge observed: "Neither side left any stone unturned on the forgery issue; there can be no doubt the jury had all available information on which to make its finding." Given that finding, the judge reasoned that a postponement for purposes of investigation inevitably would have "validated" Paul's allegations. A warning flag would have gone up as a result of an unexplained postponement of the deposition. A Jones, Day lawyer testified that postponement would have made them "suspicious" and that there was "not a chance in the world" his firm would have foregone taking Paul's deposition before any settlement. With Jones, Day's knowledge of the forgeries, the jury would have had no basis for finding that Firestone would have paid more than the nuisance amount of $100,000 it had, in fact, paid to settle Breezevale's claim. Judge Graae granted Gibson, Dunn's motion for judgment for lack of a proximate cause relationship between its malpractice and Breezevale's losses, thus erasing the jury's award of $4,930,000.

Following the jury verdict, Judge Graae heard Gibson, Dunn's counterclaim against Breezevale alleging bad faith litigation for relying on false documents. The jury had found that the documents in issue were forged under the "preponderance of the evidence" standard, but since bad faith litigation must be proved by the higher "clear and convincing evidence" standard, it was necessary for the judge to made an independent determination, based on the record already made before the jury.

Focusing on Paul's credibility, Judge Graae found nothing to suggest that she had a motive to lie. "Moreover, it is difficult, is not impossible, to believe she would invent a story so deeply implicating herself in serious misconduct and so rich in odd detail." Abou Jouade's credibility was destroyed by the evidence. His story that the offer letters had emanated from the Beirut office and had been hand-carried to Baghdad was at odds with Breezevale's practice and made no commercial sense. Abou Jouade disavowed the multiple signatures on the paper Paul had brought to her deposition from her home, but Gibson, Dunn's handwriting expert testified to the contrary. Gibson, Dunn's computer expert "conclusively proved" (Judge Graae's phrase) that an offer letter introduced by Breezevale was a forgery. Committing perhaps his most obvious blunder, Abou Jouade signed two fake offer letters which had been mistakenly typed on a Breezevale letterhead that had not existed in 1987.

Judge Graae found that Breezevale had litigated in bad faith and held a separate hearing to determine Gibson, Dunn's damages. Having represented itself, the law firm claimed $2,970,000 for its attorneys' time and $1,091,000 for expenses incurred in defending against Breezevale's bad faith litigation. It had called on the services of eleven of its lawyers and numerous support personnel for thousands of hours of work. Judge Graae rated the lawyers performance "among the best" and allowed in full the claims for fees and expenses. Gibson, Dunn also claimed $295,000 for unpaid fees and expenses associated with the Firestone litigation which the judge also allowed.

Gibson, Dunn asked for $8 million in punitive damages to punish Breezevale for its bad faith. Judge Graae wrote: "The evidence at trial was absolutely clear and convincing that the documents were forged, thereby exposing the sworn testimony of Messrs. Habib, Awit, and Abou Jouade as cynical lies. The court cannot imagine a worse abuse of the judicial process or a more deserving cause for punishment." The judge concluded, however, that Gibson, Dunn's $8 million figure was "arbitrary, high, and bore no relationship to Breezevale's ability to pay." He awarded

$1 million in punitive damages, an amount he believed "will hurt, but is not so great as to be beyond Breezevale's ability to pay."

On November 24, 1997, Judge Graae entered final judgment in the case, awarding Gibson, Dunn a total of $5,356,000 which, compared to the jury's verdict for Breezevale, improved the law firm's position by some $10 million.

Breezevale appealed to the Court of Appeals of the District of Columbia, raising numerous issues in addition to Stratton's decision to go forward that Monday morning in London. On September 21, 2000 (the wheels turn slowly) the Court of Appeals unanimously reversed the trial court's decision in major part. The court held that Judge Graae had applied the wrong legal standard in granting Gibson, Dunn's motion to set aside the jury's damages award in Breezevale's favor (except for a relatively minor part relating to the proposed tire factory in Nigeria). The court also reversed the trial court's bad faith litigation finding and damage award in Gibson, Dunn's favor on the ground that the erroneous ruling on the jury's award to Breezevale was "inextricable" from the trial court's finding of Breezevale's bad faith. The Court of Appeals directed reconsideration of a Gibson, Dunn motion for a new trial which, it ruled, would turn on a less stringent standard than the erroneously granted motion to set aside the jury's damages award—potentially putting the whole complex and protracted matter back to square one.

Gibson Dunn petitioned for rehearing *en banc*, arguing that, as a matter of law, Breezevale should be completely barred from suit as a sanction for its forgeries and the perjured testimony of its witnesses. Gibson, Dunn's rehearing petition was granted, but on October 18, 2001, the full court rejected the "clean hands" argument, reaffirmed the panel decision, and once again remanded the case to the trial court. As this book went to press, a Gibson, Dunn renewed motion for sanctions was pending. If, as seems likely, that motion were to be denied, the parties may explore other options, but settlement seems unlikely.

\* \* \*

# Comments and Questions

1. Expert witness Sherman Cohn took the position that the Breezevale plaintiffs legally could, and should, have postponed Rebecca Paul's depo-

sition—unilaterally, if necessary—in order to investigate her forgery claims before proceeding. Thomas Morgan, the defendant's expert, argued that the plaintiffs were legally obligated to proceed with the deposition as scheduled. Under the circumstances, postponement of the deposition would have resulted in some inconvenience and expense to Jones, Day; proceeding as scheduled almost inevitably would have revealed Paul's forgery claims and severely damaged, even destroyed, Breezevale's case, even if they were later proved to be false. Apart from the tactical considerations Stratton cited—not appearing to be hiding something, avoiding a court order compelling Paul's deposition—would Stratton have been justified in weighing the comparative costs and benefits to the parties in deciding whether to postpone or proceed with the deposition?

2. Did Breezevale have the authority to direct Stratton to postpone the deposition and investigate Paul's charges? Under Model Rule 1.2, "Scope of Representation," did that question involve "objectives of the representation" or "means" by which objectives are to be achieved? Casting the issue in different terms, was it a matter of "strategy" or "tactics"? By going ahead with Paul's deposition, whose primary interest was Stratton serving—Breezevale's or Gibson, Dunn's?

3. The *Breezevale* case bristles with issues of ethics which exhibit the tension between the advocate's duty of loyalty and the bedrock ethical duty to tell the truth. United States District Court Judge Marvin Frankel once complimented a lawyer appearing before him, saying that he "would lie down in front of a train" for his client. Does the duty of loyalty extend to keeping quiet about evidence suspected, or known, to be false—the dilemma which confronted Gibson, Dunn's Stratton?

4. Stratton went into the deposition having been told by Paul that critical documents given to Jones, Day in discovery were forgeries and knowing that those documents would be a major subject of the deposition. He had not investigated her charges at that point, but he thought she was sincere and he found her story plausible. Stratton did not volunteer Paul's charges to the Jones, Day lawyer, nor did he seek to withdraw the alleged forgeries. Instead, he "hoped the story would not come out. It was up to them to dig it out, not up to me to give it to them." Is this proper advocacy, jerking the opposition around, or both? Model Rule 3.4, "Fairness to Opposing Party and Counsel," provides that: "a lawyer shall not unlawfully obstruct another party's access to evidence, or unlawfully alter, destroy, or conceal a document...having potential

evidentiary value." Stratton had reason to believe that documents his firm had previously represented to the opposition as genuine were, in fact, false. By keeping silent at the deposition, hoping that the Jones, Day lawyer would not "dig it out," is Stratton "unlawfully obstructing access" or "concealing" evidence? If not, should Rule 3.4 be amended to reach this situation? Does Model Rule 4.1(b), "Truthfulness in Statements to Others," apply?

5. Rule 26(e)(2) of the Federal Rules of Civil Procedure (and similar rules in many state courts) requires a party who *knows* that a discovery response was incorrect when made to amend the response. Model Rule 3.3, "Candor Toward the Tribunal," provides that: "A lawyer shall not *knowingly* offer evidence that the lawyer knows to be false. If a lawyer has offered material evidence and comes to know of its falsity, the lawyer shall take reasonable remedial measures." When does a lawyer "know" that evidence is false within the meaning of these rules? The Model Rules define "knows" and "knowingly" as "actual knowledge," adding that "knowledge may be inferred from the circumstances." A philosopher might ask: when does one ever "know" anything? As a practical rule of conduct, the rule seems to contemplate a person's actual state of mind, as inferred from what she says and does, and from the surrounding circumstances—not always an easy standard to apply. Referring to the banana-peel hypothetical, Sherman Cohn testified that the lawyer didn't "know" he had been sent the wrong x-ray after the orthopedist told him that but the client denied it. Who is more likely to be telling the truth under those circumstances—the orthopedist or the client? Is it a matter of weighing the evidence when "knowing" something is in controversy? Do you "know" something if a preponderance of the evidence points in that direction? A lawyer might well be suspended, even disbarred, for knowingly offering false evidence in court. Should the standard under Model Rule 3.3 be "clear and convincing" —the rough equivalent of "pretty damn sure"—to reflect the severity of the consequences? Cohn points out that Rule 3.3 has been construed by the courts to be inapplicable at the discovery stage. Should the rule apply only at trial, leaving lawyers free to lie and send false documents to the opposition during discovery? During mediation or other forms of alternative dispute resolution?

6. Assume that Stratton does postpone the deposition without revealing that the documents are forgeries and the interrogatory answers based

on them are false. Sherman Cohn testified that, before investigating further, Stratton could proceed to settle the case because he doesn't "know" the documents are false. Thomas Morgan disagreed, saying that "a lawyer may not intentionally prevent himself from becoming knowledgeable." How should the balance be struck between Cohn's dedication to his client and Morgan's dedication to discovering the truth?

7. Judge Graae found the evidence "absolutely clear and convincing that the documents were forged, thereby exposing the sworn testimony of Messrs. Habib, Awit, and Abou Jouade as cynical lies." In light of the evidence and the judge's finding, is it fair to conclude that Breezevale's lawyers knew before trial that the documents were false and that their clients' stories were lies? If so, under Model Rule 1.16 would they have been permitted, or obligated, to withdraw? By going to trial, offering false documents, and calling their clients to testify, did the Breezevale lawyers violate Model Rule 3.3 and thereby subject themselves to disciplinary action—including suspension, perhaps disbarment? *Compare Nix v. Whiteside*, 475 U.S. 157 (1986) concerning the obligations of counsel for a criminal defendant who proposes to lie on the stand. Should counsel's obligations in a civil case be lesser, greater, the same?

# Chapter 2

# The Case of the Frozen Broccoli

"Miguel Rodriguez considered the payment of attorneys' fees for his employees as a cost of doing business."
— Francisco Laguna, Esq., testifying in
*United States v. Rodriguez-Orejuela*

On April 15, 1992, the motor vessel *Colleen* docked at Port Everglades, Florida, north of Miami. Her cargo included three refrigerated containers that, according to the ship's manifest, held cases of frozen broccoli consigned to Southeast Agrotrade, a Miami wholesaler in fruits and vegetables. In fact, under layers of broccoli the cases contained thousands of foil-wrapped packages of cocaine. The containers cleared customs the next morning and were loaded onto trucks that headed south, followed at a discreet distance by federal agents.

The agents were members of an interagency task force drawn from the United States Department of Justice, the Drug Enforcement Administration, Customs, and the Immigration and Naturalization Service. After a lengthy investigation, the agents had reason to believe that the frozen broccoli camouflaged a large shipment of cocaine from the Cali, Colombia cartel, a criminal organization engaged in cocaine trafficking worldwide. They watched as containers were off-loaded at the Southeast Agrotrade warehouse. Search warrants in hand, the agents kept the warehouse under surveillance for several days, observing the comings and goings and taking down license plates. Shortly after 5 a.m. on April 22, a cargo van left the warehouse. A few miles down the road, Florida Highway Patrolmen, acting in concert with federal agents, pulled the van over and searched it. A large quantity of cocaine was found, confirming the presence of cocaine under the *Colleen's* broccoli shipment.

The federal agents had learned that the head of Cali cartel operations for south Florida was one Harold Ackerman, a Colombian national living in Miami. They had obtained court authority to tap Ackerman's home and cell phones, enabling them to obtain the names and (through the telephone company) addresses of several cartel employees in the Miami area. On April 23, Ackerman, his employee Carlos Giron, and two others were arrested for unlawful possession and conspiracy to import a controlled substance: to wit, cocaine. A search of the Southeast Agrotrade warehouse produced 1,352 kilos of cocaine with a purity of 92 percent. A larger quantity was seized at a second location. The seizures totaled 6,673 kilos—approximately seven tons—processed to powder form and ready for consumption. A search of Ackerman's residence yielded $480,000 in cash and extensive records of drug operations, including detailed reports to Cali. The federal agents found a custom-built vault in Giron's residence that contained cash, plastic explosives, .357 magnum revolvers, Gloch and Baretta pistols, and Uzi submachine guns.

The men arrested in Miami in April 1992 formed one part of a far-flung organization in the business of smuggling and selling cocaine and laundering the proceeds. Those arrests represented a step in "Operation Cornerstone," the federal government's campaign to destroy the Cali cartel's operations in this country. In a two-hundred page, multi-count indictment returned in June 1995, a federal grand jury charged seventy-two defendants, most of them Colombian nationals, with offenses under sixteen federal criminal statutes. The indictment also charged two American lawyers for the cartel, William Moran and Michael Abbell, and the other defendants with knowingly and wilfully conspiring to participate with the Cali cartel, through a pattern of racketeering, in the illegal importation and distribution of cocaine from 1983 to 1995 (the "RICO" count). The indictment alleged five hundred fifty-six "overt acts," in many of which Moran and Abbell had been directly involved. The two lawyers were also charged with conspiracy to launder drug proceeds. The laundering count alleged that under cartel direction they had knowingly accepted narcotics proceeds in payment of their fees, for client bail money, and for subsistence payments that they channeled to incarcerated cartel employees and their families.

Four other American lawyers—Francisco Laguna, Donald Ferguson, Joel Rosenthal and Robert Moore—had been working with Moran or Abbell on related cases. The four were arrested and initially charged with obstruction of justice and money laundering. Faced with the prospect of long prison terms—twenty years or more—they decided to cooperate with the government by pleading guilty to reduced charges and testifying against Moran and Abbell. In the spring of 1998, Moran and Abbell were tried together and convicted of conspiracies under RICO and money laundering laws. This chapter focuses on the conduct of William Moran, Michael Abbell and the lawyer-witnesses against them in representing a corrupt, ruthless, and fabulously wealthy client who paid them handsomely for crossing lines.

In June 1991, *Time* magazine's cover story featured the Cali cartel, describing it as the world's largest producer and distributor of cocaine, eclipsing the long-dominant Medellin cartel. Confirming that assessment in the trial of Moran and Abbell, a government expert estimated that in the period 1983-1994, the cartel had smuggled some 200,000 kilograms of cocaine into south Florida. With the wholesale price per kilogram in Miami averaging $13,000, those shipments represented revenues approaching $2 billion dollars.

The *Time* cover pictured the four heads of the Cali cartel—Miguel and Gilberto Rodriguez-Orejuela, Jose Santacruz Londono, and Helmer Herrara-Buitrago, over the caption "The Kings of Coke." Each headed a faction of the cartel, operating in different territories—Miguel Rodriguez (aka "El Senor") in Florida and Texas. According to Francisco Laguna, an associate in Michael Abbell's law firm, Abbell was "really excited" about the story when it appeared; having three clients on the cover of *Time* was "pretty big stuff." But when he showed the *Time* cover to Miguel, the drug lord was "not too happy." Miguel was "in constant denial of his true profession," preferring to be known as the owner of a Colombian drug store chain, radio station, and soccer team.

Miguel Rodriguez exercised tight control over operations from his headquarters in Cali. Senior members like Harold Ackerman reported to him daily by telephone. It was Miguel who made major decisions, such as allocations of smuggled product—usually 2,000 kilograms or more—among wholesalers. Candidates for high-level jobs were flown to Cali for personal interviews. All new hires in Florida, including those for menial jobs, spoke to Miguel by telephone, giving him the names and addresses of relatives in Colombia and a promise to adhere to a code of silence. Under the code, if a member were arrested, he would be provided with a lawyer at the cartel's expense and his family would be supported financially. For his part, the member would not cooperate with the authorities.

The penalty for violating the code was well understood: retribution against members of his family, possibly including death. Fear of retribution was reinforced in ways both subtle and blunt. Gonzalo Paz, a Colombian lawyer, sometimes doubled as code enforcer. Ending a prison visit to Harold Ackerman, he touched his forefinger to his lips, then drew it across his throat. American attorneys Moran and Abbell had a less direct role in enforcing the code of silence. They persuaded their jailed clients to sign affidavits falsely stating that they did not know Miguel Rodriguez. The false affidavits acted as forceful reminders to keep silent.

## The Trial of William Moran and Michael Abbell

William Moran and Michael Abbell were first tried with four other cartel employees. (Miguel Rodriguez and several others under indictment remained in Cali, shielded from extradition by Colombian law.) Two defendants were convicted, but the jury could not agree on verdicts for Moran and Abbell and the judge declared a mistrial. The Department of Justice had been attempting for several years, with little success, to convict lawyers for major drug trafficers who, they believed, had crossed the line between legitimate representation into criminal activity. Confident they had a strong case, the federal strike force lawyers made it a priority to retry Moran and Abbell.

On April 21, 1998, the retrial began in Miami before William M. Hoeveler, Senior Judge of the United States District Court for the Southern District of Florida. Edward Ryan and William Pearson were the prosecutors. Moran represented himself, with Holly Skolnick, a Miami criminal defense lawyer, as co-counsel. Abbell was represented by Henry Asbill and William Moffitt, criminal defense lawyers from Washington, D.C. In a real sense, lawyers Laguna, Ferguson, and Rosenthal were also on trial. Their testimony as witnesses against the defendants would largely determine the prosecutors' recommendations on their pending sentences. Judge Hoeveler stated that he would be virtually bound by the prosecutors' assessments of their testimony.

The trial proceeded almost continuously until July 21, when the jury returned verdicts of guilty against both defendants. The transcript of the forty-six day trial runs to 8,427 pages and voluminous written exhibits were received into the record. Dealing with all of the issues and evidence in this complex case is beyond the scope of this chapter, which focuses on the conduct that got Moran and Abbell in so much trouble.

# The Case Against William Moran

William Moran was an able, experienced, rather flamboyant defense lawyer, generally respected by his peers in the Florida criminal defense bar. In her opening statement, defense lawyer Holly Skolnick conceded that Moran was "a little rough around the edges," and that the nature of his practice meant he was "in the government's face." Prosecutor Pearson called Moran a "street-smart trial lawyer."

The indictment alleged that Moran had been retained by Miguel and Gilberto Rodriguez in the late 1980s "to represent arrested members of their factions of the Cali cartel." Further, that he had agreed to support the cartel's objectives "by impeding and obstructing investigations of the [cartel] and prosecution of its leaders." The indictment went on to list actions Moran had agreed to undertake, including "relaying offers to pay legal fees from the leaders of the [cartel] to jailed members in exchange for their silence" and "preparing, presenting and arranging for the execution of affidavits designed to falsely exculpate Miguel Rodriguez-Orejuela from drug trafficking."

Moran's involvement with two arrested cartel employees—Carlos Giron and Gustavo Naranjo—were typical of his work for his real client, Miguel Rodriguez.

## Carlos Giron

Giron had grown up in Colombia, graduating from college with a degree in economics. He worked as a personnel manager in a brewery, then became a factotum for Miguel Rodriguez, responsible for handling payrolls and managing bank accounts. Senora Giron became a secretary to Miguel's wife. The Giron family moved to Florida in 1990 when their son needed medical treatment not available in Colombia. An illegal immigrant, Giron was unable to find work and the family was sleeping on the floor. When he learned of their plight, Miguel instructed Harold Ackerman, his man in Miami, to give the Girons $10,000, find them a decent place to live, and put Carlos to work. Giron went to work at Southeast Agrotrade as a processor of cocaine shipments. He was working on the frozen broccoli shipment when he was arrested. Giron was charged with drug trafficking and, based on the cache of pistols and submachine guns found in his home, with illegal possession of weapons.

William Moran represented Giron through his trial. In accordance with the usual arrangement, Miguel paid Moran's fee. Moran and the lawyers retained for Giron's co-defendants concentrated their efforts on motions to suppress the cocaine and other evidence obtained, they claimed, as a result of illegal searches. The federal agents had filed detailed affidavits in support of the searches and, after a two-week hearing, those motions were denied. Giron went to trial but, having been arrested hip deep in cocaine, his conviction for drug trafficking was virtually foreordained. (Surprisingly, he was acquitted on the weapons charges.) Under the federal guidelines, he was sentenced to twenty-two years, eight months in federal prison. Then thirty-eight, with time off for good behavior, Giron could expect to be released from prison in his mid-fifties. Lacking any promising grounds for appeal, Giron's only key to earlier freedom was cooperation with federal prosecutors.

Giron had known before his trial that he had the option of pleading guilty and cooperating with the government in exchange for a lesser sentence. Unlike many other cartel members who had gotten caught, however, Giron kept silent in prison "out of loyalty and fear" for four years, much longer than most cartel members initially sentenced to comparable prison terms. He testified that, early on, Moran "personally told me not to cooperate with the United States Government. That I was going to be acquitted." Giron never cooperated when Moran was his lawyer.

After a year in prison, with his appeal pending and understandably upset about his long sentence, Giron wrote a letter to Miguel Rodriguez because "he was the one with the money and the one in charge." He asked for Miguel's support "so that I can terminate the services of the attorney Moran." As Giron saw it: "The friendship [Moran] had with Miguel Rodriguez-Orejuela was more important than to defend Carlos Giron." Miguel allowed Giron to switch from Moran to a team of Francisco Laguna, Michael Abbell, and Donald Ferguson. Giron probably believed that his new defense team represented an improvement. From Miguel's perspective, the case was being safely kept in the cartel's family of lawyers.

In September 1994, one year after Giron, Ackerman, and others had been convicted following the frozen broccoli seizure, government agents armed with search warrants searched the law offices of William Moran in Miami, Michael Abbell and Fernando Laguna in Washington, D.C. and Miami, and Donald Ferguson in Boca Raton, Florida. The agents hauled away dozens of boxes of documents, including correspondence, bills, and, most significant, copies of affidavits exculpating Miguel Rodriguez from drug trafficking.

A draft affidavit downloaded from the hard drive of a computer in Moran's office was identified in court by Giron as identical to an affidavit he had signed. Its text is repeated almost verbatim in affidavits signed by other cartel members. It read in part:

> "My name is Carlos Giron. I was born in Pasto, Colombia on February 13, 1954. Prior to my arrest on April 23, 1992, I had never met Miguel Rodriguez-Orejuela. I had never had business dealings of any kind or been involved in any transaction of any kind with Miguel Rodriguez-Orejuela under his own name or any alias. I had never spoken or conspired with Miguel Rodriguez-Orejuela to import cocaine into the United States, or elsewhere, to possess cocaine, or to distribute cocaine. I have studied the photograph attached to this affidavit. I have never met, spoken, transacted business, or conspired with the man in that photograph."

Asked at the trial whether the affidavit were true, Giron replied: "It was a complete lie." He stated that he had signed it "because it was an order" and "out of fear."

The experience of Carlos Giron and his family provides an example of the code of silence in operation. After arranging for Moran to represent Giron, Miguel Rodriguez telephoned Señora Giron from Cali and told her it was "not good" for her and the children to remain in the United States. As hostages to Carlos' continued silence, it would be more convenient for the cartel to have his family in Colombia. Señora Giron went, as instructed, to Moran's office and was given $5,000 in cash. In order to avoid detection by federal agents, rather than a direct flight from Miami Miguel instructed her to take an indirect route, with the children in disguise. Señora Giron flew to Cali from Orlando, by way of Aruba, Barranquilla, and Bogota. She recalled how the younger boy had worn a scoopneck blouse and that she had "combed his hair like a girl."

Señora Giron and her children settled in Cali and she continued to receive payments from Miguel Rodriguez. The code operated as expected until 1995, when Giron read in a newspaper that William Moran, his former lawyer, had been indicted. He heard through the prison grapevine that Ackerman and other former co-workers were cooperating with the government, expecting to have their sentences reduced—in prison parlance, "jumping on the bus." After his family was returned to the United States and given places in the government's witness protection program, he agreed to cooperate. Giron testified against Moran and his sentence was later reduced by almost two-thirds—from twenty-two years, eight months to eight years, one month—demonstrating the value of cooperation.

## Gustavo Naranjo

Naranjo had grown up in Colombia and emigrated to the United States in 1973. He worked for a time in a steel mill before turning to smuggling cocaine from Mexico. Operating on a modest scale with small planes and trucks from a warehouse in Tyler, Texas, he earned some $2 million, tax free, over ten years. He met Miguel Rodriguez in Cali in 1989 and was recruited to head the cartel's activities in Texas. He was to be paid $500 for each kilogram of cocaine smuggled past customs—representing $500,000 for a single 1,000 kilo shipment. Naranjo would be responsible for salaries; Miguel would pay for warehouses, trucks, and other expenses.

Naranjo ran the cartel's Texas operations until November 17, 1991 when two truckloads of hollow concrete posts arrived at his warehouse from Miami. The trucks and several warehouses in Miami had been under surveillance by federal agents who proceeded to arrest Naranjo and several other cartel employees. The concrete posts contained 12,250 kilos—over twelve tons—of cocaine, one of the largest seizures to that time by federal agents. Naranjo was charged with drug trafficking and lodged in the Tyler County jail.

Shortly after his arrest, Naranjo was visited by Joel Rosenthal, a criminal defense lawyer from Miami. Testifying against Moran as a government witness, Rosenthal recalled telling Naranjo that he represented Miguel Rodriguez and that he was there to help him find "the best lawyer money can buy" at no expense to him. Rosenthal had made a cautionary reference to cooperation, to the effect that it "might impact negatively on my client." Naranjo had responded that he would "never cooperate," that if he did "he and his family would be killed." That message was reinforced by Miguel in a phone conversation: "If you cooperate you are dead. Nobody does that to me."

Rosenthal contacted Frank Jackson, a prominent Dallas criminal defense lawyer, who agreed to represent Naranjo. Jackson received $290,000 for defending Naranjo in a four-day trial after which Naranjo was convicted and sentenced, like Carlos Giron, to twenty-two years and eight months. Rosenthal never appeared in court for Naranjo. Nevertheless he paid himself $130,000 for securing Jackson's services, visiting Naranjo's family in Colombia, and doing some research during sentencing. The $430,000 to pay Jackson and Rosenthal was sent from the cartel's cash drawers to Rosenthal's office. As Rosenthal recalled the procedure: "I would receive a call that there were 'documents' coming to my office. Someone would come with cash in various containers, sometimes a paper bag, sometimes a gym bag, sometimes a box." Concerned that a cash payment might later be forfeited as narcotics proceeds, Jackson asked Rosenthal to pay him by check. Having run cartel cash through his bank account, the check to Jackson became the basis of Rosenthal's later plea to money laundering.

Rosenthal and Jackson flew to Cali after Naranjo's conviction to report to Miguel Rodriguez and break the news to Naranjo's family. Rosenthal recalled Miguel saying to them that "he had his problems in Colombia and that some affidavits from the people in Texas [Naranjo and his employees] would be helpful to him." According to Rosenthal, Jackson commented that Naranjo—then languishing in jail under a twenty-two year sentence—was "so grateful, he will give you any affidavit you want." Jackson had gone on to suggest that a "not entirely accurate" affidavit would be harmless as long as it would only be used in Colombia.

Miguel Rodriguez called on Bill Moran to obtain an exculpatory affidavit from Naranjo. Moran prepared a draft and sent it to Miguel for his review. Miguel was displeased with one sentence that read: "I know Mr. Miguel Rodriguez-Orejuela as an honest businessman in Cali who was a casual acquaintance of mine." Miguel wanted that sentence revised to read: "I only know Mr. Rodriguez by reputation as an honest businessman in Cali. I have never met Miguel Rodriguez-Orejuela personally nor have I ever had any contact with him directly." Gonzalo Paz brought the revised affidavit back to Moran in Miami and Naranjo subsequently signed it.

# The Case Against Michael Abbell and his Associate, Francisco Laguna

Henry Asbill, Michael Abbell's defense lawyer, sketched a sympathetic outline of his client in his opening statement. Born in Chicago in 1940 the youngest of five children, Abbell was fifty-eight when he went to trial, married and the father of three sons. He graduated from high school at 16, from Harvard University in 1961, and from Harvard Law

School in 1964. After a two-year stint in the Army, he served for twenty years as a federal prosecutor and senior official in the United States Department of Justice. Abbell rose through the ranks to become head of the Criminal Division's Office of International Affairs which was responsible for international extradition matters. In 1984, he entered private practice with a Washington firm. He later formed a partnership with another Justice Department alumnus which was dissolved when he was indicted.

Francisco Laguna, a citizen of Colombia, was born in Bogata in 1962 and moved with his family to the United States at age four. He earned a BA degree in English at the University of California in 1983 and a law degree from the University of Arizona in 1986. Laguna is fluent in Spanish and English and has a working knowledge of Italian, German, and French. He met Abbell during a student clerkship at Abbell's firm. After law school graduation, Laguna returned as a combination associate, independent contractor, and errand runner.

## The Cow in the Sugar Cane

Jose ("Chepe") Santacruz Londono, a member of the Cali cartel, suffered a reversal of fortune in the fall of 1990. He had attempted to launder some $64 million in drug proceeds through bank accounts in Luxembourg, seven other European countries, Panama, and the United States. Three Colombians had been arrested in Luxembourg and charged with laundering. Miguel Rodriguez also had an interest in the Luxembourg seizure because one of the Colombians arrested there had laundered money for him in the past, giving him potentially damaging information. Alleging that the $64 million were drug proceeds which belonged to Santacruz, drug enforcement authorities had moved for forfeiture of the entire amount. Santacruz retained a German lawyer to fend off forfeiture in the European countries, except for Luxembourg; he tapped Gonzolo Paz, the Colombian lawyer and sometime code enforcer, for Panama. Miguel Rodriguez and Santacruz together retained Abbell and Laguna to handle the forfeiture cases in Luxembourg and in federal district court in Brooklyn.

In order to defeat forfeiture, Abbell had to surmount two hurdles. First, he had to find someone other than Santacruz to claim ownership of the accounts. He settled on Heriberto Castro Meza, Santacruz' father-in-law. Laguna was assigned the task of drafting false affidavits to support Meza's ownership, insulating it from Santacruz.

Second, Abbell's claimant couldn't be just anybody; he had to be a credible owner of $64 million in cash. Senor Meza wasn't worth anywhere near $64 million, so Abbell had to manufacture evidence of greater wealth. He hired Gentil Rojas, a Colombian economist, to prepare a false report showing that Meza's business interests were generating large amounts of cash and that the foreign accounts represented "flight capital" — money generated in an unstable economy (Colombia) and moved to a stable economy to protect its worth. In reviewing Rojas' draft report, Abbell saw that some of the figures were obviously artificial, as he put it, "too clean." He directed Laguna to send the report back to Rojas to get the problem fixed. Laguna first took the report to Santacruz, who reacted angrily and phoned Rojas, saying: "Look, I paid good money for these documents and you screwed up." He then gave Rojas "marching orders to prepare a new set of phony documents."

There were other problems. The Rojas report represented that three businesses putatively owned by Castro Meza — a cattle ranch, a sugar plantation, and a clothing manufacturing company — were responsible for generating the $64 million in excess cash. On the basis of talks with Santacruz's wife and mother-in-law, Laguna believed that the clothing company, at least, existed, but he never saw it. He and Abbell asked repeatedly to be taken to the three properties to take pictures and obtain title deeds — something tangible to show authorities in Luxembourg and the United States — but nothing came of those requests. False documents were provided for each company. Supposedly representing businesses thirty years old, the papers appeared to be fresh off a copying machine. The head of a cow appeared, appropriately, in a logo on the cattle ranch stationery. The same cow also appeared on the stationery of the sugar plantation.

In September 1991, Laguna filed the Rojas report in Luxembourg and in federal court in Brooklyn. He supplied copies to the European attorneys representing Santacruz in the other countries, without telling them the report was false. In addition, Laguna filed an affidavit in federal court stating that the $64 million belonged to Castro Meza and represented flight capital. Abbell reviewed that affidavit and, knowing its falsity, raised no questions. Laguna later commented: "The purpose was to get the money back. Nobody cared about any false aspects." By the fall of 1993, Abbell and Laguna had lost the forfeiture cases in Luxembourg and in federal court in Brooklyn. Santacruz berated them for incompetence, fired them, and hired new lawyers.

## Harold Ackerman, the Cartel's Man in Miami

Ackerman was born and raised in Colombia. He married into a close group of wealthy families who owned a sporting clothes factory, eighty retail stores, and the exclusive franchise for Levi-Strauss products in Colombia. Ackerman managed the retail stores and enjoyed an affluent lifestyle. One son became a doctor, another an accountant. Unfortunately, the families' wealth attracted the unwelcome attention of M-19, an urban guerilla organization engaged in kidnapping and extortion throughout Colombia. After Ackerman's family was threatened, they moved to Miami.

Ackerman hadn't been involved in drugs while in Colombia. Drawing on family resources, he arrived in Miami with enough money to buy a $500,000 house. He opened a clothing store where he began laundering drug money—exchanging checks for cash—for some of his best customers, one of whom introduced him to Jorge Lopez, then chief of the cartel in south Florida. Lopez invited him to come to work for the cartel. The two flew to Cali to meet with Miguel Rodriguez and Ackerman passed muster. Later asked why he had joined the cartel, Ackerman replied simply: "It was for the money." After their return to Miami, Ackerman was given cash, a Lexus, a cell phone, and a false birth certificate. Lopez directed Ackerman to set up a corporation, Southeast Agrotrade, ostensibly to receive imported vegetables. Shortly thereafter, Lopez was arrested and Ackerman succeeded him as cartel chief, only to be arrested himself while overseeing the shipment of frozen broccoli.

After his arrest, Ackerman was first represented by Robert Moore, a Miami criminal defense lawyer he had met previously through other cartel employees. Ackerman soon had questions about where Moore's loyalty lay. Moore brought Gonzalo Paz for a jail visit, leaving the room while Paz related the consequences of cooperating with the government. Moore had traveled to Cali to discuss fees for himself and other lawyers he had lined up to represent Ackerman's subordinates. Ackerman testified that Moore, upon his return, had conveyed a threat from Miguel: the cartel "would finish off my family, even the family dog, if I cooperated." Ackerman consulted with his family and decided to retain an independent lawyer.

Edward Shohat is an experienced criminal defense lawyer in Miami with a deserved reputation for integrity. He has represented high-profile clients, including Carlos Lehder, former head of the Medellin cartel. Shohat has been a writer and lecturer in law schools and criminal defense seminars through a twenty-five year career, and has served as a Director of the Dade County Bar Association. He agreed to represent Ackerman through trial for a flat fee of $250,000, plus $200,000 for any appeal, payment to be made by Ackerman's relatives.

Shohat reviewed the government's evidence and concluded that the case against Ackerman was "extremely strong." As he saw it, motions to suppress the evidence derived from wiretaps "were really the only chance we had." Despite a major effort by Shohat and the other defense lawyers, their motions to suppress were denied. Shohat then advised Ackerman that his chances of acquittal were poor, but Ackerman rejected the option of pleading guilty and went to trial with his former subordinates. Seeking to portray his client sympathetically as an expendable cog in a ruthless organization, Shohat called Ackerman to the witness stand to answer one question: "Can you tell the jury why you became involved in the cocaine business?" Ackerman's responded: "No, I can't tell the jury that because too many people will be killed." Moran (who was representing co-defendant Carlos Giron) approached Shohat and Ackerman at counsel table and asked: "Did you guys get permission to do that?"

Ackerman was convicted on six felony counts, each carrying a twenty-year sentence. At age fifty-eight, this meant he would die in prison unless his sentence were reduced in return for cooperating with the government. Cartel lawyers like Moran, Moore and Laguna advised against cooperation directly, or discouraged it by veiled threats of retaliation. Shohat discussed the pros and cons of cooperation with Ackerman "because as his attorney it was my responsibility to advise him as to all the options available to him." Although Ackerman would change his mind later on, he rejected the cooperation option when Shohat raised it. As Shohat saw it: "He was scared he would be killed. His brother was a doctor in Cali. His mother lived alone in Cali."

Miguel Rodriguez instructed Abbell to obtain exculpatory affidavits from Ackerman and other cartel employees charged following the broccoli seizure. Abbell gave Laguna the lead role in that project. Working from a sample obtained from Moran, Laguna prepared a draft affidavit for Ackerman that he gave to Abbell for review. Laguna testified: "Both Michael and I knew that the content of the affidavit was false. So I asked him, well, what is our responsibility about presenting a false affidavit to somebody for their signature? And Michael Abbell told me that our job as attorneys was not to worry about the content of the affidavit. It was just to draft it and if the person who was going to sign it was comfortable with the content, that was it." Abbell approved Laguna's draft and told him to draft identical affidavits for Ackerman's co-defendants.

Abbell visited Ackerman in jail, without Shohat's permission, to discuss the affidavit. He then telephoned Shohat, informing him that, contrary to Shohat's understanding with Ackerman's relatives, Miguel Rodriguez would be paying his fee. In return, Ackerman would be expected to sign an affidavit exculpating Miguel, the text of which was being faxed to him. Shohat rejected the idea of receiving payment from Miguel Rodriguez, telling Abbell the government would call it money laundering. Upon receiving the affidavit, he immediately realized it was false and telephoned Abbell. Shohat testified: "I was very angry. I told Mr. Abbell there was no way Harold Ackerman could sign that affidavit. That the affidavit was false. And that I thought he had crossed the line into obstruction of justice." Abbell became apologetic, stating that the affidavit was only intended for use in Colombia. Shohat questioned that limited purpose; if so, why was it written in English? He pointed out that if extradition were reinstated in Colombia (as it later was) bringing Miguel to the United States would be a high priority and exculpatory affidavits would be used by the defense in a federal court. He also told Abbell that such an affidavit "would be viewed as an effort to buy silence."

Shohat told Abbell to stay away from Ackerman and visited him in jail to urge him not to sign an affidavit. He explained that a false affidavit would undermine Ackerman's credibility with government prosecutors who might decide not to call him as a witness, costing him his only leverage for a reduced sentence. Concerned about his family's safety, Ackerman wanted to sign, but reluctantly agreed when Shohat threatened to withdraw as his counsel.

Abbell and Laguna flew to Cali to obtain Miguel's approval of draft affidavits before presenting them to Ackerman and his co-defendants for signature. Attached to the affidavits was a photograph of Miguel Rodriguez under which he was identified by name. Miguel was displeased to find his name directly linked to the photograph and Abbell removed the name from the photo attachment. Returning to Miami, Laguna again visited Ackerman and several co-defendants in jail and obtained their signatures. Laguna then flew back to Cali to present the finished products to Miguel Rodriguez. Miguel still was not satisfied. As Laguna testified: "The affidavits were deficient because the persons signing them did not put their right index fingerprints on the documents." Miguel directed Laguna to have them signed again. The affidavits were duly signed and then authenticated at the Colombian consulate in Miami.

Ackerman eventually signed a false affidavit, contrary to Shohat's advice and without telling him. Working both sides of the street, Ackerman began to cooperate with the government. Testifying at the trial, Ackerman estimated that he had informed on over forty cartel members and employees. In return, the government filed a motion to reduce his six twenty-year sentences. The court granted the motion and reduced Ackerman's sentence to less than ten years.

In August 1994, more than a year after the false affidavits had been procured, the sky began to fall on the cartel lawyers, and a cover-up ensued. Donald Ferguson telephoned Laguna to ask whether he had hard copies of the affidavits from Ackerman and other Cali cartel defendants. Laguna replied that copies were in their satellite office in Miami. Ferguson suggested that Laguna shred the affidavits to which Laguna responded: "That's a good idea." Laguna then called Abbell for approval of the shredding and Abbell concurred. Abbell told him that he intended to "delete" records related to Miguel Rodriguez from the Washington office files. Laguna shredded the affidavits in the Miami office about a week before federal agents arrived to search. The agents found plastic bags full of shredded affidavits in the office.

The government's direct case was supported by detailed witness testimony and extensive records. Defense attorneys for Moran and Abbell called a parade of witnesses to their good character, but no serious attempt was made to rebut the governments' cases with direct evidence. Neither Moran nor Abbell testified in his own defense. They must have realized that the government had made strong cases against them, so they had nothing to lose. Neither had a prior criminal record that might have been used to impeach his testimony, making their decisions to stand mute difficult to understand.

## Closings, Verdicts and Sentences

Prosecutor William Pearson made the initial closing argument for the government, first sketching the dimensions and gravity of the Cali cartel's activities. The United States is the world's biggest market for cocaine. Pearson compared cocaine to "a plague that came to our shores." Of the plague carriers, "you have heard about the biggest and the very best" at what they did. In its heyday, the Cali cartel imported some

4,000 kilos of cocaine a month, representing about $40 million American dollars going to the cartel in Colombia. (After the Cali cartel declined in the late 1990s, Mexican smugglers assumed a dominant position in the American market.)

Pearson focused on Miguel Rodriguez-Orejuela, the one who "called the shots." Miguel's most feared enemy was American law enforcement. Realizing it was inevitable that some of his employees would be arrested in the course of business, Miguel sought to prevent them from implicating him. Miguel needed someone to monitor cartel employees in American jails, to represent them and arrange support payments for families in exchange for their silence, and to threaten them with the consequences of cooperation. He couldn't leave Colombia and do those things himself without risking arrest. "So he had to get somebody to do that for him. He found lawyers. He used crooked lawyers for that purpose. It's obstruction of justice. It's money laundering. But it sure isn't the practice of law."

Holly Skolnick described her client, William Moran, as "a little different. He wears cowboy boots with three-piece suits. He is impatient, temperamental, and stubborn." But he "is a hell of a trial lawyer." She walked selectively through the evidence, suggesting, for example, that the $5,000 in cash Moran gave Senora Giron might not have been proceeds of drug trafficking, that it may have come from Miguel's chain of drug stores in Colombia. Skolnick contended that Moran couldn't have been in a conspiracy with the other cartel employees because they had different objectives: "The problem is the other folks in the conspiracy — the guys in the boats, the unloaders, the packagers — really wanted to import and distribute cocaine. Bill is a defense lawyer. He doesn't want the conspiracy to succeed. He wanted people to get arrested because that's how he got business." Of course, the conspiracy had to succeed much of the time if it were to provide Moran with a steady source of clients.

Henry Asbill and William Moffitt made closing arguments for Michael Abbell. Asbill did his best to blame everything on Francisco Laguna. According to Asbill, the false affidavits — the crux of the government's racketeering case — were obtained by Laguna in Miami where he went to escape Abbell's supervision. He claimed that Laguna was working for Miguel Rodriguez behind Abbell's back, and was paid under the table. Asbill told the jury: "Mr. Laguna is a total liar and perjurer." Moffitt supplied the rhetorical flourishes. He spoke of the country's "internal enemies" — Communists in the 20s, unions in the 30s, Japanese-

Americans in the 40s — "and now our enemies have become the people who walk in the courtroom and defend people accused of crime," meaning criminal defense lawyers like William Moran, Michael Abbell, Henry Asbill, and himself. Overzealous prosecutors in the war on drugs were, he contended, the real enemy.

Prosecutors Pearson and Ryan had the last word with the jury. Pearson spoke briefly, concentrating on the credibility of key witness Francisco Laguna, stressing that his testimony had been corroborated by a dozen witnesses. Countering Asbill's portrayal of Laguna as a loose cannon beyond his client's control, Pearson pointed to records of telephone calls between Washington and Miami. Abbell had spoken with Laguna several times daily—1,200 calls over fifteen months. Ryan addressed the necessity of using convicted cartel members as "cooperators" in order to reach higher-ups in a complex criminal organization. In recognition of that practical problem, the law authorizes prosecutors to plea bargain in exchange for useful testimony, to defer sentencing until after testimony, and to file a motion to reduce the sentence in exchange for solid information. While such testimony may be suspect standing alone—the cooperator has an incentive to lie to please the prosecutors—it can be credible when substantiated by other witnesses and documentary evidence, as it was in this case.

After listening to five lawyers deliver over eight hours of closing arguments, the jurors must have been tired. Judge Hoeveler followed by reading them seventy-six pages of instructions. Many were boilerplate instructions on the respective roles of the judge and the jurors, on reasonable doubt, and the weight to be given evidence. Others were more complex, for example, the definitions of "racketeering activity" and the "financial transactions" involved in money laundering. Acknowledging that his reading of instructions "gets kind of numbing at points," the judge promised to send copies to the jury room "so that you will have them to consult."

The jury found both Moran and Abbell guilty on two counts: a RICO conspiracy to import and sell cocaine through a pattern of racketeering activity, and conspiracy to launder narcotics proceeds. Thereafter, the defendants' lawyers filed motions for judgments of acquittal on both counts. Judge Hoeveler granted the defense motions as to the RICO conspiracy, explaining his reasons in a post-trial order. As the judge viewed it, "this case presents an important question: under what circumstances does a lawyer representing a client who is involved in illegal activity...become complicit with him? When, if ever, in representing him, does he become a part of the venture, a *partner* in the enterprise [italics by the judge]. Any set of facts which demonstrates a lesser connection with the enterprise may show some type of criminality but it will not provide the needed basis for a conspiracy conviction." The judge observed that the question is complicated "when an attorney engages in a representation with the same client over and over again—particularly when the charges against the client are of the same nature." But ongoing representation "by itself is not a crime."

Judge Hoeveler "found an absence of competent proof that the defendants either were asked to, expected to, or intended to join the conspiracy." Like other lawyers, Moran and Abbell regularly billed Miguel Rodriguez for services rendered, on an itemized basis. Both had other clients. Reviewing specific actions, the judge found no fault with their drafting affidavits exculpating Miguel—merely noting the government's contention that the affidavits were, to the lawyer's knowledge, false—or with making payments to arrested cartel employees and their families, payments the government contended were hush money. As a further indication that Moran and Abbell were "not involved in an agreement to pursue the same criminal objective," Judge Hoeveler cited a lack of profit sharing or "any participation in planning the various routes and methods of bringing in cocaine or laundering money." The judge let the guilty verdict for money laundering stand, noting that "what laundering was done was isolated and was in relatively small amounts, supporting the conclusion that [Moran and Abbell] were not part of the enterprise."

Both Moran and Abbell had been released on their own recognizance following their convictions. Moran had then fled to Mexico but he was apprehended and returned to Miami for sentencing. In June 1999, Judge Hoeveler sentenced both defendants for conspiring to launder drug money—Abbell to eighty-seven and Moran to sixty months imprisonment. Both defendants appealed, and the government cross-appealed Judge Hoeveler's grant of the motions to set aside the jury convictions for racketeering.

In November 2001, the United States Court of Appeals for the Eleventh Circuit affirmed the money-laundering convictions of both defendants and reinstated the jury convictions for racketeering. The court's opinion did not directly address Judge Hoeveler's narrow reading of the racketeering statutes, but rejection of his reasoning was clearly implied. The court held that an agreement to participate in a RICO conspiracy may be proved in different ways, including where "a defendant agreed personally to commit two predicate acts and therefore to participate in a single objective conspiracy"—such as the importation and sale of cocaine. The court had no difficulty concluding that the defendants' activities in money laundering and soliciting false affadavits, among other things, qualified as "predicate acts."

As this book went to press in March 2002, sentencing of both defendants on the reinstated racketeering convictions was expected to take place in May. In addition, Bar Counsel for the District of Columbia had moved before the District's Board on Professional Responsibility that Abbell be disbarred without a hearing on the basis of his racketeering conviction. That motion was pending.

Miguel Rodriguez and his brother Gilberto were arrested and imprisoned in Bogota in 1995, but according to DEA authorities they have continued to run their cocaine enterprise from behind bars. Under pressure from the United States, Colombia reinstated extradition in December 1997, but only for crimes committed after that date. In November 1999, Fernando Jose ("Fat Man") Flores, a crony of the Rodriguez brothers, became the second alleged drug smuggler to be extradited to this country. In a published interview, Flores stated: "With threats, psychological torture...I will sign whatever [U.S. officials] put in front of me so that they get what they want—the extradition of the Rodriguezes."

* * *

## Comments and Questions

1. "*Frozen Broccoli*" illustrates some of the perils of defending members of criminal organizations. How involved can the lawyer become before crossing the line from legitimate counseling to participation in the client's illegal activities? Model Rule 1.2(d) provides that a lawyer "shall not counsel a client to engage, or assist a client, in conduct that the lawyer knows is criminal or fraudulent." He may, however, "discuss the legal consequences of any proposed course of conduct..." The drafters' notes to the rule show that these distinctions are not always easy to draw. Since Abbell and Moran were being prosecuted criminally, the Model Rules were not directly implicated, but the evidence could have formed the basis for disciplinary action.

Did Abbell and Moran cross the line and "assist" the Cali cartel in its drug operation? Abbell clearly did so when he manufactured false evidence and filed it in federal court in his unsuccessful effort to defeat the government's forfeiture claim against Santacruz Londono's drug proceeds. Likewise, Moran was "assisting" when he gave $5,000 in cash to Senora Giron to help her leave the country. Assistance to criminal activity was perhaps less clearly involved in their procuring of false affidavits. Was Frank Jackson correct in saying that procuring a "not entirely accurate" affidavit would be harmless if it would only be used in Colombia? Do you agree with lawyer Edward Shohat that procuring false affidavits might involve obstruction of justice if they were eventually used as defense evidence in a prosecution of Miguel Rodriguez in the United States? Isn't that result speculative because the false affidavits were procured when there was no extradition treaty with Colombia? Assume that the affidavits would never be used in any court. Would Moran and Abbell's involvement in procuring them nevertheless assist the Cali cartel in some realistic sense? In that regard, what would be the likely reaction of an incarcerated cartel employee when he is asked to sign a false affidavit stating that he does not know Miguel Rodriguez? Should the knowing procurement by a lawyer of a false affidavit, even if it never left the lawyer's file, be grounds for disciplinary action? See Model Rule 8.4(c), "Misconduct," making it "professional misconduct for a lawyer to...engage in conduct involving dishonesty, fraud, deceit, or misrepresentation."

Incarcerated cartel employees got the message in multiple ways—through Abbell, Moran, and others—that they were to keep silent in exchange for payment of their legal fees and support for their families. An article in *The American Lawyer* about an unsuccessful federal prosecution of a San Francisco criminal defense lawyer reports that the indictment included "discouraging cooperation with the government" as a form of obstruction of justice. *See* 18 U.S.C. 1512. The article goes on to state, however, that "many premier defense lawyers consider it a badge of honor to keep their clients from becoming informers." Recall that Edward Shohat, the criminal defense lawyer who represented Harold Ackerman, took a different view. Shohat discussed with Ackerman the pros and cons of cooperation with the government in exchange for lenient treatment "because, as his attorney, it was my responsibility to advise him as to all the options available to him." Which approach do you agree with—the premier defense lawyers' or Shohat's? Could you defend the ethics of a lawyer who discouraged her client from cooperating in the honest, but mistaken, belief that her client would be acquitted? Compare Moran's representation of Carlos Giron whom he urged not to cooperate when his conviction was a near certainty.

Prohibited "assistance" under Model Rule 1.2(d) is similar in concept to the RICO conspiracy charges against Abbell and Moran which were dismissed by Judge Hoeveler. According to the judge, a RICO conspirator must become a conscious "partner" in the illegal enterprise. Judge Hoeveler "found an absence of competent proof that the defendants either were asked to, expected to, or intended to join the conspiracy. Like other lawyers, Moran and Abbell regularly billed Miguel Rodriguez for services rendered, on an itemized basis." They had no profit sharing agreement with the cartel. Nor had they participated "in planning the various routes and methods of bringing in cocaine or laundering money." Given the logic of his ruling, would Judge Hoeveler have upheld the jury's RICO convictions if Abbell and Moran had helped to weigh and package cocaine in addition to filing pleadings?

There appears to be a disconnect between the mass of evidence of obstruction of justice by Abbell and Moran—much more in the 8,000-page record than can be related here—and the conviction for the comparatively minor offense of money laundering. The government might have made a tactical error in alleging obstructions as part of its umbrella RICO counts rather than as separate offenses. Or Judge Hoeveler's ruling may simply reflect the reluctance of one lawyer to send other lawyers to prison, perhaps for life. Some answers to these questions may come in the government's pending appeal of the ruling dismissing the RICO counts.

2. It is not uncommon for criminal organizations to pay lawyers to represent arrested members. Such payments—viewed as a routine cost of doing business—are not, in and of themselves, unethical for lawyers to receive, but they often raise conflict-of-interest questions. Model Rule 1.8(f) provides that a lawyer shall not accept compensation for representing a client from one other than the client unless: (1) the client consents, (2) there is no interference with the lawyer's independent judgment or the lawyer-client relationship, and (3) client information is protected as required by Rule 1.6. Apart from the main concern—compromising the lawyer's independence—payments, particularly large cash payments, may represent proceeds from the criminal enterprise, making the lawyer vulnerable to a charge of money laundering.

Perhaps the clearest indication of independence and its lack in *Frozen Broccoli* occurred when Shohat called Ackerman to the stand

and asked him one question—why had he become involved in the co-caine business. Ackerman answered: "No, I can't tell the jury that be-cause too many people will be killed." The question and answer obvi-ously had been rehearsed, and were calculated to paint Ackerman as a victim of coercion and worthy of some sympathy, while at the same time portraying Miguel Rodriguez as a murderer. Shohat was not be-holden to Miguel, so he was free to elicit that testimony. Recall that Moran was representing another cartel defendant in the same case and being paid by Miguel. Moran turned to Shohat and asked him: "Did you guys get permission to do that?"

The lack of independence demonstrated by Abbell and Moran by acting in the interest of their source of payment, and contrary to the in-terests of their nominal clients, would have made an unusually strong case for violation of Model Rule 1.8(f). In other situations where puta-tive criminal organizations pay the legal fees of their employees, the lawyer may demand independence and the organization may (more or less) grant it. It seems inevitable, however, that such fee-payment arrangements would generate strong pressure for inappropriate involve-ment by the payor. Should Rule 1.8(f) be enforced strictly against the criminal defense bar? Would a case-by-case, rule of reason approach be preferable? Would it be possible to enforce the rule consistently?

3. Recall that Abbell visited Shohat's incarcerated client, Ackerman, about signing a false affidavit, without first obtaining Shohat's permis-sion. Thereafter, Shohat told Abbell and Laguna to stay away from Ack-erman, and he urged Ackerman not to sign a false affidavit. Ignoring Shohat's directive, Laguna revisited Ackerman with a false affidavit which Ackerman signed, without telling Shohat. Model Rule 4.2 pro-vides that "in representing a client, a lawyer shall not communicate about the subject of the representation with a person the lawyer knows to be represented by another lawyer in the matter" without the other lawyer's permission. Ackerman was a defendant in a criminal prosecu-tion. The rule would have applied to non-consensual contacts with Ack-erman by federal prosecutors because they were "representing a client" (the United States) in the same "matter." Would this rule have applied to Abbell and Laguna's visits to Ackerman? If not, should a similar rule apply in those circumstances?

4. Edward Shohat charged $250,000 for defending Ackerman at trial, and another $200,000 for any appeal. Frank Jackson charged $290,000

for defending Naranjo at trial. Joel Rosenthal charged $130,00 for hiring Jackson, visiting Naranjo's family in Colombia (incident to other business), and some legal research. According to Model Rule 1.5, "Fees," a lawyer's fee shall be "reasonable," subject to a non-exclusive list of pertinent factors. Applying the listed factors, are these fees reasonable? Those factors do not include the depth of the client's (or his employer's) pocket, or the seriousness of his plight (here, likely life imprisonment). Do those factors make these fees reasonable? Bear in mind that the rule does not allow contingent fees and that it is the practice of criminal defense lawyers to collect their fees up front. Unless set by statute or the court, is there any real limit on fees lawyers can charge their clients?

* * *

The author strove for objectivity in telling the stories in this book. Neverthe less, a pro-prosecution bias surfaced in this chapter. The following letter to the author from criminal defense lawyer John Villa provides another perspective and better balance.

LAW OFFICES

## WILLIAMS & CONNOLLY LLP

725 TWELFTH STREET, N.W.

WASHINGTON, D. C. 20005-5901

(202) 434-5000

JOHN K. VILLA
(202) 434-5117
FAX (202) 434-5705
jvilla@wc.com

EDWARD BENNETT WILLIAMS (1920-1988)
PAUL R. CONNOLLY (1922-1978)

September 26, 2000

Mr. James L. Kelley
217 Spring Avenue
Takoma Park, Maryland 20912

Dear Jim:

I have reviewed your chapter. I have also spoken to people with personal knowledge of Abell and to a lesser extent, Moran. Abell was not a criminal defense lawyer and was not viewed as a particularly cunning person. Let me make a few observations.

First and most importantly, you seem to accept the drug members' testimony that they were in effect victims. While the verdict was against Abell and Moran, one must recognize the possibility that the witnesses – confessed narcotics traffickers, money launders, perjurers and probably much worse – embellished their accounts to curry favor with the prosecutors who were now the people that made the life-and-death decision for them and their families in the witness protection program. In fact, the "clients" had a compelling incentive to provide false affidavits totally apart from the alleged pressure that their lawyers placed on them – and that incentive was to protect themselves and their families. This motivation would, no doubt, exist irrespective of who their lawyer was.

Second, I am somewhat confused about the significance of the affidavits. Since they are clearly hearsay, they would presumably not be admissible in any American court. So is their significance that they could be used to impeach the "clients" if they turned on Miguel? Is it an insurance policy that these people will not turn or at least a basis for impeachment if they do?

Third, I think you demonize the criminal defense lawyer who is not pro-plea bargain. In fact, most successful criminal defense lawyers understand that they must be willing to try cases to have credibility with prosecutors and achieve favorable deals. Those who plead all clients degrade the profession. The fact is that the lawyer has no obligation to push his client toward a plea bargain – only to evaluate honestly the risk of conviction. In fact, most clients cling to irrational beliefs that they will be acquitted or will receive light sentences. Few will trade

WILLIAMS & CONNOLLY LLP

Mr. James Kelley
September 26, 2000
Page 2

100% certainty of a stiff sentence for some uncertain chance of a very harsh
sentence. It is often the criminal defense lawyer who pushes the client to see
reality. There is certainly no ethical or legal obligation to take that extra step.
Once they are convicted, however, it is a different matter. Now they heap criticism
on their lawyer.

    I am surprised that you do not discuss the single most important
impact of this case to the Florida bar – the chilling effect that prosecutions like this
can have on the defense bar. This case was brought by their courtroom adversaries.
Once Abell and Moran's files were seized and they were indicted, they were
through. They would be on the defensive for years; all their clients would leave
them; and professional death would be all but assured – conviction or acquittal.
Does this deter zealous advocacy by the criminal defense bar in Miami – the
jurisdiction that features more drug cases than anywhere else? Yes.

    In the final analysis, narcotics traffickers have the right to counsel
under the Sixth Amendment. Your discussion of Rule 1.8 should include
recognition that it is routine, and in many situations required by law, for one person
to pay for the criminal defense of another. Corporate indemnity provisions
permitted, and in some situations required, by law allow a corporation to advance
legal fees to its corporate directors, officers, employees and agents in criminal cases
involving corporate misconduct. Is this presumptively unethical or obstruction?

    Your analysis of Judge Hoeveler's ruling on the narcotics conviction
seems wrong on the law. Under Falcone and other aiding and abetting cases,
individuals become part of the enterprise by sharing in the profits. Receiving legal
fees, even generous ones, would not seem to qualify. The ruling seems right.

    Why do you criticize Abell and Moran for not testifying? If you believe
their guilt – as you clearly do – then their testimony would either be perjurious or
incriminating. Assuming they are guilty of some offense, the only reasonable tack
may have been silence. Besides, prosecutors often have great evidence that they
can't use on direct but is usable as impeachment. By keeping the client off the
stand, the defense attorney can outfox a prosecutor. Finally, a lawyer may not be a
good witness before a Miami jury. Maybe the character witnesses portrayed him
better than he could have presented himself.

WILLIAMS & CONNOLLY LLP

Mr. James Kelley
September 26, 2000
Page 3

The notion that obstruction of justice is less severe than money laundering is contrary to the statutory maxima and to every instinct of the defense lawyer.

What is missing here is a recognition that there is a slippery slope and that allowing your adversary to push you down that slope can inhibit your zealous advocacy. This is very dangerous stuff.

Call if you have questions.

Best regards,

John K. Villa

# Chapter 3

# Breaking Up Is Hard To Do

"Were you aware that on or about July 16, 1992 your company's law firm was considering whether Admiral Murphy could divert business to a new company, allowing your company to wither?

No. Why would I think that? They were our lawyers."

— Colloquy between examining attorney and
Margot Bester of Murphy & Demory,
in *Murphy & Demory v. Admiral Murphy.*

Murphy & Demory, Ltd., a Washington, D.C. public relations firm, was founded in 1987 by Daniel Murphy, a former Admiral and Deputy Director of the Central Intelligence Agency, and Will Demory, a lawyer and economist. The firm prospered, generating $2.5 million in revenues in 1991, from which the Admiral (as he was called) and Demory took home $340,000 apiece. The Admiral as the rainmaker while Demory ran the office seemed to be a winning formula. Unfortunately, the firm's success was accompanied by growing tensions between the two owners over the kinds of business they should cultivate, over their respective roles, and—from the Admiral's perspective—over Demory's performance. With each owning fifty percent of the company's stock, neither was in a position to assert control. Power was also shared through corporate offices, with the Admiral as chairman of the board and Demory the CEO.

Demory responded to a worsening situation by standing apart and keeping his own counsel. The Admiral took a more aggressive approach. Without consulting Demory, he began to explore ways he might take over the firm, or, failing that, start his own firm, taking along the clients he had brought in. This chapter tells the story of how Murphy & Demory, Ltd. ("M&D") was broken up, leading to court judgments against the Admiral and Pillsbury, Madison & Sutro—M&D's corporate counsel which took sides with the Admiral.

In June 1992, the Admiral met with Deanne Siemer, a partner in the Washington office of Pillsbury, Madison & Sutro, a national law firm based in San Francisco. The Admiral's relationship with Siemer went back to 1977 when he was Deputy Undersecretary of Defense for Policy and Siemer, not yet forty, was General Counsel of the Defense Department. He had continued to seek her advice from time to time after leaving Defense. Seimer's work for M&D had begun shortly after the firm was founded in 1987 and Siemer was a partner at Wilmer, Cutler & Pickering. She continued to represent M&D on a variety of matters after she moved to the Pillsbury firm in 1990. She also worked for the Admiral on personal matters, like his will, and on matters involving both personal and firm interests which were not readily separable. However, all Pillsbury bills, whether related to M&D or the Admiral, were sent to and paid by M&D.

After their meeting, Siemer directed Frazer Fiveash, an associate, to do research and write a memorandum on the law governing dissolution of Virginia corporations, the state in which M&D was incorporated. In July, Siemer asked Fiveash for a memorandum concerning whether the Admiral would have the right to divert business from M&D to a new company to be controlled by him alone, allowing M&D to "wither." Fiveash expressed concern about a conflict of interest, but did as she was told. Siemer reviewed the Fiveash memoranda and conveyed their substance to the Admiral by phone. In August, another young associate was assigned to draft a complaint for the judicial dissolution of M&D, with the Admiral as plaintiff and M&D as defendant. Demory was to learn of the memoranda and complaint only after M&D sued the Admiral.

The Admiral and Demory had always operated their firm informally, more like a partnership than a corporation. Board meetings had been viewed as a formality, with no real business transacted. By this time, however, the Admiral had learned enough corporate law from Deanne Siemer to know that a vote of the board of directors could shift control to him, despite the equal shareholdings of himself and Demory. There were three board members: the Admiral, Demory, and Margot Bester, a lawyer who had been with the firm from the beginning. The Admiral believed that if he could persuade Bester to join forces with him, together they could activate a dormant board and vote effective control to him.

Apparently assuming that the husband could control the wife, in late August the Admiral directed Jeff Grieco, an M&D employee, to meet with Bester's husband, Bruce Markowitz. Grieco immediately phoned Markowitz and arranged an appointment at his law office for later that day. As Grieco described his mission: "The Admiral asked me to get a pulse from Bruce as to what Bruce thought Margot would want to do" if the Admiral "had to restructure the firm or start a new company."

Grieco and Markowitz knew one another socially. Both were avid Buffalo Bills fans, the kind who debate the merits of draft choices. Following pleasantries of the "how 'bout them Bills" sort, Grieco outlined the Admiral's concerns about M&D and his plans for either taking control or leaving. Grieco charged Demory with various faults and transgressions, personal and professional: Demory was involved in illegal transactions with Lybia and Iraq; he had opened foreign bank accounts to evade income taxes; he wasn't developing business for M&D and was undermining clients of others to win them over to himself. As if that weren't enough, Grieco claimed that Demory was on anti-depressant medication.

Markowitz thought Grieco had come to him "to convince me to persuade Margot to leave Will [Demory] and join the Admiral in a new firm and to poison my mind against Demory." Markowitz was "extremely concerned and upset" by Grieco's statements and, believing his wife might be in professional jeopardy, phoned her right after Grieco left. She told him Grieco's charges were baseless and that she would side with Demory in any struggle for control. In hindsight, Markowitz found it "rather humorous that [Grieco] thought I would have that kind of influence over her. She's a lawyer and her office was two doors down from the Admiral's. All he had to do was ask her himself."

Frances Gray was the office manager at M&D during the breakup. Several days before the Admiral resigned, Grieco asked Gray to copy the contents of the safe. Gray made the requested copies—including client contracts, income tax returns, balance sheets, income statements, and current bank and money market balances—and sent them by messenger to the Pillsbury firm, as Grieco had requested. After the breakup, Gray had to decide whether to stay with M&D or join the Admiral's new company. It was "one of the hardest decisions I've ever had to make, but I just didn't think Will was going to be viable."

As the break-up became imminent, the legal work involved in making it happen fell primarily to Keith Mendelson. Mendelson had come to Pillsbury, Madison & Sutro as an associate in 1984. He was promoted to "senior counsel" in 1991 and was under consideration for partner in August 1992 when Siemer drew him into the problems at M&D. Mendelson first became involved on Friday, August 28, when he was called into meetings with other Pillsbury lawyers, Grieco and another M&D employee, ostensibly for his expertise in corporate law. Mendelson's notes included the statement that he was "uncomfortable that what we were trying to do was find out information about a client of ours," but he was not uncomfortable enough to decline becoming involved. After that meeting, Siemer asked Mendelson to accompany her to talk with Demory the next day in response to the Admiral's request.

Siemer and Mendelson met with Demory at M&D the next morning, a Saturday. As Mendelson recalled the meeting, Siemer opened on a conciliatory note, saying they were there to "help you guys work out your problems." At that point, Mendelson recalled that Demory "looked like he was going to cry" as he said: "Deanne, I can't tell you how happy I am that you are taking that approach." But as the meeting progressed, Demory's answers to Siemer's questions (according to Mendelson) became evasive and defensive. Siemer closed the meeting by urging Demory to meet with the Admiral over the weekend to "see if they could sort things out."

Demory remembered the meeting with Siemer and Mendelson somewhat differently. Siemer had begun by saying that she was representing M&D, neither Demory nor the Admiral individually. The meeting proceeded on a cordial note with general discussion of company business and prospects. Siemer went on to comment, however, that she had met with the Admiral several times in the past year to discuss "restructuring" or breaking up M&D, a disclosure which "came as pretty much of a shock" to Demory. After that, the tone of the meeting changed. Demory sensed that he was being interrogated, that Siemer was becoming accusatory and implying he might be involved in illegal dealings.

After Siemer and Mendelson left his office, Demory phoned Margot Bester to report what had been said and his impression that Siemer was acting at the Admiral's direction. Putting that meeting together with what Grieco, the Admiral's agent, had said to Bester's husband earlier that week, Demory and Bester decided to fire the Pillsbury firm and hire new corporate counsel. They called John Dowd of the Washington firm of Akin, Gump, Strauss, Hauer & Feld, still on Saturday morning. Dowd then called Siemer's office and left a message informing her of his firm's representation and that Demory would not meet with the Admiral over the weekend. Siemer interpreted Dowd's message to mean that he was representing Demory individually. As far as she was concerned, the Pillsbury firm still represented both M&D and the Admiral.

That afternoon, Mendelson helped the Admiral draft a letter to Demory proposing that he be given control of M&D. The letter was delivered by messenger and Demory found it on his front stoop on Sunday morning. In the meantime, the Admiral renewed his efforts to gain the support of Margot Bester for his takeover proposal. He phoned her and she agreed, reluctantly, to meet with Mendelson at her home. Mendelson went to Bester's home in Potomac, Maryland on Sunday around noon. Bester's husband, Bruce Markowitz, joined the discussion. Mendelson began by saying he was there as counsel for M&D, not for the Admiral personally. That got him a cool reception. Bester told him that, in her view, the Pillsbury firm had a conflict of interest and that, as a director of M&D, she did not acquiesce to his presence in their home as counsel for the firm. Markowitz, an experienced corporate bankruptcy lawyer who dealt with conflict of interest problems routinely, added his opinion that the Pillsbury firm "had a blatant conflict." Markowitz later testified: "I found that outrageous. I couldn't believe that this was happening in my living room. It was something you learn about in law school, Ethics 101." The meeting went nowhere, and Mendelson departed.

Mendelson had expressed concerns about a conflict of interest to Siemer before his Sunday meeting with Bester. Demory was strongly opposed to the Admiral's takeover plan, and he did own half of M&D and was its CEO. Immediately after leaving Bester's home, Mendelson called Siemer from a phone booth to restate his concerns. She reassured him that they didn't have a conflict. Siemer flew to California that afternoon on other business and later to Europe, leaving Mendelson to cope with a rapidly unraveling situation.

That Sunday afternoon, Demory drove to the Admiral's home and handed him a letter rejecting the Admiral's restructuring proposal. The two sat at the kitchen table while the Admiral read the letter. There was no discussion and Demory departed to fax a letter to Siemer firing the Pillsbury firm as counsel to M&D. When the Admiral learned of that the next day, he purported to rehire the firm, even though that authority was vested in Demory as CEO.

The Admiral, a former commander of the Sixth Fleet, would later refer to that Monday as "D Day." In the morning, accompanied by Mendelson and armed with a statement Mendelson had written for him, he met with the M&D employees. He stated that he and Demory "have drifted apart over the last three months." The Admiral expressed regret for having "delegated too much of the management" but asserted that he "cannot accept this situation any longer." He outlined his proposal to transfer a controlling stock interest and management authority to himself, the proposal Demory had rejected the day before. The Admiral expressed his willingness to "try to work things out" with Demory. Failing that, however, he would "seek to dissolve M&D and form a new company of my own." And if that were to happen, all the employees would be invited to join his new company.

Over the next three days, the Admiral and Demory met several times in fruitless attempts to resolve their differences. Then on September 4, Demory fired Grieco, the Admiral's factotum, without consulting the Admiral. Grieco went directly to the Admiral who rehired him on the spot. Demory took the position that "in light of what Mr. Grieco has done over the preceding week or so," it was necessary to fire him before there could be "constructive discussions." But as the Admiral saw the firing of Grieco: "That's a deal breaker; that's the end of it."

The board of directors was to meet on the afternoon of September 9. Mendelson met with the Admiral, Grieco, and several other employees in the morning to review their resignations and letters to M&D clients soliciting their business for the new company. Mendelson also drafted a resignation letter and a statement for the Admiral to deliver at the board meeting. Before the meeting, Mendelson discussed his conflict-of-interest concerns once again with another Pillsbury lawyer. As he recalled: "I wanted to be sure in my own mind what capacity I was going in. It was pretty clear by that time that Admiral Murphy was our client and our only client."

The board meeting was brief, its outcome foreordained. The Admiral brought the meeting to order and moved that M&D be "voluntarily dissolved." As expected, that motion failed for want of a second. The Admiral then submitted his letter of resignation, along with the resignations of several employees who moved out that afternoon to new office space in the same building. The next day, articles of incorporation for Murphy & Associates were duly filed in Richmond.

Margot Bester stayed with M&D. She described the breakup as "devastating." Within a short time, "the employees left, the majority of the clients left, which really affected our income stream. That in turn affected our ability to hire new people who could bring in new business."

Making a bad situation worse, M&D had recently entered into a lease for new space which called for payments of $1.5 million over seven years. The Admiral's new firm could have made effective use of that space, but the Admiral declined to assume the lease.

A few months after the breakup, M&D sued the Admiral, Siemer, Mendelson, and Pillsbury, Madison & Sutro in the Circuit Court for Fairfax County, Virginia. The complaint alleged breach of contract and violation of fiduciary duty by the Admiral and legal malpractice by Siemer, Mendelson, and the Pillsbury firm. The Akin, Gump firm represented M&D. The Pillsbury firm hired another firm to defend it against the malpractice claim. The Admiral opted for local representation, possibly on the theory—mistaken, as it turned out—that Fairfax lawyers would connect better with a Fairfax County judge. Following a period of discovery, the case went to trial on April 25, 1994 before Judge Jane Roush, sitting without a jury. The trial lasted six days; fifteen witnesses testified; some four hundred exhibits were offered in evidence.

Winston Churchill once summoned a waiter, saying: "Pray remove this pudding. It has no theme." A court case, like a pudding, needs a theme, a compelling message to shape the facts and impress the judge with the justice of your cause. The plaintiffs would speak of betrayal. They were the innocent victims of a treacherous scheme. The Admiral, assisted by the Pillsbury lawyers, destroyed the firm he and Demory had worked so hard to build. For their part, the Admiral's lawyers would portray him as the practical businessman, the one who had sought a constructive compromise, the reasonable one. It was Demory, they said, who had shown a "remarkable lack of common sense," who had "dropped a bomb on himself" and M&D.

As the plaintiff, M&D had the burden of proving that the Pillsbury firm had deviated from the standard of care—the basis of a legal malpractice claim. Stated another way, the issue was whether the firm had acted like hypothetical "reasonable lawyers" would have acted under similar circumstances? And in a case like this, where rules of legal ethics prescribe conduct in some detail, those rules may go far in determining the standard of care.

M&D relied on its expert witness, David Epstein, to establish the standard of care and to prove that Siemer and Mendelson had breached it. Epstein's qualifications were impressive. A graduate of Harvard Law School, he was a founding member of the District of Columbia's Board of Professional Responsibility. He had taught professional responsibility at the Georgetown University Law Center and had served as an Assistant United States Attorney before entering private practice. He had represented lawyers charged with ethics violations and served as an expert witness in cases involving professional misconduct.

Epstein's testimony was elicited by hypothetical questions incorporating the basic facts of the plaintiff's case. He was asked to assume that the Pillsbury firm had an attorney-client relationship with M&D when the Admiral went to Siemer for advice on restructuring or leaving the firm; that the Pillsbury lawyers provided the Admiral with the requested advice; that neither the Admiral nor the lawyers disclosed to M&D that the Pillsbury firm was working for the Admiral; and that they assisted him in carrying out a strategy to break up the firm.

The principle is embedded in Western culture: "No man can serve two masters" (*Bible*, Matthew, 6:24). "Whose bread I eat, his song I sing" (German proverb). Conflicts of interest are among the most pervasive, difficult, and consequential problems faced by lawyers. The Model Rules of Professional Conduct, in force in Maryland and over forty other jurisdictions, contain no fewer than eight conflict-of-interest rules, far more attention than the Model Rules devote to any other topic.

All parties agreed that the law of the District of Columbia, where most of Pillsbury's work for the Admiral had been done, would govern the malpractice issue. Epstein cited Rule 1.7 of the District of Columbia's Rules of Professional Conduct—adapted from the ABA's Model Rule—as the best evidence of the applicable standard of care. That rule prohibits simultaneous representation of two clients whose interests are "adverse"—the classic, direct conflict of interest. Textbook examples include the lawyer who represents both husband and wife in a divorce, or both buyer and seller in a real estate sale—situations where it's impossible to fully represent one side without compromising the other.

In Epstein's opinion, when Admiral Murphy set out to explore a takeover his objective was adverse to M&D—a corporate entity represented by its CEO and its board of directors. Epstein reasoned: "Once the third party [the Admiral] starts moving off in a direction that is serving only his interests, and the CEO of the corporation [Demory] and the board are not kept informed of that divergence, the law firm should advise the president and the board that there's a conflict." Unless both sides then consent to its continued participation, the law firm should then withdraw from the matter altogether, leaving both sides free to retain separate counsel.

Here, the conflict should have been apparent back in June, when Siemer assigned Fiveash to research the Admiral's options without telling Demory. According to Epstein, the Pillsbury firm's failure to withdraw at that point began a continuing violation of the rule, until the firm was fired in late August. And even if the situation in June were viewed as not involving a present conflict, the lawyer is expected to look ahead and see that—as Judge Roush expressed it—"this situation is fraught with potential adversity."

After Demory fired the Pillsbury firm and hired Akin, Gump, Pillsbury ceased to be in violation of Rule 1.7 because that rule applies only to *present* clients. However, Pillsbury went on to violate a separate conflict-of-interest rule by continuing to represent the Admiral against its *former* client, M&D. The District of Columbia's ethics rules prohibit a lawyer from switching sides during a controversy, unless the former client consents. According to Epstein, the rule is aimed at the law firm that switches clients after learning confidential information from the former client—information that may now be used against it. Pillsbury had obtained a wealth of inside information about the company while claiming to represent M&D and secretly helping the Admiral to break it up. In addition to violating the Rules of Professional Conduct, Epstein pointed to the common-law principle—a precursor of more recent rules of ethics—that a fiduciary (a lawyer or a trustee, for example) owes a duty of "undivided devotion and attention" to the client. In Epstein's opinion, the Pillsbury firm had violated that principle by covertly assisting the Admiral against its own client.

Counsel for the Pillsbury lawyers didn't call an expert witness of their own to controvert Epstein's opinions. It fell to Deanne Siemer to convince the judge that the Pillsbury lawyers, following her lead, had not committed malpractice. Siemer was a veteran trial lawyer with an abrasive manner. During her years at Wilmer, Cutler & Pickering and later at the Pillsbury firm, she was widely respected but disliked by some opposing counsel. Exceptionally gifted, energetic and ambitious, she had written a book, *Understanding Modern Ethical Standards*, for the National Institute of Trial Advocacy, of which she was chair-elect at the time of trial. Siemer might well have qualified as an expert on legal ethics in a case in which she wasn't herself a defendant.

Siemer began by describing herself as the Admiral's long-time lawyer, downplaying her work for M&D as "discrete matters" and suggesting that there was no lawyer-client relationship between the Pillsbury firm and M&D when the Admiral began to explore abandoning ship. It was shown, however, that Siemer had done significant work for M&D on numerous occasions and that Demory and Bester considered the Pillsbury firm to be counsel for their company. In any event, Epstein laid that question to rest when he testified that the comparative duration of two concurrent representations was irrelevant—a conflict would remain "if you've been representing one client for fifty years and a second one for three weeks."

Siemer testified that she had become aware of a possible conflict of interest problem when the Admiral had asked her about restructuring M&D in June 1992, and again in July when she asked Fiveash to look at diverting business to a new corporation, allowing M&D, in Siemer's words, "to wither." As Siemer had seen it then: "I had been asked to provide information. It was my judgment that [it was] in Admiral Murphy's interest he should receive correct information, then he knows what to do, and he'll act correctly. It was [also] in the corporation's interest that he receive accurate information....They had the same interest." Seemingly incredulous, counsel asked Siemer: "You didn't possibly think, did you, that the corporation had an interest in having its business diverted elsewhere and it withering up?" Unfazed, Siemer responded: "That wasn't the question that was asked. Whatever information needed to be delivered to Dan Murphy so that he could make a decision, that was in the corporation's interest." As long as the Admiral hadn't made a final decision to leave, she thought it proper to assist him, without informing Demory—even to the point of preparing a formal complaint for dissolution of M&D which she termed "a housekeeping matter."

Siemer didn't recall considering the conflict of interest issue again until after her somewhat confrontational meeting with Demory on August 28—a meeting she had arranged at the Admiral's request but in which she claimed to be representing M&D. By that time the Admiral, with Mendelson's help, was drafting his restructuring proposal and Grieco was meeting with Pillsbury lawyers to work out the details of setting up a new firm. In this advanced stage of the Admiral's plans, Siemer discussed the conflicts issue with Mendelson and other Pillsbury lawyers. Nothing had happened to that point to change her mind. "We thought it was really quite clear there was not a conflict," adding, however: "I made the judgment."

Mendelson hadn't found Siemer's judgment completely reassuring. On September 1, after Demory had fired the Pillsbury firm but it was still representing the Admiral, Mendelson telephoned Ben Vandegrift in Sweden. Vandegrift was Mendelson's supervisor and head of the corporate group in the Washington office. Mendelson had come to recognize that they were dealing with "a thorny, hard issue" and he wanted to get Vandegrift's judgment on it. Mendelson described the facts to Vandegrift who concluded that they didn't present a problem. Vandegrift added that "ultimately, the partner in charge [Siemer] has to make that decision." Mendelson also sought out George Sugiyama, a member of the firm's professional responsibility committee. Sugiyama had acknowledged that it was a "tough call" but he, too, saw it as Siemer's decision.

Judge Roush asked Epstein whether there are distinctions in the potential malpractice liability of a partner like Siemer, compared to Mendelson, the senior counsel, and to associates. The judge expressed particular concern about the exposure of a young associate like Fraser Fiveash. "She's raised the issue and she's been overruled and she's a year and a half out of law school." Under the District's Rule 5.2 subordinate lawyers are bound by the rules "notwithstanding that the lawyer acted at the direction of another person." Epstein responded: "Today is the funeral of former President Nixon [which recalls] a situation where many people were doing what they were asked to do, but knew that it was wrong, and they got into a lot of difficulty and were disbarred for following orders." Subordinate lawyers may avoid responsibility only if they acted " in accordance with a supervisory lawyer's "reasonable" resolution of an "arguable" question of professional duty. In Epstein's opinion, Siemer's resolution of the question had not been reasonable, nor had the question itself been arguable.

The plaintiffs called a certified public accountant with extensive experience in business valuations in support of their claim of damages. Using alternative methods, the accountant came up with pre-breakup values ranging between $1.5 and $2.5 million. He testified that after the break-up M&D's assets exceeded its liabilities and therefore its worth was $0.

Judge Roush rendered her decision from the bench in June 1994, about a month after the trial ended. She found that, prior to his resignation on September 9, the Admiral had breached his employment contract with M&D "by devoting his energies to activities other than those in the corporation's best interest." Among other things, the Admiral had formed a new company "whose primary purpose is to offer consulting services in direct competition with M&D" and induced its employees to leave and join his new company. She assessed compensatory damages of $1 million against the Admiral for breach of contract.

The judge also found that the Admiral had breached his fiduciary duty as an officer and director of M&D. She acknowledged that "some amount of pre-departure planning is permissible. A fiduciary need not wait until he is out in the street until he looks for other work." She concluded, however, that Admiral Murphy's "preresignation planning crossed the line by a considerable amount into impermissible acts of disloyalty to M&D." Before embarking on that course, he "should have disclosed his intentions or resigned to form his new company."

Judge Roush turned to the malpractice claim against Siemer, Mendelson, and the Pillsbury firm. She ruled that the Pillsbury defendants had committed malpractice at every stage of their involvement with the Admiral in the breakup of M&D, listing numerous specifics, among them:

- by accepting representation of the Admiral in his efforts to take control of M&D or to form a new corporation, before resigning from M&D;
- by simultaneously representing the Admiral in matters adverse to their client M&D without disclosing the dual representation;
- by meeting with director Margot Bester to enlist her support in the Admiral's takeover plans;
- by inducing M&D employees to resign and to join Murphy & Associates;
- by drafting the Admiral's restructuring proposal;
- by drafting letters for M&D clients terminating their relationships and directing that their files be sent to Murphy & Associates;
- by filing a lawsuit seeking judicial dissolution of their then-former client, based in part on confidential information obtained from M&D employees during their representation of M&D.

Judge Roush found that Deanne Siemer's testimony—that the interests of the Admiral and M&D had been the same—"lacked credibility." She expressed agreement with Epstein that M&D "had no interest in Admiral Murphy's knowledge of how to undermine the company." She concluded that "Ms. Siemer willfully ignored the District of Columbia Rules of Professional Conduct with which she was well familiar, having written a treatise on legal ethics."

Judge Roush was disturbed that "the Pillsbury defendants ignored the warnings of associates at the law firm that the dual representation of Admiral Murphy was rife with conflicts of interest. Every inquiry by an associate into the propriety of the firm's actions had been referred back to Ms. Siemer for resolution. Clearly, Pillsbury, Madison & Sutro's internal mechanisms for resolution of ethical issues are seriously deficient. The partner in charge of the client relationship who is least likely to be objective is the ultimate arbiter of whether the firm has a conflict of interest."

That left the question whether Keith Mendelson, a senior counsel at the time, was liable for malpractice equally with Siemer and the firm. Siemer had been in charge and had, as she put it, "made the call." Normally, Mendelson would be expected to take directions from Siemer, the responsible partner. Should he refuse to take orders, he might jeopardize his chances for partnership for which he was under consideration at the time. Such pressures are not always subtle. Mendelson recalled Siemer saying to him as she was getting on an elevator: "Keep in mind you are a senior counsel, sort of pushing partner on this." Judge Roush noted that she was "not unsympathetic to Mr. Mendelson's difficult position," but found that "he was equally responsible for the legal malpractice. Simply put, Mr. Mendelson was senior enough that he should have put a stop to the undisclosed dual representation by disclosing it to the board in obtaining their consent of, failing that, by withdrawing from the representation."

Judge Roush found that the Pillsbury defendants' malpractice had damaged M&D in the amount of $500,000. How she arrived at that figure (or, for that matter, the $1 million damage awards against the Admiral) she did not explain. Some forms of damage, such as hospital bills, can be calculated to the dollar. In a case like this, however, damage awards are often highly judgmental. A few weeks after the trial, the parties settled all claims in the lawsuit for undisclosed amounts, foreclosing any appeals.

Keith Mendelson made partner at Pillsbury, Madison & Sutro in January 1995. Deanne Siemer and her lawyer husband had worked in the Trust Territory of the Pacific Islands in the 1970s. She left the Pillsbury firm and they returned to establish Siemer & Willens, a civil practice firm, on Saipan, the Mariana Islands.

\* \* \*

# Comments and Questions

1. This chapter introduces the subject of conflicts of interest with a direct and blatant conflict in violation of Model Rule 1.7(a), which states the general conflicts rule. (The substance of the District of Columbia rule, as relevant here, is the same.) Note that Judge Roush found multiple acts of malpractice, based on conflict-of-interest violations, from the

time the Admiral first sought Siemer's advice about his "options" until he resigned to form his own firm. According to an article in *Of Counsel* (August 15, 1994, p. 20) "some observers have publicly marveled at the obviousness" of the conflict. The article cites Professor Stephen Gillers' suggestion that "there doesn't seem to have been anything subtle, much less waivable, about this particular conflicts charge." By contrast, the two chapters that follow raise difficult questions about former-client and non-waivable conflicts.

One can only speculate why Deanne Siemer, a veteran litigator and author of a book on lawyer ethics, could have gotten into this conflict, and stayed in it, especially after an experienced lawyer like Keith Mendelson kept questioning her decision. Could she have convinced herself, as she claimed, that her services were beneficial to M&D as well as to the Admiral? Judge Roush flatly rejected that explanation, finding that it "lacked credibility." Did her long-term professional relationship with the Admiral, perhaps unconsciously, divert her loyalty in his direction at M&D's expense? Or did she commit a deliberate violation of Rule 1.7, as Judge Roush found? If the judge was right, why might a lawyer in Siemer's position commit such a violation?

2. Keith Mendelson, the senior associate up for partner, was in a bind. He was uncomfortable helping the Admiral dismantle M&D, a client of the firm, and he expressed conflict-of-interest concerns to Deanne Siemer, the partner in charge of the matter. She kept telling Mendelson there was no conflict. She also implied that his performance on the matter would be considered in his bid for partnership. Not reassured, Mendelson voiced his concerns to a member of the firm's ethics committee and to his regular supervisor, then in Sweden. Both deferred to Siemer. His concerns thrice rejected, Mendelson soldiered on and eventually had a malpractice judgment entered against him. Under the circumstances, what should Mendelson have done?

Judge Roush identified part of the problem: "Pillsbury, Madison & Sutro's internal mechanisms for resolution of ethical issues are seriously deficient. The partner in charge of the client relationship who is least likely to be objective is the ultimate arbiter of whether the firm has a conflict of interest." How might a firm like Pillsbury structure "internal mechanisms for resolution of ethical disputes?" Pillsbury, like most big firms, has an ethics committee to which problems are sometimes referred. Here, the committee member apparently chose not to refer Mendelson's concern to the committee. (A similar non-referral occurs in the next chapter.) Should all concerns from associates be referred to committee? Should a lawyer concerned about a conflict be permitted to report to the ethics committee anonymously? If so, how long do you think it would take for the lawyer's supervisor to figure out who raised the concern? Should a lawyer be free to decline to work on a matter because of conflicts (or other ethics) concerns if the lawyer's supervisor believes her concern is unfounded? If an associate were to exercise that option, would it be likely to affect salary increases or chances for partnership?

3. It was one thing to hold Keith Mendelson responsible for malpractice, despite his "difficult position," as Judge Roush termed it. "He was senior enough that he should have put a stop to the dual representation... or by withdrawing from the representation." But what about Fraser Fiveash, the associate less than two years out of law school? She had raised the conflicts issue with Siemer, had been reassured, and wrote memoranda on legal questions. Assuming Fiveash knew about the firm's relationship with M&D, she would be held responsible for violating Rule 1.7(a). That conclusion follows from Model Rule 5.2, under which a lawyer is held responsible for a rule violation "notwithstanding that the lawyer acted at the direction of another person," unless she acted in accordance with her supervisor's "reasonable resolution of an arguable question." David Epstein, the plaintiff's expert stated, correctly, that Siemer's position was neither reasonable nor arguable. But was it fair of Epstein to compare Fiveash to the co-conspirators in Watergate? Might someone in Fiveash's position be found in violation of the ethical rule but not guilty of malpractice? If so, on what theory?

4. Counsel for the defendants did not call an expert witness to counter the opinions of Epstein that they knew from depositions were forthcoming. Their only testimony on those issues came from Siemer whose conduct was being challenged. Can you explain that strategy, if strategy it was?

# Chapter 4

# Of Chinese Walls and Comfort Zones

"If a client ever complained to you about your representation of
a competitor, what would you do?
In polite English, I would tell him to get lost."
— Colloquy in *Martirans G.P., Inc. v. Pepper, Hamiton &
Scheetz* between counsel for Pepper and its expert witness.

J. Anthony ("Jerry") Messina was a partner in the Philadelphia law
firm of Pepper, Hamilton & Scheetz. Messina headed the firm's labor
department and represented management in labor negotiations. Stephen
Van Dyck was president of Maritrans G.P., Inc., a publicly-held company based in Philadelphia that transported petroleum products on the
East and Gulf Coasts by tug and barge. Before a dispute arose between
them in the fall of 1987, Messina and the Pepper firm had been representing Maritrans in labor negotiations for more than ten years.
Messina and Van Dyck had developed a close, if sometimes difficult, relationship. John Harkins, another Pepper lawyer, thought the two "had
a kind of love-hate relationship." Despite their difficulties, Van Dyck
admired Jerry Messina's abilities, recalling how "he negotiates with the
airline stewardesses when he gets on the plane."

During the spring of 1987, Messina began to represent four tug and
barge companies based in New York harbor in joint negotiations with
the longshoremen's union. Maritrans competed with the New York
companies for business in New York harbor, but Messina did not tell
Maritrans about his new clients. When Van Dyck learned about them
from other sources in September 1987—months after Messina had become heavily involved in labor negotiations for the New York companies—he objected to Messina's representing Maritrans' competitors.
Messina and Alfred D'Angelo, another labor partner at the Pepper firm,
met with Van Dyck and attempted, unsuccessfully, to allay his concerns.
As D'Angelo recalled the meeting, Van Dyck "felt that Messina had

been so close to them that somehow they had a right to Messina, exclusive of others." Messina took offense at Van Dyck's objections. "Steve, what you're saying is you don't trust me." Van Dyck responded: "Damn right I don't." Van Dyck demanded that Messina withdraw from representation of the New York companies.

Pepper, Hamilton & Scheetz, like most major law firms, maintains a professional responsibility committee to resolve conflict-of-interest and other ethics questions that arise from time to time. After Van Dyck objected to Messina's representing Maritrans' competitors, Messina asked D'Angelo "to run the issue past the committee." D'Angelo went to Jon Baughman, chairman of the professional responsibility committee, and described the situation. As Baughman understood Van Dyck's objections: "Jerry was using his considerable abilities the same way for other clients as he was for Mr. Van Dyck—that was the concern." Van Dyck had expressed that objection—perhaps his primary objection—succinctly: the Pepper lawyers were "his lawyers" and, having bought and paid for their loyalty, they shouldn't work for the opposition. The litigation to come would bring to the fore a different concern: that Messina might disclose to the competition confidential information he had acquired while representing Maritrans.

The Pepper firm's consideration of Van Dyck's objections was cursory at best. D'Angelo and Baughman met for about one half-hour. Neither put anything in writing. Baughman did not inquire further into the facts, did no research, and did not even refer the question to the full professional responsibility committee. As he saw it: "There was no need to." Baughman advised D'Angelo that there was "no general prohibition on representing the competitors of a client." The only question was whether Pepper, on a hard-headed business basis, was prepared to lose Maritrans to gain other, quite probably more profitable, clients.

Maritrans had been a valuable client, generating more than $2 million in fees over the years. Although its labor business had been declining, Pepper management decided to make a final effort to work things out with Van Dyck. Peter Hearn, a senior partner (and godfather of one of Van Dyck's children) was designated to attempt a compromise that would keep Maritrans in the fold. Hearn met with Van Dyck on November 3. The two reached a tentative compromise under which Messina would withdraw from representation of the New York companies after the current round of negotiations and would not undertake representation of other New York tug and barge companies. Specifically,

Messina and Pepper would not represent Bouchard Transportation, Maritrans' most formidable competitor. In the meantime, two other Pepper lawyers, D'Angelo and Anthony Haller, would represent Maritrans. In order to protect any confidential information D'Angelo or Haller might learn from Maritrans during that period, it was further agreed that a "Chinese wall" would separate them from Messina—in theory, preventing any exchange of information about their respective clients. Hearn and Van Dyck sealed the tentative compromise with a handshake.

The compromise of November 3 proved fragile. It hadn't been reduced to writing and resolution of several points had been deferred. Messina, a rainmaker and power in the firm, was opposed to giving up representation of other tug and barge companies. Hearn wrote a draft agreement which Van Dyck rejected. Van Dyck responded with a draft which Hearn rejected. Van Dyck's draft suggested a compromise that would have allowed Pepper lawyers, other than Messina, to represent the New York companies, indicating that Van Dyck was not seriously concerned about disclosure of confidential information. On December 1, Hearn abandoned the effort at compromise and wrote to Van Dyck, terminating Pepper's representation of Maritrans.

# Maritrans G.P., Inc. v. Pepper, Hamilton & Scheetz

On February 1, 1988, Maritrans' new counsel filed suit against the Pepper firm and J. Anthony Messina, individually, in the Court of Common Pleas of Philadelphia County. Richard Sprague, a former Philadelphia District Attorney, represented Maritrans. Messina was represented by Arthur Raynes, another seasoned trial lawyer. Sprague and Raynes would spar throughout the trial—sometimes with barbed humor, sometimes with thinly veiled hostility. Counsel for the Pepper firm were joined by Stephen Gillers, a professor and prominent scholar of legal ethics. The case was heard by Judge Abraham Gafni.

Maritrans' complaint sought an injunction to bar Pepper and Messina from "continuing their conflicting legal representation of Maritrans' New York-based competitors." The crux of its claim was that Pepper, as a result of representing Maritrans for ten years, was privy to a broad range of information considered confidential throughout the industry. If Pepper continued to represent the New York competitors that information would inevitably be disclosed to them, whether intentionally or unintentionally, and Maritrans would suffer serious competitive injury.

Trial began on December 20, 1988 and continued over several months, generating a massive transcript with voluminous exhibits. As it developed, the case involved four basic issues:

- Did the Pepper firm have confidential information about its former client, Maritrans, which, if disclosed to its competitors, would harm Maritrans?
- Had Pepper lawyers disclosed confidential information to Maritrans' competitors, or was disclosure likely unless representation of the competitors were enjoined?
- Did Pepper's representation of Maritrans' competitors violate Pennsylvania's conflict-of-interest rules?
- Under the circumstances, was Maritrans entitled to an injunction barring Pepper from representing its competitors?

The first two issues were exclusively factual. The third issue presented legal questions which would produce a classic clash of experts. The last issue involved application of traditional tests for injunctive relief.

## Did the Pepper Firm Have Confidential Information of Maritrans?

Maritrans called Heyward Coleman, its executive vice president of sales and marketing, as a witness on these issues. Coleman's educational background included an MA degree in nuclear physics from Duke and an MBA from Harvard. An articulate witness, Coleman testified concerning a 1987 public offering of Maritrans securities in which the Pepper firm had represented the company. In preparing disclosure documents for the Securities and Exchange Commission, representatives of Pepper became "intimately familiar with the cost structure of our company," including labor costs, the largest variable cost in the tug and barge industry and among the most sensitive information in labor negotiations. Pepper had also represented the company in securing loans through a private placement. That transaction included "a very detailed prospectus that went into a great deal of sensitive, confidential information concerning our market shares. It consisted of our revenues broken down by regions, statements of our long-term strategy, and a long-term financial forecast."

The parties disputed whether Maritrans' business strategies and forecasts would become stale in the near term and therefore useless to competitors. According to Coleman, that information is projected out as far as ten years, "particularly in regard to our strategy—how you are going to position yourself over the long term—is something that tends to change very, very little over time." Asked if strategy information could be used by Maritrans' New York competitors, Coleman replied: "Absolutely." As he explained: "I would love to have similar statements of strategy from our competitors. It would be of enormous use to me to know what markets they plan to concentrate on, how they plan to manage their cost structure, what types of competitive advantages they currently hold and expect to gain."

John Burns, manager of labor relations, had dealt extensively with Messina for a decade. The company had multiple labor agreements, union and nonunion, which Messina had for many years negotiated. Burns treated the agreements, which contained terms and conditions of employment and pay rates, as confidential. He gave an example of how knowledge of Maritrans' labor costs would be useful to a competitor: "If my total labor costs are $3,000 a day and my competitor wants to better me in the marketplace, he has to shoot for some figure under $3,000 a day. But if he knows I'm paying $3,300 a day to attract good employees, he may have to pay $3,400 a day to do the same. That's a decision he has to make, but he's got the information on which to base the decision."

Maritrans called Robert Bray—an attorney who, like Messina, had worked exclusively for management in labor negotiations since 1966— as an expert witness. Bray supported the testimony of Coleman and Burns from his perspective as lawyer-negotiator for scores of clients in hundreds of labor negotiations. On the need for information: "There is no labor counsel around who would not become intimately involved with all the information available to a client in terms of its economic future and its economic life blood. His whole job is to improve the competitive condition of his client." He described Maritrans as "the key player in the industry—the company competitors would be highly concerned with in their strategies for dealing with labor."

Ironically, some of the strongest evidence for Maritrans came from the mouths of its competitors. One towing company president confirmed the value of knowing a competitor's labor costs when he declined to reveal his company's estimates of Maritrans' recent labor costs. An official of Bouchard Transportation, Maritrans' most formidable competitor, provided (perhaps unintentionally) proof of the importance competitors attached to keeping business information confidential. The President of Maritrans was in the room during the official's deposition when Richard Sprague, counsel for Maritrans, asked: "Who is your largest customer?" The official replied: "I'm not going to tell you." Sprague asked why. The official responded: "Tell him to leave the room. He's my competitor."

Witnesses for the Pepper firm sought to rebut Maritrans' case, point by point. Pepper partner Alfred D'Angelo described the firm's contractual arrangements with Maritrans. Pepper did not have a retainer agreement with Maritrans. Nor had the firm ever agreed to represent it exclusively in the tug and barge industry. As with most of its clients, Pepper had done work for Maritrans when called upon, at their regular hourly rates. "We weren't prepared to allow Maritrans or anybody to foreclose us from representing other companies in the industry."

D'Angelo denied that Pepper lawyers had received a broad range of information about Maritrans during labor negotiations, including cost and price structures, financial forecasts, and overall corporate strategy. Asked if such information was "essential to function adequately as labor counsel," D'Angelo replied: "They are not essential to representing the client either adequately or superiorly or any other adverb you want to put in there." D'Angelo also denied it would be helpful in negotiations to know another company's competitive situation or its labor costs. While he occasionally found the labor agreements of other companies useful, D'Angelo had been able "to get collective bargaining agreements virtually any time I needed them or wanted them"—usually from a union representative.

The Pepper firm called H. Thomas Felix II as a labor law expert to rebut the testimony of Gray, the Maritrans expert. Asked what information he would request of a client when negotiating a labor contract, Felix listed personnel policies, fringe benefits, labor costs, and any specific goals in the negotiation. By contrast, in a renewal contract—such as the tug and barge company contracts involved here—less information would be needed. He would want to know how much the client is willing to spend on wages and benefits, and whether it is in a position to cope with a strike. Felix was asked whether or not he would ask the client for the other types of information that Maritrans had claimed were important in negotiations—such as cost and price structures, corporate strategy, revenues by customer and market segment and financial forecasts. Felix replied: "It's not only not necessary, but my client would never pay me to learn that information."

The evidence at that point was conflicting. It was fairly clear, however, as Judge Gafni would find, that over the years Maritrans had provided a range of information to Pepper lawyers which Maritrans expected to be kept confidential. Although some of that information, such as collective bargaining agreements, may have been available outside the company, other sensitive information was not. Moreover, there was evidence, supported by common sense, that some information—for example, labor costs—could be useful to a competitor and harmful to Maritrans.

## Had the Pepper Firm Disclosed Confidential Information? Were They Likely to Disclose?

Disclosure of information in a situation like this can be difficult to prove. A customer list may be considered confidential, but a Maritrans tug pulling a Mobil petroleum barge through New York harbor becomes public information. The source of the leak may be unknown; it may have been an outside lawyer, or it may have been a company employee. Usually there will be no record of oral disclosures—only faded, and perhaps selective, recollections.

There was testimony indicating disclosures of information that might be termed "borderline confidential" because it was not closely held, or had somehow become general knowledge. A single, more serious, disclosure would weigh heavily in the court's decision. The "Chinese wall" erected to prevent D'Angelo and Haller from disclosing Maritrans information to Messina had been a key part of the November 3 compromise. Although that compromise had failed after a month, it was in place on November 5 when D'Angelo and Haller met with two Maritrans officers, Vice President Heyward Coleman and John Burns, manager of labor relations. The subject of the meeting was an impending strike by the longshoreman's union in New York harbor.

Those present at the meeting gave differing recollections of what had occurred. Judge Gafni summarized the testimony: "D'Angelo and Haller contend that the only thing discussed was a very general labor law question concerning the legal implications of attempting to obtain new work during a strike in New York harbor, since Maritrans was considering such action. Moreover, they insist that no strike plans, no operating plans, and no potential customers were discussed; rather the legal advice given was all generic." Contradicting the Pepper lawyers, Coleman testified that "Maritrans proposed options, strategy, and intentions in the event of a strike by [employees of the] New York-based competitors. [This information] was conveyed to D'Angelo and Haller for the purpose of securing both legal and practical advice. They also discussed how aggressive Maritrans intended to be in seeking new business."

Judge Gafni was satisfied that the meeting was "closer to Coleman's version" of what had taken place. "D'Angelo and Haller had conceded that the information conveyed at the meeting was considered by Maritrans to be confidential and was not to be conveyed to Messina, who was then representing the New York competitors. If only generic legal advice had been given, there would have been no reason for Maritrans to be so concerned that the information would be told to Messina." Despite that explicit understanding of confidentiality, in late December Peter Hearn, architect of the short-lived compromise agreement, convened a meeting of D'Angelo, Haller, and Messina in which the information provided to D'Angelo and Haller at the November 5 meeting was disclosed to Messina and Hearn, in violation of the compromise agreement.

That disclosure violated Pennsylvania Rule of Professional Conduct 1.6 which broadly prohibits a lawyer from revealing information about a present or former client's case, not only to competitors, but to anyone other than co-counsel. Beyond that, Judge Gafni found Hearn's trial testimony concerning the circumstances of the disclosure more disturbing than the disclosure itself. Hearn testified that in the late December meeting he had been acting as counsel to Maritrans, along with the company's designated lawyers, D'Angelo and Haller, and that, therefore, notes of the meeting were covered by the attorney-client privilege. (He claimed not to recall that Messina had been present.) Hearn was first allowed to testify with the notes before him without disclosing them to Maritrans counsel Sprague, who was cross-examining him. Sprague asked Hearn: "Is there anything [in those notes] indicating the assigned attorney?" Hearn replied in the negative. Following Sprague's cross-examination, Judge Gafni reviewed the notes and discovered that Hearn was not named among lawyers assigned to Maritrans labor matters. Reversing himself, the judge ruled that Hearn had not been acting as counsel for Maritrans as he had claimed; as a result, the attorney-client privilege was lost when D'Angelo and Haller told Hearn what had transpired in their November 5 meeting with the Maritrans officers.

Judge Gafni was sharply critical of Hearn's response to Sprague's question which, as he saw it, "could be interpreted as reflective either of an absence of candor or, at best, a disregard of fairness, when considering the disability under which Mr. Sprague was conducting his cross-examination." Stopping short of calling Hearn's response "a purposeful misstatement or a lie," it was, as the judge saw it, not something which "can inspire confidence in Maritrans as to Pepper's good faith or, at the very least, what careful attention and weight will be given to their assurances of what they will do with confidential information in the future." Hearn's disingenuous response to a single question showed how a lack of candor from a witness—particularly a lawyer from a blue-chip firm—can color a judge's view of an entire case.

## Had the Pepper Firm Violated Conflict-of-Interest Rules?

Courts commonly say that violating a rule of ethics is not, of itself, a basis for an enforceable claim in court. The stated purposes of the rules are to provide guidance and, where appropriate, to enforce discipline against lawyers. Nevertheless, as Judge Gafni recognized: "In determining the fiduciary duty an attorney owes his client, the courts will inevitably look to the ethical rules." Four leading experts on legal ethics became involved in the Maritrans litigation: Charles Wolfram and Geoffrey Hazard for Maritrans; Stephen Gillers and Marvin Frankel for the Pepper firm.

The expert witnesses focused on Rules 1.7(a) and 1.9(a) of the Pennsylvania Rules of Professional Conduct—identical in all relevant respect to the corresponding Model Rules—dealing, respectively, with concurrent and successive conflicts of interest. Rule 1.7(a) prohibits a lawyer from representing two present clients whose interests are "directly adverse." According to Maritrans, the Pepper firm violated that rule from the spring of 1987 until December 1, 1987—the period during which it represented Maritrans and its New York competitors concurrently.

Rule 1.9(a), the "former client" rule, addressed the situation after the Pepper firm terminated its relationship with Maritrans on December 1. The rule provides:

A lawyer who has formerly represented a client in a matter shall not thereafter represent another person in the same or a substantially related matter in which that person's interests are materially adverse to the interests of the former client unless the former client consents after consultation.

The rule implicates sometimes conflicting policy considerations. A former client should have confidence that its former lawyer will not disclose its secrets to competitors. This consideration relates not only to the former client's "comfort zone" (Judge Gafni's phrase) about future disclosures, but also to the willingness of clients generally to share fully with their lawyers information they need to provide effective representation.

On the other hand, law firms should not be completely foreclosed from taking on competing clients when they have information—in their files or in their memories—about former clients in the same field. This is a major concern for big law firms with specialized departments and for smaller (boutique) firms which specialize, for example, in representing television stations or airlines. A related concern, reflected in subpart (b) of the rule, is with the young lawyer who wants to move to another firm which happens to represent clients with interests adverse to clients of his present firm. If knowledge gained from his work at his present firm is to be attributed ("imputed") to the new firm, costing them clients, that firm will probably be unwilling to hire him. The drafters of Rule 1.9 attempted to balance these competing considerations.

## Maritrans' Legal Position

Charles Wolfram was called as the ethics expert for Maritrans. Wolfram had practiced with Covington & Burling in Washington, D.C., joined the faculty at Cornell Law School, and serves as Reporter for the American Law Institute's *Restatement of the Law Governing Lawyers*. Wolfram, an industrious witness, had prepared thirty-nine pages of direct testimony. He was cross-examined by Stephen Gillers, also a professor and author of a widely-used textbook on professional responsibility.

Wolfram testified that the Pepper firm's representation of the New York competitors was not permissible under the "substantial relationship" standard of Rule 1.9(a). Under that standard, the issue is whether the former and present representations are factually related. Wolfram contended: "There is probably no information that a competitor might wish to know about Maritrans' labor policies, strategies, practices, or plans that Mr. Messina did not know or possess in documentary form." That same information is relevant to the labor negotiations work which Messina and other Pepper lawyers are performing for the New York operators.

Generally speaking, if a matter is "substantially related" under Rule 1.9(a), the interests of the former and potential new client are, in Wolfram's opinion, likely to be "materially adverse." Here, the evidence of adversity was strong. Maritrans and the New York competitors were both working the New York harbor—a shrinking market—and competing for some of the same customers. In these circumstances, competitors would want to know "as much as Messina knows about Maritrans in order to shape their labor relations." Wolfram did not, however, interpret the rule to impose a flat ban on working for a former client's economic competitor. As an example, he cited the lawyer who specializes in suing for delinquent accounts; that lawyer can work for Walmart and Sears, simultaneously or successively. The "matters"—different bills and different people—are not related, "substantially" or at all, and there is little danger that Walmart's commercial secrets will be passed on to Sears, or vice versa.

Wolfram rejected the Pepper lawyer's claims that they, "as honorable lawyers, would not use or disclose any information relating to their former representation of Maritrans." Without questioning the integrity of Pepper lawyers or lawyers generally, Wolfram nevertheless viewed those claims as "irrelevant" under the substantial relationship test—irrelevant because, in legal language, Rule 1.9(a) is a "prophylactic" or "per se" rule. Its application does not depend on a showing of abuse (disclosure of information) in a particular case. If a substantial relationship exists, looking only to the factual commonalities between the former case and the new case, the representation is barred, regardless of a lawyer's good conduct and honest intentions.

Nor does a prophylactic rule merely reflect a Caesar's wife approach. There are practical reasons supporting such rule. As Wolfram saw it, "no lawyer in Mr. Messina's situation could have forgotten all of the mass of confidential Maritrans information known to him. At the very least, the subconscious impulse to employ that information, when relevant in the interests of the competitor clients, would be very difficult, if not impossible, to resist." In addition to psychological realities, serious practical problems arise when the former client seeks to prove that disclosures *have* been made. Here, for example, Pepper took the

position—which the judge rejected—that Maritrans should be required
to reveal in court the very information for which it was claiming confidentiality, effectively destroying that claim while trying to save it.

## The Pepper Firm's Legal Position

Pepper called Marvin Frankel as its expert witness on the ethics rules.
Frankel, a New York City practitioner, had behind him a distinguished career in the law. As a young lawyer he served under the Solicitor General of
the United States, arguing cases before the Supreme Court. In private practice he specialized in labor litigation. For thirteen years, Frankel served as a
United States District Judge. Most relevant here, Frankel was a member of
the American Bar Association's "Kutak Commission" (after its chairman,
Robert Kutak) which drafted the Model Rules of Professional Conduct.

Frankel's testimony also focused on Rule 1.9(a)—specifically, on
whether the interests of the New York companies were "materially adverse to the interests of the former client." Drawing on his knowledge of
the Kutak Commission's deliberations, he advocated a narrow reading
of "materially adverse" under which the rule would not be applicable to
Pepper's representation of the New York companies. "We were aware
that lawyers commonly represent competitors, concurrently and successively, especially if they are specialists, and we weren't about to include
adversity between competitors, whether the clients were concurrent or
successive." Frankel contended that lawyers should be free to work successively for economic competitors, for example, for Anheuser Busch,
then Miller; for General Motors, then Ford.

Competition between big companies takes place in a national market among millions of potential customers. According to Frankel, the
rule was intended to apply *only* in situations where client and former
client were competing, head to head, for the same business—a situation
he illustrated hypothetically: The City of Philadelphia is planning a
bond issue and is looking for an investment banker to underwrite it.
Goldman, Sachs and Morgan, Stanley compete on an ongoing basis for
the city's bond business, and both bid for the upcoming bond offering.
The Pepper firm represents Goldman, Sachs, which is initially selected
as underwriter and later fired before the offering. Whereupon, Pepper
terminates its relationship with Goldman, Sachs. Morgan, Stanley de-
cides to resubmit its bid and approaches the Pepper firm to represent it.
Can the Pepper firm accept the representation? Frankel answered in the
negative.

Frankel and Wolfram were in agreement on several points. Rule 1.9(a) is "prophylactic;" its application does not depend on proof that the former client's confidential information has, in fact, been disclosed. Wolfram agreed with Frankel's position that head-to-head competition meets the rule's "materially adverse" requirement. The practical difference between the two came down to this: does the rule cover situations like the present case which lie between very broad, sometimes national competition (General Motors versus Ford) and head-to-head competition where only one can win. To repeat, Wolfram said that it does. Frankel first conceded that "at some point between the only-one-can-win [situation] and Adam Smith's marketplace where you have a million competitors there may be a problem with two competitors." When pressed by Judge Gafni, however, Frankel stated that the rule only applies to head-to-head competition.

The case before the court was closer to head-to-head competition than to the world of Adam Smith. Maritrans and the New York companies were competing in one market area, New York harbor, with a limited number of potential customers. There was direct competition for some of the biggest customers, notably oil companies like Mobil and Sun. The unwillingness of executives from the New York towing companies to disclose information provided graphic evidence of real competition with Maritrans.

# Judge Gafni's Decisions

On April 21, 1989, two years after the Pepper firm began representing Maritrans' New York competitors, Judge Gafni rendered his decision from the bench. He found that the Pepper firm had "become intimately familiar with Maritrans operations in the course of rendering legal services, including detailed financial and business information," and that some of that information "is still current and would be useful to Maritrans competitors if it were disclosed to them."

Judge Gafni dealt with "adversity" and "substantial relationship" as closely related issues. He held that "the mere possession of Maritrans confidential information by Pepper does not bar Pepper from representing economic competitors of Maritrans. Standing alone, the interests of Maritrans are only *generally adverse* with respect to its New York competitors (italics added)." Moreover, the fact that both representations involved negotiations with the same labor union would not, in Judge Gafni's view, have been enough to create a substantial relationship. He reached the same conclusion where, as in this case, the two representations involved different unions. Those scenarios lacked significant facts in common. Although the judge did not refer explicitly to the testimony of Maritrans' expert Wolfram who had found "substantial relationships" in similar situations, he implicitly rejected Wolfram's approach.

Judge Gafni turned to the November 5 meeting of Pepper's D'Angelo and Haller with the Maritrans officers who were seeking advice on the company's options for responding to the impending strike in New York harbor. Judge Gafni found: "At that point, a link was established between the simultaneous representations of Maritrans and the New York competitors." The opposing parties became "competing economic enterprises" with interests "more than merely generally adverse. Rather, their interests became *directly adverse* as specific counsel was being sought from Pepper as to how Maritrans might directly compete with the New York companies." The competition had, in Frankel's phrase, become head-to-head.

On November 5, Pepper's representation of Maritrans had not yet been terminated; Pepper was concurrently representing the New York companies with the consent of Maritrans, pursuant to the short-lived compromise agreement of November 3. That consent, however, had been limited by a Chinese wall provision to insulate Maritrans information from Messina. Judge Gafni ruled: "Pepper breached the limited consent of Maritrans when it subsequently allowed the information from the November 5 meeting to be conveyed to Messina in late December at the meeting called by Hearn. Such breach was a violation of Rule 1.7(a) of the Pennsylvania Rules of Professional Conduct." The later December disclosure to Messina, in effect, vitiated the consent Maritrans had given. The judge rejected Pepper's argument that all obligations under the compromise agreement lapsed on December 1, when Pepper ceased to represent Maritrans. As he saw it, obligations under the Chinese wall continued indefinitely to protect whatever sensitive information had been disclosed in reliance on it.

Judge Gafni went on to find a violation of Rule 1.9(a), the "former client" rule, but on a narrow ground. He noted that D'Angelo, the Pepper partner designated to work for Maritrans under the short-lived compromise, had later joined Messina as an attorney for the New York competitors and was participating in their labor negotiations. The linkage necessary for a "substantial relationship" under the rule was supplied by the November 5 meeting in which information about Maritrans' plans for responding to the impending New York harbor strike had been disclosed to D'Angelo—the same linkage which supplied the "directly adverse" element under Rule 1.7(a).

Having found violations of the Pennsylvania Rules of Professional Conduct, Judge Gafni turned to "the more difficult problem" whether a preliminary injunction should be granted, a remedy which he characterized as "extraordinary, to be granted only after careful deliberation." The judge attempted to weigh the harm that would result from denying Maritrans an injunction against the harm to the Pepper firm and its New York clients if an injunction were to be granted. D'Angelo of the Pepper firm had testified that an injunction would have "a devastating effect" on their labor law practice, in Philadelphia and beyond.

Judge Gafni focused once more on the disclosures that had occurred in the late December meeting about Maritrans' plans for getting new business during the strike against its competitors. "Since the strike has been ongoing for over fourteen months, it is likely that [Maritrans'] plans have already been implemented" and probably are not "of present-day importance." The judge concluded: "Hence, the future injury to Maritrans cannot be deemed to be irreparable." He gave no explicit consideration to harm that might flow from future disclosures by Messina or other Pepper lawyers. Maritrans' request for an injunction was denied.

Five days later, on April 26, 1989, Judge Gafni called the lawyers back to court to tell them he had changed his mind; he was going to issue an injunction, after all. As he explained: "This is one of those rare situations where I started to look back and to have a sense of disquiet and a lack of ease about whether I had done the right thing." The judge had come to believe that his decision "did not fully account for the special relationship between attorney and client and the comfort level and confidence to which a client is entitled both during and subsequent to his representation by an attorney." Judge Gafni referred once more to Hearn's lack of candor on the witness stand and to the "absence of sensitivity" by D'Angelo and Haller to issues of ethics in the late December meeting with Hearn. Most important, he had not given full weight to the fact that "Rule 1.9(a) is prophylactic in nature. As information was disclosed casually once before, so may it be disclosed in the future. The possibility of disclosure, even inadvertent, is a significant concern."

On May 1, 1989, Judge Gafni enjoined the Pepper firm from representing Maritrans' competitors in collective bargaining negotiations and from communicating Maritrans information to any successor counsel for the New York competitors. Pepper sought a stay of the injunction pending appeal that was denied. Pepper appealed to the Superior Count of Pennsylvania, the Commonwealth's intermediate appellate court.

The case was argued before a three-judge panel of the Superior Court in December 1989 and decided in March 1990. Its opinion was remarkably obtuse. Noting the Judge Gafni had based his decision on violations of the Pennsylvania Rules of Professional Conduct, the court held that those rules are not themselves a basis for injunctive or other civil relief. So far, so good; the rules themselves so state. It is, however, the practice of courts to look to rules of ethics as evidence of the content of general legal obligations—such as the fiduciary obligations of lawyers. That, as he had made clear, was what Judge Gafni had done. There remained the question whether injunctive relief could be justified on some other legal basis, apart from the rules of ethics. The Superior Court rejected that possibility perfunctorily, stating that: "Our independent review of the record reveals no basis upon which an injunction could have been issued."

Maritrans filed a petition for review with the Supreme Court of Pennsylvania. It acquired a powerful ally in Geoffrey Hazard, a Professor at Yale University School of Law and formerly Reporter for the Kutak Commission's Model Rules, who filed an amicus curiae brief in support of Maritrans' position. Hazard pointed out that the Superior Court "badly confused the relationship between duties under the rules of ethics and legal rules that create actionable liabilities apart from the rules of ethics. The court [incorrectly] held that the trial judge's reference to violations of the rules of *ethics* somehow negated the existence of a *legal* duty by the Pepper firm to its former client." In so doing, "it stood the correct analysis on its head." Hazard called for correction of "the egregious and unprecedented error committed by the Superior Court."

On January 29, 1992, the Pennsylvania Supreme Court decided the case in Maritrans' favor, reversing the Superior Court in a sometimes scathing opinion. "The Superior Court emasculated common-law principles, turning the ethics rules governing lawyers into a grant of civil immunity which has been condemned from time immemorial." The Supreme Court borrowed, at length and verbatim (but without attribution), from Hazard's amicus brief, observing that the Superior Court had "badly confused" the relationship between ethics rules and legal rules and had "stood the correct analysis on its head." The Supreme Court agreed with Hazard that, long before modern ethics rules were adopted, "the common law recognized that a lawyer could not undertake a representation adverse to a former client in a matter substantially related to that in which the lawyer had previously served the client." The Court stopped short of creating a blanket rule that a lawyer may not represent the economic competitor of a former client. On the facts of this case, however, "it was perfectly reasonable to conclude that Maritrans' competitive position could be irreparably injured if Pepper and Messina continued to represent its competitors." The Court reinstated Judge Gafni's injunction, five years after the Pepper firm undertook representation of Maritrans' New York competitors.

In November 1992, the Pepper firm agreed to pay $3 million to Maritrans—somewhat less than Maritrans' legal fees in the case—in settlement of its conflict of interest claim and Maritrans agreed to dismissal of its lawsuit.

* * *

# Comments and Questions

1. The *Maritrans* case is a complex example of the "former client" rule, originally judge-made and codified in 1983 as Rule 1.9(a) of the Model Rules. The classic formulation of the rule is found in Judge Weinfeld's opinion in *T.C. Theatre Corp. v. Warner Brothers Pictures, Inc.*, 113 F. Supp. 265, 268-69 (S.D.N.Y. 1953):

> I hold that the former client need show no more than that matters embraced within the pending suit wherein his former attorney appears on behalf of his adversary are *substantially related* to the matters or cause of action wherein the attorney previously represented him, the former client. The Court will assume that during the course of the former representation confidences were disclosed to the attorney bearing on the subject matter of the representation. It will not inquire into their nature or extent. Only in this manner can the lawyer's duty of absolute fidelity be enforced and the spirit of the rule relating to privileged communications be maintained (emphasis added).

Judge Posner elaborated on the Weinfeld formulation in *Analytica, Inc. v. NPD Research, Inc.*, 708 F.2d 1263 (C.A. 7, 1983), shortly before State and Federal courts began to adopt the Model Rules. According to Posner, "substantially related" means:

...if the lawyer *could* have obtained confidential information in the first representation that would have been relevant to the second. It is irrelevant whether he actually obtained such information and used it against his former client (emphasis added).

Interpreting Rule 1.9(a) in *Maritrans*, the expert witnesses and Judge Gafni agreed that the rule is "prophylactic"—that neither actual receipt nor subsequent disclosure of confidential information from the first representation need be shown. Factual inquiries into receipt of information and its possible disclosure would be time-consuming, perhaps more time-consuming than the merits of the case. Furthermore, as Judge Posner pointed out in *Analytica*, inquiry into receipt and disclosure may result in revealing the very information the rule is designed to keep confidential.

2. Nevertheless, considerable time was devoted to proving that confidential information *had* been received by the Pepper lawyers and later disclosed to the New York competitors, perhaps because proof of *access* to information—required for a "substantial relationship"—would often involve testimony about phone calls, meetings with and documents sent to lawyers. As a practical matter, therefore, proof of *receipt* of information would come into the case through proof of access. However, proof of subsequent *disclosures* of confidential information is clearly not required under Rule 1.9(a). Disclosures are separately prohibited by Rules 1.6 and 1.9(c). So why did Judge Gafni attach such significance to incidents of disclosure in *Maritrans*—especially the disclosures to Messina at the late December meeting. Was it because he viewed entitlement to an injunction as a question separate from a proven violation of Rule 1.9(a)? Or is this an example of facts being more important than law? Recall Hearn's evasive testimony about the late December meeting and the casual attitudes of the other Pepper lawyers in attendance toward their obligations to keep Maritrans' information confidential. If a judge ceases to trust witnesses for one side, that loss of confidence may be more significant to the outcome than abstract legal elements.

3. Maritrans involved both a conflict with a present client under Rule 1.7(a) and a former client under Rule 1.9(a). Attention focused on the former-client conflict since the Pepper firm had terminated its representation months before the lawsuit was filed. Maritrans still might have argued that it was a present client because Pepper had represented it con-

sistently on many matters for ten years, even though it may not have been working actively for it when the dispute arose, and that it could not drop Maritrans like a "hot potato" when more lucrative clients came its way. *See Unified Sewerage Agency v. Jelco, Inc.*, 646 F.2d 1339, 1345 n.4 (C.A. 9, 1981).

During the 1980s, several large companies had an arrangement with Joseph Flom of Skadden, Arps, Slate, Meagher & Flom under which they paid an annual retainer to Skadden, in part to be assured of his services if faced with a hostile takeover, but primarily to prevent Skadden from representing other companies that might want to launch a takeover attempt against them. The arrangement drew criticism and Skadden eventually discontinued it. *See* Caplan, *Skadden: Power, Money, and the Rise of a Legal Empire*, pp. 81-86 (1993).

4. Model Rule 1.6, "Confidentiality of Information," prohibits disclosure of "information relating to representation of a client." It would have prohibited the Pepper lawyers' disclosure to the New York competitors of information they learned in representing Maritrans. Judge Posner noted in *Analytica*: "This prohibition has not seemed enough, by itself, to make clients feel secure about reposing confidences in lawyers, so a further prohibition has evolved." Why not? Shouldn't Pepper's duty to abide by Rule 1.6 allow the firm to take competing businesses as clients? But is it realistic to expect that lawyers could completely block out information from a former client that would be useful to a competitor?

5. The existence of a substantial relationship is generally understood to depend on a commonality of facts between the former and a subsequent representation. Identity of legal theories or objectives is usually not required. For example, in the *Analytica* case Judge Posner was faced with a situation in which the former representation involved restructuring a company's stock — a non-litigation setting — followed by representation of the same company's opponent in an antitrust case. Despite the different legal contexts, Judge Posner found a substantial relationship because the information the lawyer could have received in the stock restructuring matter "might have been relevant" to the antitrust case. The overlap of facts should be substantial, but may be much less than complete. Judge Posner's *Analytica* opinion for the Seventh Circuit represents a broad approach to former-client disqualification questions. Courts take varying approaches to these questions, however. In *Government of*

*India v. Cook Industries, Inc.*, 569 F.2d 737, 739-740 (C.A. 2, 1978), the Second Circuit took a narrow approach to disqualification based on a former representation, saying that it would be granted only when the issues in both cases were "identical" or "essentially the same." What are the likely advantages and disadvantages of a broad, versus a narrow approach to former-client disqualification in promoting clients' feelings of loyalty and confidence in their lawyers? From the lawyers' perspective, how do those differing approaches affect their ability to represent new clients? According to expert witness Frankel, a member of the Kutak Commission which drafted the Model Rules: "We were aware that lawyers commonly represent competitors, especially if they are specialists, and we were not about to include adversity between competitors." And from the judge's perspective, which approach would better avoid protracted litigation over collateral issues?

6. The Model Rules (except to a limited extent in Rule 1.11 relating to government employment) and most jurisdictions do not recognize "Chinese Walls" as a mechanism for avoiding present—or former—client disqualification problems. If Chinese walls were recognized, what practical effect might that have on a broad approach to such problems, as illustrated by the *Analytica* decision? Would the narrow approach taken by the Second Circuit in *Government of India* be necessary to avoid such problems? Even in a jurisdiction which recognizes Chinese walls, they must be better constructed and observed than the short-lived wall in *Maritrans*. For a well-constructed Chinese wall, *see Cromley v. Board of Education*, 17 F.3d 1059 (C.A.7, 1994).

7. As expert witness Wolfram stated, the key concepts in Rule 1.9(a)— "substantially related" and "materially adverse"—are closely related and tend to turn on the same facts. His testimony stressed a substantial relationship between Pepper's representation of Maritrans and its competitors for New York harbor business. Frankel, the opposing expert, emphasized a lack of "material adversity" between the two. In his oral decisions, Judge Gafni seemed to equate the two concepts. Verbal formulas aside, the practical heart of the experts' disagreement was on whether a law firm should be allowed to successively represent two competitors in a market in which competition is sometimes (or usually) not head-to-head, but much more direct than in an "Adam Smith," *Ford v. General Motors*, market of virtually infinite customers. How did Judge Gafni resolve that disagreement? Under his ruling, how free

would other law firms be to represent competitors of former clients; to represent competitors of present clients under Rule 1.7(a)?

The value of professional independence—in this context, the freedom of lawyers to take on new clients, including clients who compete to some degree with present clients—is in some tension with an expansive reading of conflict of interest. The issue is not simply that expansive conflicts rules would make it economically harder to practice. It is also that powerful private interests should not be able to monopolize access to legal services by invoking conflict rules to prevent lawyers from representing actual or potential competitors. This appears to be the concern that underlies comment [3] to Rule 1.7: "...simultaneous representation in unrelated matters of clients whose interests are only *generally adverse, such as competing economic enterprises*, do not require the consent of the respective clients." However, it is sometimes difficult to draw the line. Should the *Maritrans* case have been decided differently if the parties had been competing all along the East and Gulf Coasts in addition to New York harbor? What about representation of different clients in a fledgling industry with a small number of firms, as in some high-tech areas? In some practice areas, such as patents and bankruptcy, the bar is specialized and relatively small. Bankruptcy judges tend to treat potential conflicts leniently in order to avoid conflicting out the relatively few available lawyers experienced in large-scale corporate bankrupcies.

Conflicts of interest are becoming more of a problem as law firms become larger, with more branch offices, and corporations merge, establish multiple subsidiaries, and enter into alliances, such a joint ventures. These trends are giving rise to complex and Byzantine conflicts in which the stakes are high.

8. The Pennsylvania Supreme Court reinstated Judge Gafni's injunction, relying on a common-law principle that "a lawyer could not undertake a representation adverse to a former client in a matter substantially related" to that of the former client. Without attempting any greater specificity, and without reference to Judge Gafni's rationale, the court found a violation of that principle on the facts of the *Maritrans* case. Principles of legal ethics are supposed to provide helpful guidance to lawyers in problems they commonly confront. A departure from earlier ethics codes which were largely cast in generalities like the Pennsylvania Supreme Court's decision, the Model Rules of Professional Conduct represent an attempt at a mature statement of rules—based on the com-

mon law, practical experience, the sometimes competing needs of lawyers and clients, and the biases of the drafters—with as much specificity as the subject allows. Are lawyers better served by the specificity of the Model Rules, or by common-law principles and a case-by-case approach?

Theory aside, lawyers are in greater danger of being sued under a common-law, fiduciary theory than for malpractice based on violations of ethics rules. The causation standard for breach of fiduciary duty is often applied more leniently than the malpractice standard and, in many states, neither causation nor injury need be proved to obtain disgorgement of fees.

# Chapter 5

# Two Scorpions in a Bottle

"It's a wicked world, and when a clever man turns his brains to crime, it is the worst of all."
—A. Conan Doyle, *Adventure of the Speckled Band.*

The whole sordid business began with an innocent mistake at the law offices of Weinberg & Green a few days after Christmas in 1982. David Blum, a partner in the old-line Baltimore firm, was drafting a set of documents for a major client, Fairfax Savings Bank, to incorporate last-minute changes in a complex $5.7 million loan agreement scheduled to close before the end of the year. The loan, from Fairfax to developer Charles Ellerin, was to provide construction financing for "Sherwood Square," a shopping mall planned for nearby Westminster, Maryland.

In his haste to complete the drafting, Blum made a change in the agreement (as he later testified, "for clarity") which had the unintended effect of extending the personal liability of Ellerin to the full amount of the loan if the Sherwood Square project were to fail. Blum's late change should have been brought to Ellerin's attention before he signed the loan agreement; unaccountably, it wasn't.

Sherwood Square ran into difficulties early on and the loan went into default in 1985. Blum's slip of the pen set off a decade of bitter and protracted litigation—with Fairfax Savings Bank suing Ellerin to repay the loan, with Ellerin countersuing Fairfax for fraud, and, ultimately, with Fairfax turning around and suing its former lawyers, Weinberg & Green, for malpractice and fraud.

Two men were instrumental in creating the ethical morass that would grow from Blum's innocent mistake: Malcolm C. Berman, owner of Fairfax, and Stanford Hess, Berman's lawyer at Weinberg & Green. A Baltimore lawyer who knows both men calls them "two scorpions in a bottle."

Malcolm Berman was CEO and majority stockholder of Fairfax Savings Bank, a savings and loan based in Baltimore with assets in excess of $400 million. He estimated his net worth between $60 and $70 million. Something of a Renaissance man, he was a licensed private pilot and an accomplished yachtsman. A high-school dropout, Berman had gotten his start buying houses in depressed Baltimore neighborhoods. From his financial base as a landlord, he had acquired Fairfax Savings and went on to build a fortune as a banker who sailed close to the wind. Berman was ruthless in his dealings, eventually quarreling with most of his business associates. Stanford Hess thought there was a "dark side of Mr. Berman. He looked for some way to kill the other side, not just to win the case."

Stanford Hess became a member of the Maryland bar in 1966 and served for several years in the Office of the State Attorney General. In 1974, he became an associate with Weinberg & Green, one of Baltimore's oldest and largest firms. Hess rose rapidly in the firm, making partner in 1977 and becoming a member of the executive committee in 1987. Hess owed his success largely to his close personal and professional relationship with Malcolm Berman. The two had met in 1976 when Berman was attempting to qualify for a real estate license. State regulators had denied his application because Berman had in the past pled *nolo contendere* to a mail fraud charge. As a former lawyer for the state, Hess's knowledge of regulatory requirements and those who administered them helped him obtain a license for Berman. Berman soon began calling on Hess with more profitable assignments.

Outside the office, Berman and Hess and their wives were, for a time, frequent dinner companions. Berman recalled that later: "When Stanford was going through his divorce, we would talk every night." Hess asked Berman to serve as trustee of a trust for his children. Hess had the use of Berman's vacation home in Florida and of his private plane that he used to visit his children away at college. And yet, as Hess would testify, he sensed something was lacking in their relationship: "It's my impression that Mr. Berman didn't really trust anybody." As will be seen, Malcolm Berman would have reason to distrust Stanford Hess.

By the late 1970s, Berman had brought most of his considerable legal business to Weinberg & Green; his various interests were generating over $1 million annually in fees. The Berman billings represented about half of Hess's total billings. Hess's profit share was—as is customary in law firms—tied directly to what he brought in ("eat what you kill"). As a result, Hess stood to profit, proportionally more than his partners, if Berman's bills were to increase.

# The Ellerin Litigation

What started as a routine lawsuit to collect on a defaulted loan mushroomed into major litigation extending over ten years—through three jury trials, two appeals, and finally ending in a settlement. The Sherwood Square project had been constructed as planned, but few tenants had signed up, not enough to make the project viable. Under the loan agreement as Blum had revised it, Ellerin was liable for the full amount of the loan—a slam-dunk case until Ellerin counterclaimed for fraud, alleging that Fairfax Savings Bank had slipped critical wording into the agreement without his knowledge.

The first trial began in September 1987, with Weinberg & Green representing Fairfax. The jury found that Fairfax had committed fraud but that Ellerin had forgiven ("ratified" in legal jargon) the fraud. The jury went on to award Fairfax a judgment for $7.5 million to repay the loan. Ellerin appealed that decision which was later reversed on a technicality—that the judge had given the jury erroneous instructions on the law of ratification.

While Ellerin's appeal was pending, however, Berman directed Weinberg & Green to collect the $7.5 million judgment as soon as possible, by any legal means. Steven Caplan, a Weinberg & Green lawyer, directed the Sheriff of Baltimore County to seize and sell Ellerin's property, including the furniture in his office and home. On the Friday evening after Thanksgiving 1987, Ellerin was hosting a dinner for his extended family when (according to Ellerin) the Sheriff and his deputies pounded on the door, shouted, intruded on the premises, and began to inventory the furniture—including the chairs on which the guests were seated. A little later, as the dinner grew cold and the children wept, Caplan arrived on the scene, adding to the commotion. Caplan would later give a more decorous account of the incident but, by either account, it made for bad blood between borrower Ellerin and banker Berman.

The appeal process delayed a second trial until 1990. That trial ended in a hung jury. The third trial began in April 1991 and ended in a total victory for Ellerin. The jury found that Fairfax had committed fraud and that Ellerin was not obligated to repay the Sherwood Square loan. In addition, Ellerin was awarded compensatory damages of $2.6 million, plus $6 million in punitive damages designed to punish Fairfax for "malicious conduct." (Testimony from Ellerin about the Thanksgiving weekend sheriff's raid had undoubtedly helped the jury to find malice.) This time, Fairfax appealed. In 1993, an appeals court upheld the jury's decision on compensatory damages and the loan repayment issue, but reversed the $6 million punitive damages award and sent the case back for yet another trial.

A fourth *Ellerin* trial was scheduled to begin in September 1995 when Berman decided to cut his losses by settling the case for an undisclosed amount (as is customary in settlements). Settling appeared to be the prudent course. If his Fairfax Savings Bank were to lose again—as seemed likely, given the verdict in the third trial—Berman might have been saddled with a court judgment for some $15 million, plus legal fees.

In any event, Berman had already begun to implement a different strategy for salvaging the Sherwood Square fiasco. Upset about the adverse verdict in the third *Ellerin* trial, he had fired Weinberg & Green and, in October 1992, had sued the firm for malpractice, citing Blum's drafting of the Sherwood Square loan documents. (Paradoxically, Berman was at the same time defending Blum's drafting in the second *Ellerin* appeal, through new legal counsel.) The suit also charged conflicts of interest in connection with Weinberg & Green's representation in the *Ellerin* case. In June 1994, Berman expanded the pending suit by alleging fraud in the firm's overbilling scheme. We turn next to the origins of that scheme, to its implementation, and how it was finally disclosed to Berman, its victim.

## The Scheme to Inflate Berman's Bills

Malcolm Berman was by far the biggest billing client of Weinberg & Green, paying millions in fees over the years. Despite competent legal work, however, Berman was a slow-pay client. After receiving a bill, he would hold it for months, sometimes years, and then try to negotiate a discount. Berman, of course, profited by paying late. As the billing partner, Hess was responsible for dealing with Berman and seeing that his bills were paid. Hess grew weary of the incessant haggling with Berman. In early 1986 the two finally cut a deal: Weinberg & Green would give Berman a fifteen percent discount on legal bills for Fairfax and several other Berman accounts. For his part, Berman agreed to pay all his bills on time, without requesting further discounts.

Neither Berman nor Hess kept his end of the deal. Berman continued to delay payments and ask for discounts. From time to time, as far back as 1983, Hess had padded some of Berman's bills by manually increasing the hours on other lawyers' time sheets. Frustrated and angry over Berman's refusal to live up to their deal, Hess's episodic bill padding now became systematic. He devised a scheme to erase the fifteen percent discount Berman had bargained for, without telling Berman. Hess discussed his scheme with Howard Miller, chairman of the firm's finance committee, who approved and helped to implement it. Miller directed the firm's bookkeeping staff to put in place a computer program that would automatically increase Berman's bills by fifteen percent—equal to the discount Berman mistakenly thought he was getting.

The effect of Hess's scheme was to charge Berman for hundreds of hours of lawyer time that had not been worked—conduct which the judge in the later malpractice and fraud trial against Weinberg & Green would label "outrageous" and "reprehensible." Put simply, Hess was stealing from his client. He nevertheless insisted that his motives had not been corrupt. Hess testified at the malpractice trial that the purpose of his computerized mark-ups had been "to recoup the losses Mr. Berman caused the firm to suffer." He denied engaging in "a billing fraud." When it was pointed out that the mark-ups had increased his compensation because of the credit he received as billing partner on the Berman accounts, Hess responded: "Well, that wasn't really in my mind as the reason for doing it." He acknowledged, however: "That was the effect of it." Whatever Hess's motivation, the computerized mark-ups were effective. Over a period of some sixteen months, Weinberg & Green overcharged Malcolm Berman by about $475,000.

Hess's computerized scheme implicated others in the firm, in addition to finance committee chairman Miller. The involvement of computer and other administrative personnel in the billing department might be rationalized, if not excused, by their subordinate positions. But the firm's ethical stance was compromised when, months before the fraud was disclosed to Berman, knowledge of it came to Ronald Craemer, managing partner of the firm, to most members of the executive committee, and to a few other partners in the firm. None of those in a position to take corrective action did anything. A few months after Berman was told of the fraud, Craemer resigned from the firm to pursue opportunities in business. Miller, who had participated in the billing fraud almost from its inception, became the new managing partner.

Lawyers who acquire knowledge that another lawyer has violated a rule involving dishonesty or untrustworthiness are ethically required to inform bar disciplinary authorities—here, the Attorney Grievance Committee of Maryland, an arm of the Maryland State Bar Association.

It's hard to imagine an ethics violation falling more squarely within that rule than Stanford Hess' scheme to systematically overbill Malcolm Berman. Yet neither managing partner Craemer, nor Miller, chairman of the finance committee, nor any other lawyer at Weinberg & Green having knowledge of the scheme took it to the grievance committee. Craemer, *ex officio* chairman of the executive committee, recalled that committee discussing whether the firm had any duties to the bar association in connection with the overbilling; that committee somehow managed to answer that question in the negative. So anxious was the firm's management to keep a lid on the scandal that several months passed before the executive committee decided to inform the other partners in the firm about the overbilling, a fraud for which they could be held personally liable.

Despite management's efforts at secrecy, it was probably inevitable that word of the overbilling would leak outside the firm. In September 1987 the first *Ellerin* trial was starting and Fairfax Savings Bank, represented by Weinberg & Green, was seeking to collect the legal fees it had previously incurred attempting to collect on its loan to Ellerin. In preparing a fee petition for filing in court, the lead lawyer for Weinberg & Green, Judith O'Neill, became aware that Hess had been inflating the lawyer time billed on the case. O'Neill went ahead and filed an inaccurate fee petition, including some time not worked, but then found herself in an awkward position when lawyers for Ellerin demanded supporting documents — documents which would have revealed the fraud.

O'Neill reported her dilemma to her boss, James Carbine, head of Weinberg & Green's litigation department and a lawyer of undisputed integrity. Carbine went immediately to Miller and Craemer, demanded an end to the billing fraud and authority to conduct an internal investigation — authority quickly granted by the executive committee. A day or two later, Carbine ran into Hess at an Oriole game at Camden Yards. He said to Hess: "Stanford, what we've done is wrong. You have to tell Malcolm and we have to pay him what we owe him." Hess replied: "We can't do that. If we tell Malcolm what we've done, that will be the end of the firm. We're in this boat together." To which Carbine responded: "Stanford, not only are we in the same boat, but you've got one oar and I've got the other." Carbine kept pulling his oar.

With Carbine's investigation going forward and an increasingly pressing need to withdraw the false fee petition in the Ellerin case, the executive committee held a Sunday meeting on September 13, 1987.

The committee decided to send a delegation—including Hess, but not Carbine—to Berman's home later that afternoon. There, for the first time, Berman was told something about the firm's overbilling. The extent of the disclosure that Sunday afternoon, and in the months following, would form the crux of Berman's fraud case against Weinberg & Green, with the firm maintaining it had made a full disclosure and Berman claiming he hadn't been told the half of it.

In any event, Berman's initial reaction to be billing fraud was somewhat surprising. Far from being outraged, he seemed amused, soon thereafter remarking to another lawyer that Weinberg & Green had "outsmarted itself." Berman urged the firm not to take any disciplinary action against Hess. Berman may have wanted to bide his time, storing his knowledge of the billing fraud as leverage in future dealings, or as a basis for a suit against Weinberg & Green if the firm should lose the Ellerin case (which it later did). For their part, possibly fearing loss of Berman as a client as much as exposure of the theft, Weinberg & Green took no action against Hess.

## The Malpractice and Fraud Claims Against Weinberg & Green

*Fairfax Savings Bank v. Weinberg & Green* was tried before Judge Ann Harrington, sitting without a jury, during the spring of 1995 in Montgomery County Circuit Court in Rockville, Maryland. The trial lasted six weeks. Fifty-five witnesses testified, generating over 7,000 pages of testimony; thousands of exhibits were placed in evidence. Fairfax was represented by a Baltimore firm. Sparing no expense, Weinberg & Green retained Brendan Sullivan, Jr. of Washington's prominent litigation firm, Williams & Connally. Sullivan, Oliver North's lawyer during the Iran Contra hearings, had gained a measure of fame with his "I am not a potted plant" retort to a Congressional committee chairman who thought he was objecting too much.

The trial dealt, first, with the claim that Blum had "slipped something into" the Sherwood Square loan agreement to extend Ellerin's liability without his knowledge. Judge Harrington decided that claim in Weinberg & Green's favor. As she saw it, Blum had indeed committed malpractice, but Ellerin still could not prevail because it had failed to prove that Blum's actions had directly caused damage to the bank. Beyond that, Fairfax's malpractice claim had arisen in 1987 but suit had not been filed until 1992, two years late under the statute of limitations.

The trial focused primarily on Hess's fraudulent billing scheme, the existence of which was conceded. Weinberg & Green set out to prove that full disclosure of the scheme had been made and that Berman had been fully reimbursed. The Sunday evening meeting at Berman's home was the starting point, although there were no records of that meeting and, at that point, no one had known the full extent of the overbilling. Shortly after that meeting James Carbine had undertaken a review of all Berman files. He concluded that it would be impossible to determine from the firm's records the exact amount of the overbilling. Carbine directed those in the billing department doing the calculations to err on the side of overcompensating Berman to ensure that he received the full benefit of a fifteen percent discount.

The staff determined that Fairfax was due payments of $275,000 for overcharges in the *Elllerin* case, $90,000 for overcharges in an unrelated *"Zurich"* case, and an additional $110,000 for other accounts—for a total repayment of $475,000. At the trial, Weinberg & Green called a "certified fraud examiner" from the Price, Waterhouse accounting firm to testify that the law firm's methods of computing overbillings "more than fully compensated" for Berman's losses. Finance committee chairman Miller testified that he had then met with Berman to explain the staff's calculations and to tell him how much the firm proposed to pay for the affected accounts. According to Miller, each of three components of the overbilling problem—*Ellerin, Zurich,* and the remaining accounts— were discussed and Berman had been satisfied with the firm's proposals.

In December 1987, Berman signed a "release of claims" whereby Weinberg & Green was absolved of any claims against it in connection with the *Zurich* case; in exchange for that release, Berman was paid $90,000. In January 1988, Berman signed another release that surrendered any claims against Weinberg & Green relating to legal fees associated with the Sherwood Square project and the related *Ellerin* litigation. Berman was paid $275,000 for the second release and, in addition, Weinberg & Green agreed to continue to represent Fairfax Savings in *Ellerin*, a condition on which Berman had insisted. In addition, Berman was paid $110,000 for overbillings in other Berman accounts. Weinberg & Green had advised Berman repeatedly to consult another lawyer concerning the proposed payments and releases, but Berman didn't take that advice.

Weinberg & Green's evidence of disclosures, payments, and releases during the period 1987-88, standing unanswered, would have barred Berman's fraud claim under the statute of limitations. Maryland has a three-year deadline for filing such claims—that is, three years after the fraud is, or should have been, discovered—and Berman had not filed suit until 1994. Berman and his lawyers were, of course, well aware of their statute of limitations problem. Accordingly, they set out to prove that Berman had been duped by Hess, that Berman hadn't discovered the extent of the fraud until 1993. That strategy depended on Berman's markedly different recollection of key events and on his self-portrayal as naive, trusting, and inexperienced, attributes not usually associated with this shrewd, manipulative, and extraordinarily successful banker.

Berman testified that Hess had come to his home that Sunday afternoon in 1987 and said: "Malcolm, I've done something wrong and I need to tell you about it. I added $20,000 to the Ellerin bill before the discount was taken off." Berman had asked: "Stanford, I need to know the extent of this. Is there anything else?" Hess, face flushed and starting to cry, had replied: "Absolutely not." According to Berman, Hess then stated that Weinberg & Green was "going to make this good" but that he needed a commitment: "You've got the swear to me that you'll never tell anyone because it could be the end of my career." Berman responded: "If this is the truth, you have my word I won't discuss it."

Berman "didn't recall" meeting with Howard Miller to go over the firm's overbilling calculations and proposed reimbursements. He testified that all of his discussions about the overbillings had been with Hess. According to Berman, Hess's explanations of the repayments had led him to believe that the only overbilling had been in the *Ellerin* case. Hess had told him that the $90,000 payment for the *Zurich* case didn't represent deliberate overbilling but an inadvertent "mistake." Hess told Berman that he was receiving $110,000 for his other accounts due to Hess's advocacy on his behalf, that Hess had insisted to his partners that Berman get a fifteen percent discount across the board, "even if he wasn't entitled to it," and that Berman "should be happy."

Berman testified that he had relied entirely on Hess's explanations of the payments. He hadn't consulted an attorney outside Weinberg & Green because he had promised Hess he would tell no one about the overbilling. Berman thus positioned himself to claim that he hadn't learned the extent of the overbilling until after he had fired Weinberg & Green and sued them for malpractice and fraud. At that point, during routine document exchanges, Berman's lawyers had obtained copies of Weinberg & Green documents concerning the overbilling which they passed on to their client. Berman recalled sitting up to read the documents until 3 a.m., feeling shock and outrage. He testified that only then, in October 1993, had he learned about the full extent of the billing fraud. If that testimony were credited, it would effectively counter Weinberg & Green's position that Berman's suit had been filed too late. But there were other reasons not to credit Berman's testimony, particularly the releases.

The three releases Berman signed in December 1987 and January 1988 were short (less than two pages each) and in plain English. The release covering Sherwood Square and the *Ellerin* litigation clearly included all related claims Fairfax might have against Weinberg & Green. As a banker, Berman frequently had occasion to read legal documents, including releases more complex than those involved here. Drafts of the releases had gone back and forth between Berman and the law firm, with Berman making numerous handwritten changes. Nevertheless, Berman testified that he had not paid much attention to the drafts, that he had not really understood them, and, again, that he had relied on Hess — all part of Berman's *persona* (adopted for the case) as the naive, trusting, and inexperienced client.

Brendan Sullivan, Weinberg & Green's lead lawyer, set out to expose Malcolm Berman as a liar, in matters large and small, beginning with his education. Berman testified under oath that his college education consisted of less than six months of accounting courses at the YMCA College of Commerce in Baltimore. Sullivan proved that in three other recent lawsuits, Berman testified that he had taken "several years" of college accounting courses. Berman, the CEO of a major bank, claimed to have "bad problems in reading" and that he couldn't write a letter without help. Sullivan proved that Berman routinely reviewed voluminous business documents and marked up drafts of letters and memoranda Hess sent to him for approval. Berman denied that an important incident established by prior testimony had ever occurred. Sullivan labeled Berman's denial an "in-your-face lie" which he compared to "that old song by the country singer, Colin Rae, *That's My Story and I'm Stickin' to It.*"

Berman was shown to be anything but naive and trusting in his dealings with lawyers — at Weinberg & Green and other Baltimore firms. Judge Harrington noted that Berman had hired "legions of lawyers" over the years. Berman had boasted to Hess that he was "his own best lawyer." A lawyer hired to write an appellate brief testified that Berman had reviewed a draft and sent back "comments on sentence structure, ordering of the arguments, strategy, and whether we should personally attack opposing counsel for conduct during the case." The lawyer came away feeling that working with Berman "was like working with a colleague in the office." Sullivan summed up, saying: "There is a point when lies become so numerous, so pervasive, so all-encompassing, so foolish on their face that together they become recognized as a corrupt effort to mislead the court. The breathtaking scope of Berman's false testimony is so stunning and so far beyond what lawyers and judges generally encounter that it warrants complete rejection."

Judge Harrington saw through Berman's pose. "The Malcolm Berman who took the witness stand in this case could not be the same meticulous, detail-oriented person who emerged from the testimony of the other witnesses. Sadly, Berman was not candid with the Court on many matters. The substance of Berman's testimony was that his decisions on matters related to Weinberg & Green were not informed, were the subject of undue influence, or were flawed because of his naivete and inability to read well. The Court does not accept this."

Judge Harrington went on to decide that Berman had been fully informed about the overbilling in 1987, that the payments had been fair, and that his fraud claim was barred by the releases, as well as by the statute of limitations. That left Berman and his legal team with one last string in their malpractice bow — conflicts of interest.

The Fairfax lawyers called Charles Wolfram, a Professor at Cornell Law School whom we met in Chapter 4, to testify about conflict-of-interest violations by Weinberg & Green. Wolfram identified several conflicts that, in his opinion, had "colored [Weinberg & Green's] representation of Fairfax." He believed that Weinberg & Green should have withdrawn from the *Ellerin* case in 1986 when Blum was first accused of malpractice in drafting documents. As Wolfram saw it, that accusation created a "divergence of interests;" it would have been natural for the firm to think of protecting itself first, rather than its client, Fairfax. He didn't, however, cite specific instances in the record where that had happened.

According to Wolfram, a second conflict had occurred when Weinberg & Green continued to represent Fairfax after the Thanksgiving weekend sheriff's raid on the Ellerin family dinner. As we saw earlier, Steven Caplan of Weinberg & Green had been involved in that incident. Caplan was slated to be the lead lawyer in the upcoming *Ellerin* retrial, but he would also be an important witness to the Thanksgiving incident—an incident which the Ellerin lawyers were expected to (and did) introduce in the retrial as evidence of malice, the basis for punitive damages. Model Rule 3.7 prohibits a lawyer from acting as both advocate and witness in the same case primarily because the dual roles might confuse the jury—a legitimate, if less than compelling, concern. However, the rule includes an exception to the imputation rule (Model Rule 1.10) which allows the lawyer to testify and another lawyer in the same firm to act as advocate. When Weinberg & Green decided not to withdraw entirely, the firm should have assigned another of its lawyers to replace Caplan as counsel.

The most serious conflict-of-interest problem arose from the billing fraud. A conflict can usually be waived if the person who might be disadvantaged by it is told all the facts, freely consents to a waiver, and the lawyer concludes that he can fairly represent the person despite the conflict. There are, however, some conflicts so fundamental, so destructive of the lawyer-client relationship, that they are considered unwaivable. The law firm must withdraw, even if the client urges it to continue.

Berman's legal team argued that the billing fraud had created an unwaivable conflict in the *Ellerin* case, and that Weinberg & Green should have withdrawn when the fraud was disclosed (whether partially or entirely) to Berman in 1987, despite Berman's insistence that it remain as Fairfax's counsel. Under those circumstances (the argument went) Weinberg & Green had to be more concerned with protecting itself from liability for the overbilling, with avoiding disciplinary proceedings by the bar association, and with guarding its reputation, than with representing Malcolm Berman's bank. As Professor Wolfram put it, the billing fraud "had to be kept under wraps." Rather than withdraw, Weinberg & Green had acceded to Berman's wishes and continued as counsel to Fairfax until it lost the *Ellerin* retrial in 1992, and Berman fired them.

The fact that Weinberg & Green lost a difficult case before a jury doesn't prove that it didn't perform competently. A major part of the jury's decision was later overturned on appeal. But there was at least a possibility that the law firm allowed its interest in protecting itself to take precedence over its duty of loyalty to its client. By the late 1980s, the billing fraud was known at Weinberg & Green and to some outsiders, but it wasn't generally known in the Baltimore legal and business communities until 1994, when Berman took it public by suing his former lawyers. By staying in the case, Weinberg & Green reduced the risks of exposure presented by other lawyers gaining access to the billing records or learning of the overbilling through Berman. Those risks aside, the Berman lawyers weren't able to identify decisions from the court record that may have been influenced more by Weinberg & Green's desire to keep the billing fraud quiet than by Fairfax's interest in winning the case. Court records, however, may not reflect the real reasons for litigation decisions. Most strategic decisions are made back at the office.

Finally, but not least, there is the question of mutual trust, the essence of the lawyer-client relationship. How is a client to trust a lawyer who has been systematically stealing from him to the tune of $475,000? Berman's insistence that Weinberg & Green stay in the *Ellerin* case was no proof of his loyalty. Quite the opposite. Judge Harrington recognized that Berman had viewed the billing fraud "as an opportunity to put a powerful weapon in his arsenal for future use, should the need ever arise." And how can a lawyer trust—give his best to—a client who is in a position to turn on him, as Berman would later do?

On behalf of Weinberg & Green, the Sullivan team took the position that no conflicts of interest had occurred. They could have attempted to rebut Professor Wolfram with an academic expert of their own. Instead, they retained Thomas Murphy, a Rockville lawyer with offices a few blocks from Judge Harrington's chambers. Murphy is a former President of the Montgomery County Bar Association and Chairman of its Ethics Committee. He served on that committee's "hotline" for two years, fielding questions almost daily. Murphy testified that the billing fraud had not presented an unwaivable conflict because it had been disclosed and Fairfax had been repaid. Asked to assume intentional and systematic overbilling, Murphy opined: "If the client is satisfied, it's their choice. There's no difference in your duty to a client whether you innocently, negligently, or intentionally overbill. People can put that behind them and move forward."

Judge Harrington ruled that no conflict of interest related to the overbilling had occurred. She could find no evidence that Weinberg & Green had "intentionally lost" the *Ellerin* case. (No such claim had been made). She further believed that their lawyers had given "reasonable advice to Fairfax throughout the *Ellerin* trials." (No basis for such a sweeping conclusion was stated.) Judge Harrington made it clear that she was inclined to accept the views of local attorney Murphy—"a trial

lawyer with substantial experience in the application of ethical principles to the practice of litigation—rather than those of Wolfram—a law
professor who has not practiced law since the early 1960s." She adopted
Murphy's position that once the billing fraud was disclosed and repayment made, the alleged unwaivable conflict "ceased to exist," adding:
"The Court is not persuaded that, despite the cure of the conflict, a
lawyer would be forever barred from further representation of a client
in this situation." (No one had suggested that Weinberg & Green
should stop representing Malcolm Berman's interests forever, only that
they should have withdrawn from the *Ellerin* case.)

In August 1995, Judge Harrington wrote a seventy-five page opinion and entered judgment for Weinberg & Green across the board. Fairfax appealed to Maryland's Court of Special Appeals. In December
1996, the appellate court affirmed Judge Harrington's decision in all respects, ending a chain of disputes that had begun fourteen years earlier
with a slip of a lawyer's pen.

# Post Scripts

Weinberg & Green had its share of ethics problems in the 1990s.
The firm hired a young lawyer, Mark Tomaino. Tomaino brought
clients with him, including Genesys, a rapidly growing company with an
estimated market value of $35 million. As a relatively new associate,
Tomaino structured a complex deal designed to return stock to the company's founders and former owners. The deal went sour and ended up
in court where the judge spoke of "some very serious wrongdoings" by
Tomaino. His clients had lost their company altogether while Tomaino,
their lawyer, had received a payment that looked very much like a kickback. Almost none of Tomaino's work had been supervised by a senior
Weinberg & Green lawyer, and no corrective action had been taken
when problems came to light. Quite the contrary. When Tomaino's actions were reviewed after the fact and he agreed to leave the firm voluntarily, Weinberg & Green rewarded him with a $55,000 departure
bonus.

The former owners of Genesys sued Tomaino for conflict of interest.
Looking for a deeper pocket, they also sued Weinberg & Green for failing to supervise their associate. In July 1996, they won a $24.9 million
verdict against the law firm, all in compensatory damages. A separate
trial was scheduled on punitive damages—the jury had found actual

malice on the part of the law firm—when the case was settled for an undisclosed amount.

Weinberg & Green had paid a price for its ethics scandals. In August 1996, one year after Judge Harrington's decision, James Carbiner, head of Weinberg & Green's litigation department since 1985 and the partner principally responsible for uncovering and terminating the billing fraud, resigned from the firm to become a sole practitioner. Carbiner reportedly left because of a shrinking firm and declining referrals brought on partly by the billing fraud. At that time, the firm numbered about 130 lawyers, most of them associates. By 1998, the firm's roster had been cut in half—42 partners and only 14 associates. Howard Miller, who participated with Hess in the billing fraud, continued as managing partner of Weinberg & Green until 1992. In 1999, Weinberg & Green merged with Saul, Ewing, Remick & Saul which became Saul, Ewing, Weinberg & Green. Stanford Hess left Weinberg & Green in 1994, seven years after his billing fraud scheme came to light, to became a partner in the Baltimore firm of Neuberger, Quinn, Geilen, Rubin & Gibber, specializing in banking law. The Attorney Grievance Commission of Maryland finally caught up with Hess and, in 1999, his license to practice was suspended for three years. Also in 1999, Hess was disbarred from practice before the United States Supreme Court.

* * *

# Comments and Questions

1. Stanford Hess' overbilling scheme did not violate any specific provision of Model Rule 1.5, "Fees," but it presumably would not have met the rule's overall "reasonable" standard. The overbilling did represent a clear case of "professional misconduct…involving dishonesty" within the meaning of Rule 8.4(c). Lacking the element of asportation (physical movement of the stolen item), it wasn't common law larceny. But under modern theft statutes that modify and merge such common-law offenses of larceny, larceny by trick, and embezzlement, Hess probably could have been prosecuted for a theft offense. In the event, however, neither Hess nor those in league with him at Weinberg & Green were prosecuted criminally.

One would like to think that overbilling and its near relative, expense fraud, are isolated phenomena. Expense fraud involves fictitious or inflated bills for airplane tickets, hotels, restaurants, etc. purportedly incurred in representing the client. An exhaustive study by Professor Lisa Lerman of Catholic University Law School, "Blue Chip Bilking: Regulation of Billing and Expense Fraud by Lawyers," 12 *Geo. J. Legal Ethics* 205 (2000) describes in detail 16 cases of major billing and expense fraud in the 1990s, most of them in large firms. All but a few of the offending lawyers stole more than Stanford Hess—the top seven each took $1 million or more. The law firms included Winston & Strawn and Brown & Platt, Chicago; Akin, Gump, Strauss, Hauer & Feld, Washington, D.C.; Thompson, Hine and Flory, Cleveland; Latham & Watkins, San Francisco; Hunton & Williams, Richmond; and, famously, The Rose Law Firm, Little Rock, where Webster Hubbell had been managing partner. Most of the offenders were senior partners in their firms; five were managing partners. A few were prosecuted criminally; most were either disbarred or voluntarily resigned from the bar. Stanford Hess got off comparatively easy with a three-year suspension of his license to practice. The sixteen cases Lerman studied were high-visibility, involving mostly prominent firms, big money, and, of course, those who happened to get caught. One wonders how much billing and expense fraud is going on that isn't caught.

2. Part of the shock power of the billing and expense fraud cases comes from the dramatically large sums of money siphoned off by a few dishonest lawyers. Viewing those amounts from another perspective, however, they add up to less than $20 million—not even a good month's revenue for a megafirm. Much larger amounts may be unjustifiably billed to clients by the near-universal practice of hourly billing.

There are conflicts of interest (different from the Model Rule variety) between lawyers and their clients when it comes to setting fees, no matter what fee arrangement is agreed to. The contingent fee lawyer may want a higher percentage of the recovery than the client will want to give up. Similarly, the lawyer performing a service for a fixed fee is motivated to set it on the high side. In either case, the lawyer will factor into her percentage or fixed fee an estimate of how long it will take to perform the service, so that hourly billing enters into her calculus through the back door. But when contingent or fixed fees are agreed upon, the client does have some control in the negotiation, and he knows what the final bill will be. Not so with hourly billing. Clients can sometimes negotiate hourly rates, but most lawyers don't negotiate their rates. Once the rate is set, the conflict between lawyer and client kicks in, demonstrating the adage: "The longer it takes me, the more money I make." A law firm's incentive, particularly with a deep-pocket client, is to work the case to a fair-thee-well, piling up as many billable hours as it believes the client will tolerate. Bills for every kind of discovery, depositions of every possible adverse witness—sometimes by teams of lawyers—and exhaustive legal research of collateral issues sometimes generate bills well beyond what a prudent lawyer would have found necessary or appropriate. Considering the potential for abuses in hourly billing, are there practical alternatives for billing? Can hourly billing be retained and its abuses reined in?

Billable hour requirements—or "expectations" as they are sometimes called—for associates present a different set of problems. Firm X, for example, may tell its associates that they are expected to log 2,000 billable hours per year, and that their raises and eventual consideration for partnership will depend significantly on whether they meet that goal. (My students tell me that 2,000 is a representative number for Washington, D.C. firms; some are higher, a few lower.) Taking into account vacations, sick leave and holidays, a 2,000-hour requirement means that the associate is expected to average over forty billable hours each week. While forty-plus hours may not sound unreasonable, in fact, it puts tremendous pressure on young lawyers to run up their hours, with little regard for the significance of the work—for example, researching tangential cases from other jurisdictions—or whether, on a Saturday afternoon when they would rather be playing soccer, the client is getting its money's worth.

More important from an ethics standpoint, there is both pressure and an incentive for associates to cheat by padding their billable hours to meet—better yet, exceed—an annual requirement. Based on my experience in law firms and on conversations with other lawyers, that is what frequently happens. Not massive cheating—more a matter of 3.2 hours becoming 3.7 hours. An hour of padded time each day by half of the associates in a big firm can mount up in a year to thousands of hours billed to clients that were not worked. An associate padding her time sheet by one unworked hour to make a slow day look a little better is not in the same moral universe with the partner who systematically defrauds clients by $300,000 or more. Still, both are guilty of "professional misconduct...involving dishonesty" within the meaning of Model Rule 8.4(c). Beyond that, the practice of padding billable hours can condition associates to think that cheating clients on a modest scale is not only acceptable, but expected, and promote cynical attitudes to other ethical standards that can impede the search for revenue. Apart from the technical rules of ethics, who has greater responsibility for false billable hours, the associates who report them or the firm that imposes a minimum billable-hour requirement on its associates?

3. The Fairfax Savings Bank (Berman) plaintiffs claimed that Weinberg & Green had been guilty of an unwaivable conflict of interest when it failed to withdraw from the *Ellerin* litigation after the billing fraud was revealed to Berman. At Berman's insistence, Weinberg & Green had stayed in the case, but later lost it. There was no evidence, however, that the law firm had conducted the litigation so as to protect themselves from further disclosure of the billing fraud at their client's expense. Testifying for the plaintiffs, Professor Wolfram stressed that the billing fraud "had to be kept under wraps," and that need would, potentially at least, prejudice the client. Thomas Murphy, the defendant's expert, testified that disclosure of the fraud, repayment, and Berman's insistence that the firm continue had effectively waived the conflict. Judge Harrington found for Weinberg & Green. Do you agree with her rationale?

Professor Wolfram seemed to imply that whenever a serious conflict arises between lawyer and client, the lawyer must withdraw from any related matter or litigation, regardless of the client's wishes. Should the conflict of interest rules protect a sophisticated client like Berman from himself? Do you agree with witness Murphy's statement that there is no difference between innocently, negligently, or deliberately overbilling a client, so long as consent is given?

Classic examples of unwaivable conflicts are representing both husband and wife in a contested divorce or both buyer and seller in a sale of property. In such situations, one can say with confidence that it is impossible to represent one, and possibly both, sides adequately. Was that true of *Fairfax Savings Bank v. Weinberg & Green*? If not, should the law nevertheless insist that in situations involving dishonesty by the law firm and rancor on both sides, the law firm should withdraw?

4. Recall that no lawyer at Weinberg & Green reported the billing fraud to the Attorney Grievance Committee of Maryland despite the Maryland counterpart of Model Rule 8.3 "Reporting Professional Misconduct": "A lawyer having knowledge that another lawyer has committed a violation of the Rules of Professional Conduct that raises a substantial question as to that lawyer's honesty...shall inform the appropriate pro-

fessional authority." Professor Lerman states: "Rule 8.3 is perhaps the most widely violated and most under-enforced of the disciplinary rules." She describes conducting a continuing legal education program for about one hundred lawyers who were asked to raise their hands if they had seen violations covered by Virginia's "tattle-tale rule" and had not reported them to disciplinary authorities. Almost all of the lawyers raised their hands; many said they had observed and not reported numerous instances of serious misconduct.

There is, of course, a tension between wishing to have misconduct reported and not wishing to be a tattle-tale or rat fink. Can you think of ways in which more reporting could be encouraged? Or would it be better to abandon mandatory reporting of misconduct on the theory that a rule so widely violated must represent unsound policy?

# Chapter 6

# The Gatekeeper

"This case gets worse as you learn more of the facts. Every time you turn over a rock something crawls out. That's not supposed to happen in a securities offering."

— Kathy Patrick, counsel for plaintiffs in *Delta Municipal Fund, Inc. v. N-Group Securities, Inc.*

The $73 million bond deal closed at a Dallas law office on October 25, 1989. The proceeds would finance construction of high-capacity jails in six Texas counties. The project had been promoted as a partial answer to overcrowded conditions in State prisons and county jails. A federal judge presiding over a constitutional challenge to conditions in the Harris County jail in Houston had found "almost a human carpet of people sleeping on the floor; they had to step over each other." The new jails would be privately operated, representing an extension of the privitization concept. The nationally-known firm, Wackenhut Securities Systems and Services Co., was slated to be the operator. Wackenhut would contract to house and rehabilitate prisoners for a fixed fee per prisoner, per day, operating more efficiently, it was thought, than government-staffed detention facilities.

The conference room where the closing took place was almost as crowded as the Harris County jail, with the major players in the deal — the mutual fund buyers, the counties, the underwriter, the construction company, the developer, and a legion of lawyers — signing stacks of documents. The buyers presented checks totaling $73 million to Drexel, Burnham & Lambert which Drexel paid over to the trustee for the bond buyers, after deducting its $2.2 million underwriting fee (representing three percent of the proceeds). Ray Hutchison received $730,000 for his law firm's services to the bond issuers. Brent Bailey, an associate at the Houston office of Chicago-based Keck, Mahin & Cate, received $294,000 for representing Drexel.

Pat Graham was operating as developer of the project through his N-Group Securities, Inc., an entity he had created for that purpose. As the man who had made it happen, Graham received $1.25 million at the closing, but that was only the first installment of what would grow to a bonanza. All parties to the transaction knew that Graham was entitled to a developer's fee of $2.25 million—half at closing, the other half after corrections officials had signed contracts for prisoner housing—in return for putting together the project team and for some ill-defined consulting services. What the other parties didn't know was that the $2.25 million represented only about one-quarter of Graham's eventual take.

Graham offered the construction contract to H.A. Lott, Inc., the builder of Houston's Astrodome, on the condition that Graham would be paid $800,000 for each of the jails—$4.8 million for all six. For his part, Graham would render services similar to those he had already agreed to perform for his developer's fee. Graham's offer was on a take-it-or-leave it basis; business was slow, so Lott took it. The arrangement, formalized in a subcontract, had the earmarks of a kickback—an under-the-table payment for steering lucrative work, without performing significant services. The existence of the subcontract was later disclosed in the preliminary official statement ("POS")—the principal sales document—but the amount of Graham's fee was not.

Both federal and Texas law require that all material facts—facts relevant to an investment decision—be disclosed in the sale of bonds and other securities. Unlike common-law fraud which requires proof of intentional deception, it is not enough that the seller's representations are true, standing alone. They must be true in context, so that the message to the buyer is, in the words of federal securities law, "not misleading." Graham's subcontract fee meant that almost $5 million of the bond proceeds—money investors were led to believe would be spent on steel bars and razor wire—were going instead into a developer's pocket. Ray Hutchison, counsel for the county agencies and an experienced bond lawyer, expressed surprise on learning, long after the closing, how much Graham had extracted from H.A. Lott as a condition of becoming general contractor for the project. "It is an enormous amount of money. It represents ten percent of the contract price. Some in the industry would suggest that a materiality factor is reached at five percent." Hutchison added: "Had I known this, these transactions would not have been closed with our participation for the very simple reason that this is, obviously, payment for something other than services rendered."

Graham's contract with Lott also gave him the right to select the subcontractor for structural steel—the largest subcontract for the project. Graham offered that subcontract to Hirschfeld Steel Co. on the condition that he would receive ten percent of the company's $15 million price — another $1.5 million for Graham. That kickback was kept secret from the other deal participants and later from investors, prompting an investor-witness at the trial to observe: "This really highlights the sleaze in the transaction." Graham had also negotiated favorable loans from underwriter Drexel and from Lott. Graham's total take from the jail project exceeded $8.5 million. And had the project succeeded as planned, he would have stood to gain an additional $2.5 million for "monitoring" prisoner contracts.

Pat Graham had entered the workforce in the early 1970s at "Graham's Men and Boys," a clothing store owned by an uncle. He left in 1986 to open his own store, a haberdashery called "Gents of Humble." Graham soon grew weary of selling suits and socks for modest profits. At about that time, overcrowding in the State's prisons and jails was becoming increasingly acute and Graham, along with others, began to visualize themselves as developers of jail construction projects. There was a lot of money to be made, or so it seemed. In the beginning, Graham knew nothing about jails and had no experience as a developer. But he learned something about the business as he went along, mostly in remodeling projects for small jails.

Pat Graham believed he had developed a breakthrough concept in detention facilities. He described with pride how he had drawn the initial sketches "on my dining room table." Graham's prototype facility was designed to house five hundred prisoners — most of them in dormitories, a few in maximum-security cells. Sketches in hand, he set about trying to sell the concept. During 1988, Graham met with James Lynaugh, then Executive Director of the Texas Department of Criminal Justice, the agency responsible for the State's prison system. The Department was then a defendant in *Ruiz v. Lynaugh*, a prison overcrowding case in which a federal judge had prohibited the acquisition of additional prison dormitory space; all new prisons were to be cell-only. Lynaugh told Graham that his facility design would not meet *Ruiz* standards and that, therefore, the Department of Criminal Justice could not legally transfer inmates to them, despite overcrowding in the State prisons. That meant the loss of a major potential prisoner market, but Graham chose not to modify his design, and he pressed ahead.

Graham offered Drexel, Burnham & Lambert the opportunity to underwrite a bond offering to finance construction of the jails on the condition that Drexel would loan Graham $50,000, ostensibly to cover expenses N-Group was incurring in putting the deal together. Such a loan to a developer from an underwriter was unusual. If Graham really needed $50,000, what was he doing in a multi-million dollar deal? But Graham's offer, like the offers to contractor Lott and Hirschfield Steel, was take-it-or-leave-it, and Drexel didn't want to pass up what looked like a profitable deal. Drexel loaned Graham $50,000 (later, an additional $50,000) and signed on as underwriter.

Mark White was elected Attorney General of Texas in 1978 and Governor in 1982. Following his term as governor, he entered private law practice with a Houston firm that later merged with Keck, Mahin & Cate, a Chicago-based firm of some 350 lawyers. Governor White (Texas governors keep their titles for life) was to be the principal rainmaker for Keck, Mahin's Houston office. Pat Graham had known White for years and had contributed to his political campaigns. In April 1989, he met with White and it was agreed that Keck, Mahin would act as underwriter's counsel for Drexel in the jail bond offering.

Governor White got credit for bringing Drexel in as a client, but the legal work would be done by Brent Bailey, an associate and the only lawyer in the small Houston office with experience in securities financing. Bailey had graduated from Baylor Law School in 1983; he was in the sixth year of the Keck, Mahin's seven-year partnership track. His work on the jail bond deal would be a major factor in whether he made partner. As principal draftsman of the POS, the document most relied on by potential investors, Bailey would be responsible under the federal securities laws for exercising "due diligence," a term of art meaning reasonable efforts to ensure that the POS disclosed all material facts about the jail project. But he was also subject to a conflicting pressure: as the deal was structured, counsel for the underwriter would receive no fee unless the deal closed. Brent Bailey, the associate-up-for-partner, was in a bind. He was expected to disclose the facts with diligence, including facts that might break the deal. At the same time, he was expected to make the deal go through so that Keck, Mahin would get paid.

Brent Bailey's work on the jail bond deal was to be supervised by Kai Nebel, a partner in Keck, Mahin's home office in Chicago and head of the firm's municipal finance group. A graduate of Princeton and Harvard Law School, Nebel had been a general litigator, had represented municipalities, and, shortly before joining Keck, Mahin in 1984, had acted as underwriter's counsel in some bond offerings. In 1988 he served as counsel to the underwriter in a $140 million municipal school bond offering—the largest offering he had been involved in. Brent Bailey had worked with Nebel on the school bond deal, making several trips to Chicago, and Nebel had formed an opinion of the young associate from the Houston office as a "first rate lawyer, very thorough."

The deal had to be sold to the counties before it could go forward. Pat Graham organized a "workshop" on May 25 at the Fairmont Hotel in Dallas. Representatives of six rural Texas counties—Angelina, Falls, LaSalle, Pecos, San Saba, and Swisher—accepted Graham's invitation, attracted by the prospect of jail payrolls being spent in their small communities. Governor Mark White made a welcoming speech, assuring the counties of a continuous supply of prisoners: "Let me tell you I have been down to Harris County [Houston] and you don't have to worry much about losing your raw materials. There is plenty of new product coming to you." (When White ran again for governor in 1990, Pat Graham, his brother Mike, and several others associated with the jail project showed their appreciation of White's efforts by contributing $225,000 to his unsuccessful campaign.) Later on the witness stand, White testified: "I was not promoting the bonds. I was telling them the truth about the product." In any event, the county representatives came away persuaded. Each agreed to establish a "jail facilities financing corporation" as a separate entity to issue the bonds and become owner of its new facility.

Brent Bailey began to write the POS—a separate document for each county facility—in early June. He distributed a first draft to members of the working group—composed of himself, Hutchison, Pat Graham, and representatives of Drexel and H.A. Lott—for comment and any proposed revisions on June 13. Bailey's draft stated: "Although constructed according to the standards of a maximum-security facility, the facility will house only minimum- and medium-security prisoners as long as it is operated by a private entity." A feasibility study prepared by an economist-consultant at Bailey's request also described the facility as "maximum security." A major issue in the later litigation would be whether the jails, as they were described to potential bond purchasers, could house maximum-security prisoners including murderers and bank robbers, or only minimum-security forgers and car thieves. The higher the level of security incorporated into the design, the more flexible, and therefore the more valuable, the facility. In his earlier meeting with Lynaugh of the Department of Criminal Justice, Graham had said that his proposed facility was designed to minimum security standards—a design which would eliminate a potential market in medium- and high-security prisoners. Graham, father of the facility design, would have been the most knowledgeable source of clarifying language for the draft POS, but the "maximum security" description remained unchanged.

Texas law requires that municipal bond offerings be approved by the State Attorney General whose staff reviews the documents for legality and feasibility of the project. Bailey's POS and the feasibility study were duly submitted for review on July 12. The day before, Mike Graham, who was active in the jail bond project with his brother Pat, purchased a $10,000 cashier's check payable to the gubernatorial campaign fund of Jim Maddox, the incumbent Attorney General. Maddox's campaign fund never received the money. Instead, Pat Graham took the check from Mike and carried it around in his wallet until October 17, when it was redeposited in an N-Group account. At that point, however, the Attorney General's office had confirmed that the bond offering would be approved. On November 7, the Graham brothers formed "Citizens for Enhanced Criminal Justice," a political action committee supporting Jim Maddox for governor, to which they contributed $55,000. Maddox would later testify, denying any impropriety: "I'm here to explain to you that the things you are suggesting are absolutely ludicrous and stupid." However, asked whether he had a conversation with Mike Graham in July 1989, he replied that was "possible." The evidence fell short of bribery, but it probably had negative connotations for the defendants in the minds of the jurors.

The POS for each county stated on its cover page: "The facility will be available to house inmates of the county, the State of Texas, other counties within the State of Texas, the United States government, and other governmental entities allowed by law to transfer inmates to the facility." The review by the Attorney General's office focused on whether that language reflected a realistic availability of prisoners (prisoner markets, or, in Governor White's term, "product") to fill the jails, a question critical to feasibility of the project. The working group had been assuming that out-of-state prisoners—those from "other governmental entities" like the District of Columbia—would be the primary market for the new jails. At that time, the District's corrections facilities were inadequate and its convicts were being farmed out to Texas and other state prisons. Brent Bailey and Ray Hutchison met with James Thomassen, Assistant Attorney General of the Public Finance Section in the Attorney General's office. They were told that the State had no authority to house prisoners from other States or the District of Columbia in the privately-operated facilities being proposed, effectively eliminating a major part of the anticipated market. Thomassen also told Bailey and Hurchison that only small numbers of federal prisoners could be housed in Texas because federal tax laws limited funding for tax-exempt projects (the federal payments for prisoners would be considered "funding"). Furthermore, there would have to be some nexus between the State of Texas and the crime so that the State wouldn't become a prisoner farm for the rest of the country.

The Attorney General's review also raised questions about "inmates of the State of Texas" as a source of prisoners. Bailey and other members of the working group knew that the facilities would not comply with the *Ruiz* court order barring additional use of dormitory beds in the State prison system. This meant that inmates already housed in State prisons did not represent a potential market, even if those prisons were overcrowded. The *Ruiz* order did not apply to convicted felons being housed temporarily ("backlogged") in county jails, pending availability of beds in State prisons. However, there was a dispute—later to become a lawsuit—over whether the State or the counties were obligated to pay for housing those inmates. Thomassen advised Bailey and Hutchison that, as a result, there was no assurance that payments would be forthcoming, even assuming State prison officials were willing to transfer prisoners to the new jails.

The POS reference to "inmates of the county" did not represent a significant market because the rural counties where the new jails would be constructed had low crime rates; existing jail space was sufficient to meet the need. That left "other counties within the State of Texas" as the primary market for prisoners. Whether those counties would transfer prisoners to privately-operated, and perhaps more expensive, facilities was an open question. Unless a county were sued and enjoined to alleviate jail overcrowding, it might opt for a less-expensive, if unconstitutional, status quo.

The discussions with Thomassen called the expected markets for prisoners, as described in the POS, into serious question. Those concerns surfaced in a working group meeting on July 20. According to Bailey's notes of the meeting, Hutchison was concerned that Drexel might not be willing to market the bonds in what was left of the market. Bailey had responded to Hutchison: "Ray, we need to get our act together." As the draftsman of the POS and the person primarily responsible for its accuracy, it fell to Bailey to make any necessary revisions in the POS. That document, as it was later distributed to investors, had been revised in some respects, but it did not reflect the concerns about prisoner markets raised during Thomassen's review. Most significant, the POS reference to "prisoners of the State of Texas" had not been qualified to exclude inmates in State prisons covered by the *Ruiz* order. Bailey would later testify that such a qualification had been unnecessary because "that was a fact that everybody knew," despite the fact that the POS seemed to say the opposite. The revised POS also failed to note that the State was refusing to pay for convicted felons backlogged in county jails. As a result, *no* "prisoners of the State of Texas" could have been transferred to the proposed new jails at that time.

On July 25, Wackenhut Securities Systems wrote to Pat Graham: "It is with deep regret that I must notify you of our decision to withdraw Wackenhut's name from consideration as the operator for the 500-bed correctional facilities.... Despite significant attempts by yourself and various Wackenhut staff to address our many operational concerns, we have yet to achieve a satisfactory level of comfort...." Three months before the closing, Graham had to find a new operator. The working group had expected that Wackenhut would supply a substantial number of prisoners. Wackenhut's withdrawal and its "operational concerns" were not disclosed to investors.

On August 22, the revised POS was circulated to some 30 institutional buyers, all managers of high-risk mutual funds. The funds were heavily invested in tax-free municipal bonds for upper-income shareholders. The jail bonds were offered at par, at an interest rate of 9.75%. Factoring in the federal income-tax break, shareholders might expect a return on investment of about 18% if premiums were paid to maturity. The jail bonds were risky, a fact noted in several places in the POS. Perhaps most significant, they were "revenue" bonds, meaning that the only source of payment would be revenues from housing prisoners. The county corporations that owned the facilities would not be liable to the bondholders if revenues proved insufficient after payment of operating expenses. Revenues, in turn, would depend on continued overcrowding in Texas prisons and jails, on the willingness of county and state officials to send prisoners and pay for them, and on a facility design appropriate for housing all types of prisoners.

On September 5, when the bond offering was still under review, Assistant Attorney General Thomassen wrote to Bailey: "I still see a significant weakness in the feasibility study in that it does not contain any information to indicate that other counties will, indeed, place prisoners in these facilities." Concerned that the deal was coming unglued, Bailey made telephone calls to several county officials, hoping to substantiate a potential market among prisoners in county jails. On September 13, Bailey responded to Thomassen's letter. He wrote that Travis County (Austin) had transferred one hundred prisoners to other counties under a federal court order to relieve jail overcrowding, and that Cullen County had transferred ninety prisoners because its jail had been decertified by the State commission. While the market represented by those two examples was less than robust, Bailey nevertheless concluded his letter with the hope they would convince Thomassen "that there are entities out there that would be willing to pay out of their pockets to house their own prisoners in another's facility." One day before the closing, the Attorney General approved the bond offering, with the standard disclaimer that he had relied on representations of the issuers, "without undertaking to verify [them] by independent investigation."

Brent Bailey's efforts—from the draft POS in June, through the revised POS in August, to the closing in October—received minimal supervision from Kai Nebel, the head of Keck, Mahin's municipal finance group in Chicago. Nebel flew to Houston for their only meeting when he also met Governor White, the Houston office's rainmaker. He did not meet any of the participants in the jail bond deal, and knew nothing of their backgrounds—specifically, that a court judgment for fraud had been entered against the Graham brothers. He asserted that such a judgment "would have been irrelevant" to an investment decision. He saw it as his role to "review certain of the critical documentation" for "consistency" and "full disclosure." In the course of his testimony, he did not point to any specific contributions he had made to the offering documents.

Nebel was asked about the failure to disclose in the POS the amount of the $800,000 fee N-Group was to receive for each of the six facilities under its subcontract. His responses concerning that issue typified his level of involvement. He had known from his review of the POS that it referred to a subcontract fee without disclosing its amount, but he had not raised questions about the amount with Bailey. Nebel had not seen the subcontract, and had not known that N-Group had refused to disclose the fee to Bailey. In any event, Nebel claimed that he had not considered the fee amount to be "material" in the sense that it could affect investment decisions and therefore had to be disclosed. He reasoned that since H.A. Lott's contract was for a fixed price, the costs of the subcontracts were irrelevant, and Lott would be required to complete construction and pay any overruns out of its own pocket (assuming its pockets were deep enough). Even if cost overruns from subcontracts were to adversely affect the quality of construction, Nebel contended that investors would be looking to the income stream, not to the facilities themselves—the concrete and iron bars—as collateral for their investment because of the speculative resale value of these single-purpose facilities (assuming there would be *any* income stream for use of a substandard facility).

The POS, the feasibility study, and related documents were reviewed by analysts for the funds more closely than by Kai Nebel. Drexel personnel, sometimes joined by Brent Bailey or Pat Graham, fielded their questions in telephone conferences, and, ultimately, the $73 million bond issue was fully subscribed. H.A. Lott commenced construction simultaneously in the six counties in early 1990. Construction was completed in the spring of 1991 and the Texas Jail Standards Commission certified the new jails for occupancy by minimum-security prisoners.

The bondholders had been led to believe that the new jails would be rapidly filled with prisoners, generating revenues to meet interest payments and, on maturity, to pay off the bonds. That did not happen. In mid-1991, the bondholders retained the Goldman, Sachs investment-banking firm, a lawyer, and a political consultant to assist in getting prisoner contracts. After several months, no contracts had been obtained, interest payments ceased, and the bondholders began negotiating to sell the jails to the State prison system. Taking advantage of the bondholders' weak bargaining position, the State offered $6 million for each jail—less than the cost of construction—a total of $36 million for all six. By April 1992, there still were no contracts for prisoners; five of the six jails were sitting empty and beginning to look like white elephants. One jail was housing prisoners from Houston's Harris County under a federal court order, but there was no assurance that situation would continue. Reluctantly, the bondholders accepted the State's offer, selling the jails for $36 million and taking a $37 million loss on their investments. They sought to recoup their losses by suing Keck, Mahin & Cate, the Graham brothers, N-Group Securities, Drexel, Burnham & Lambert, and H. A. Lott. *Delta Municipal Fund, Inc. v. N-Group Securities, Inc.* was filed in federal district court in Houston in 1992 alleging violations of federal securities laws, the Texas Securities Act, common-law fraud, and legal malpractice; it sought compensatory and punitive damages. The case was assigned to Judge Sim Lake. The bondholder plaintiffs were represented by Robin Gibbs and Kathy Patrick of Gibbs

& Bruns, a Houston firm specializing in commercial and securities litigation. Other lawyers heavily involved in the case included William Wilde of Bracewell & Patterson—among Houston's major corporate firms—for Keck, Mahin & Cate, and David Peden, a specialist in construction litigation, for H.A. Lott. After suit was filed, Drexel, Burnham declared bankruptcy (precipitated by Michael Milken's disastrous junk-bond deals) and was dismissed as a defendant. Following extensive discovery, trial began before Judge Lake and a jury on September 12, 1994 and continued over five weeks. Forty-nine witnesses generated a transcript of 5,000 pages, and thousands of exhibits were placed in evidence. A complete account of this complex case would be far beyond the scope of this chapter, which focuses on salient features of the investors' case against Keck, Mahin & Cate.

Kathy Patrick of Gibbs & Bruns called investment advisors from three of the plaintiff mutual funds to testify that they had been induced by misrepresentations in the POS and the feasibility study, and by statements of Pat Graham, Brent Bailey, and Drexel sales personnel, to buy some $50 million in jail bonds. The testimony of Jerome White, director of the municipal bond department of Delta Municipal Fund, was representative of the investor witnesses. White stressed the importance of accuracy and full disclosure in preliminary official statements, particularly in the municipal bond market. There are some 2,000 companies listed on the New York Stock Exchange, compared to some 50,000 issuers of municipal bonds. It would be wholly impracticable for institutional bond buyers to conduct independent investigations of issuers before buying their bonds.

White had been personally involved in analyzing the jail bond offering, reading the documents several times. He had understood from reading the POS that the jails would be built to maximum-security standards. "To me, that meant that any prisoner in the State of Texas could be housed in these facilities." It was important to have the broadest possible prisoner market because, as revenue bonds, payment would depend on operating the jails at profitable levels.

Patrick asked White about the POS cover-page description of prisoner markets, which referred to prisoners of "the State of Texas." He had understood that prisoners of the Texas Department of Corrections —those in the overcrowded State prisons—would be a major part of the market for the new jails. White had verified his understanding in a telephone conversation with Pat Graham and a Drexel representative, which had included discussion of the *Ruiz* case. White had come away with the incorrect understanding that the jails—with mostly dormitory beds—would nevertheless meet *Ruiz* design standards.

White was shown a copy of Assistant Attorney General Thomassen's letter of September 5 to Brent Bailey in which he had questioned whether felons temporarily housed in county jails awaiting available beds in a state prison—the "backlogged prisoners"—represented a viable market. Although Bailey had sent White a copy of his September 13 response, as well as copies of other correspondence with Thomassen, White had not been sent the September 5 letter. In that letter, Thomassen had reiterated his earlier statement to Bailey and Hutchison that the State "had no money to put prisoners in these facilities" so that "high demand for [State prison] beds does not translate into high demand for local detention facilities." White was not told that the State had no funds to pay for backlogged prisoners, the only other source of State prisoners. He testified that Delta Fund would not have bought jail bonds if he had known that State prisoners would not be an available market.

Patrick asked White about his understanding of N-Group's role in the jail project. White responded: "N-Group was to play a pretty all-encompassing role...to help develop, design, construct [the jails] and bring in prisoners through relationships with counties" for a total fee of $2.5 million. White had asked Graham the amount of the "separate fee" for his N-Group under its subcontract with Lott. He was told it would be "nominal," about $500,000, and that N-Group's total compensation for all its services would be approximately $3 million—about one-third of the $8.5 million Graham did eventually receive. Patrick showed White the description of services to be rendered by N-Group under the subcontract. In his opinion, N-Group was already being paid $2.5 million as its developer's fee "for doing the exact same thing."

On White's recommendation, Delta Municipal Fund had bought $28 million of the $73 million jail bond offering. Had he known the jails would not meet maximum-security standards, that state prisoners were not an available market, or that $8.5 million—twelve percent—of the bond proceeds were going to N-Group, Delta would not have bought the bonds. In White's opinion, the bonds had been "worthless" when they were bought. Investment advisors representing other plaintiff funds gave testimony similar to White's, one of who summarized his position in a phrase: "This deal stinks."

Plaintiff's counsel Robin Gibbs called Pat Graham as an adverse witness. Graham agreed with Gibbs that "minimum security" would be an accurate description of the facilities he had been promoting. Asked why those facilities had been described to the investors as "maximum-security," Graham first pointed to Brent Bailey, the "wordsmith" of the POS. Graham went on to contend, however, that "maximum security" had been an accurate term in the sense that the minimum-security areas in his design — the dormitory areas — could have been built "out of sheet rock" instead of the sturdier materials which had, if fact, been used. According to Graham, he had been "trying to impress on everyone that we're going above [sheet rock], that we're building [with] the same materials used in a maximum-security facility." Graham ignored the fact that the standards for jail construction materials — such as the quality of concrete and steel — are distinct from the physical features found in a maximum-security jail. A minimum-security facility constructed with steel walls instead of sheet rock, but lacking such features as constant visual surveillance, perimeter fences, and guard towers, would not be used to house maximum-security inmates.

There was a potential smoking gun in the case: whether Brent Bailey had known the amount of N-Group's $4.8 million subcontractor fee *before* the POS he had written was circulated to investors. If he had, his failure to disclose that such a large sum was being diverted from construction to Pat Graham would have represented a clear violation of federal and State disclosure requirements. Graham first testified that he had disclosed the fee amount in a meeting with Bailey and Ray Hutchison shortly after the subcontract was signed in late May.

What little remained of Pat Graham's credibility disappeared entirely when, late in the trial, Judge Lake directed counsel to disclose any payments between the parties. In response, David Peden, counsel for H.A. Lott, dropped a bombshell — a document reflecting Graham's agreement to testify favorably to Lott, following a script approved by Peden, in return for $50,000 to enable Graham to pay an attorney. Judge Lake reacted with shock: "In twenty-five years of practice as a trial lawyer and as a judge, I've never seen a document like this." There was concern that a mistrial might be required. Instead, Graham was recalled to explain. He testified that until he received the $50,000 from Lott in exchange for his testimony, he had planned to take the Fifth Amendment when called as a witness. Graham claimed that he had been broke at the time — despite having received over $8 million from the jail-bond deal only two years before — and that he didn't want to testify without a lawyer. His deal with Lott included a specific commitment to testify that he had disclosed the $4.8 million subcontract fee to Brent Bailey.

Under blunt cross-examination by Wilde, counsel for Keck, Mahin, it became clear that Graham had been willing to sell alternative versions of his story, depending on the buyer's needs. Wilde confronted Graham: "This isn't the first time you tried to sell your testimony, is it?" Graham responded: "I don't think this is selling testimony, as such, no." Graham admitted, however, that he had approached Wilde shortly after suit was filed. This colloquy ensued:

> Wilde: "Now, Mr Graham, you sat in my office and you told me that unless Keck, Mahin was willing to fund your defense...that you were going to get yourself out of it and make a deal with the plaintiffs."
>
> Graham: "I thought that was one of my options, yes sir."
>
> Wilde: "And I told you that we would have no interest in such an arrangement."
>
> Graham: "I think you left me with that impression."

Before closing his packaged testimony deal with Lott, Graham had expressed his intention to make a similar deal with Gibbs and Patrick, counsel for the plaintiff-bondholders. Had he done that, Graham would have made the rounds of *three* adverse parties expressing his willingness to testify to different versions of key events. On his lawyer's advice, Graham did not follow through by approaching Gibbs or Patrick. During a conference with counsel out of the jury's presence, Judge Lake stated: "I don't believe Mr. Graham's testimony about what he told Brent Bailey."

Brent Bailey was on the stand for two full days, longer than any other witness. He was frequently on the defensive, offering hairsplitting distinctions and evasive responses. Seeking to distance himself from the POS he had authored, Bailey stated: "This is not my document. It's the [bond] issuers' document." He went on to say, however, that the final word on the text of the POS belonged to his underwriter-client, Drexel, "because they were the ones primarily responsible for distributing it to the investors." In Bailey's opinion, he had no duty to probe his sources; he was "entitled to assume that everybody in the transaction is acting ethically unless he got information that would lead him to believe otherwise."

The origin of Bailey's characterization of the jails as "maximum security" was obscure. The authoritative sources on security standards for the project would have been the State's standards for jail occupancy and Lott's construction contract. Bailey's reviews of those documents admittedly had been cursory. Ultimately, Bailey took refuge in Pat Graham's explanation—that the phrase "maximum security" referred to construction materials, not to facility design. The feasibility study, which was incorporated by reference (made a part of) Bailey's POS, also referred to "maximum security" facilities "capable of offering several dozen levels of treatment due to its state-of-the-art design." Asked what "state of the art" meant, Bailey said he didn't know, nor had he made any attempt to find out.

Brent Bailey denied that he had known the amount of Graham's subcontract fee when he wrote the POS. He testified that he learned for the first time of Lott's subcontract with Pat Graham in a June 14 phone call from H.A. Lott. He was not told the amount of the fee and did not ask for a copy of the subcontract. In notes of a subsequent conversation with Hutchison, however, Bailey stated: "Ray and I agree that [the subcontract] could cause some problem and it is a situation which needs to be monitored closely." On June 15, Bailey wrote a letter to Graham: "In connection with our due diligence, I would appreciate it if you would provide me in writing a description of all services which N-Group Securities will provide apart from its basic role as the financial advisor/developer." Bailey did not ask specifically for the amount of the subcontract fee. As he attempted to explain, investors were entitled to know about Graham's $2.25 million developer's fee because it would be paid directly from bond proceeds, while the subcontract fee would be paid by Lott, "separate and apart from bond proceeds"(his theory apparently being that the money would lose its character as bond proceeds by passing through Lott's bank account on its way to Graham). On June 19, an N-Group employee wrote back to Bailey, enclosing a list of services to be performed, but stating that its fee for the services was "proprietary and confidential information." Bailey understood that Graham and Lott had not yet agreed on a fee, based on information he had received from Pat or Mike Graham, but he did not confirm that understanding. Thereafter, Bailey revised the POS to refer to a subcontract fee, without stating its amount. He made no further inquiry, and the fee of $4.8 million was not disclosed to investors.

Geoffrey Hazard had taught and written on ethics and related subjects, including professional standards in the sale of securities, for over thirty years at Yale and at the Universities of California, Chicago, and Pennsylvania. He had served on a New York Stock Exchange committee concerned with disclosure rules governing securities transactions and he had developed practice standards for the National Association of Bond Lawyers. When called as an expert witness for the plaintiffs, Hazard was Director of the American Law Institute that he described as a "think tank for good laws." Hazard's fees matched his credentials: $500 per hour, plus a $7,000 "engagement fee." Over objection, Judge Lake accepted Hazard as an expert on standards of care applicable to securities lawyers.

Hazard testified concerning Brent Bailey's performance as draftsman of the POS. He stated as a general principle that a securities lawyer is "required to use due diligence in investigating, and due care in expounding." The lawyer is to apply common sense and good judgment. "It's not rocket science." Hazard spoke of a "gatekeeper" metaphor commonly employed to summarize the responsibilities of a lawyer in Bailey's position. "The securities lawyer is standing at the gate between the person trying to push the securities out into the market and the recipients out there in the market. His responsibility is to make sure that the information pushed out there to induce people to invest passes muster, that incorrect or misleading information doesn't get through the gate. That's one of the reasons you have lawyers reviewing these things, because they understand the law and what a material omission is. [The securities lawyer is] supposed to frisk the thing as it goes by to make sure it doesn't violate the law." If the lawyer's "frisk" turns up false or misleading statements, his duty is to call for changes. Hazard continued: "If the promoters don't want to make those changes, you have to say: "This is not a document that I can sign, and you're either going to have to recast the proposal, abandon the project, or go see if you can find some other lawyer who will do it."

Hazard focused on the most controversial parts of the POS—the "maximum security" representation, prisoner markets, and failure to disclose the $4.8 million subcontract fee. Bailey had first convened the working group on May 12; the agenda of that meeting described the proposed facilities as "minimum security." There was testimony that after the draft POS was distributed on June 12, a lawyer for Lott had telephoned Bailey and questioned whether the "maximum security" language was accurate. Such as call was, in Hazard's opinion, "a flashing light that says, not only is this material, but this is probably inaccurate.... Bailey keeps right on going in disregard of that warning."

Patrick directed Hazard's attention to the September 5 letter from Assistant Attorney General Thomassen to Bailey that cited the lack of a realistic market among state prisoners. Hazard observed: "Bailey did not use the information conveyed therein to modify the POS, but, to the contrary, he wrote in the "no material changes" letter [required to reflect last-minute changes] that everything was okay without further change." In Hazard's opinion, "failing to disclose those points is going ahead in the face of very serious risks that are obvious and to which Bailey is just being oblivious."

Hazard testified that Bailey had acted in "reckless disregard of his obligations" in failing to determine the amount of Graham's subcontract fee and to disclose it in the POS. "That amount of money [$4.8 million] would raise a question whether it was going to be used for some other purpose, say, of greasing the skids." While Bailey's letter of inquiry to Lott was appropriate, Lott's response was to stonewall—the fee was "proprietary and confidential information." "When you get a letter like that, what you have to do it say, 'Fine, please tell me the amount of the fee. That's not a hard letter to write.'" And if Bailey had thought (as he claimed) that the fee had not yet been determined, he could have written "a fee of $_____" in the draft POS, leaving the amount to be supplied later. That would have raised a question in the minds of investors that the fee amount was, or could be, a material fact.

William Wilde's defense of Brent Bailey and Keck, Mahin & Cate stressed two themes. The plaintiff funds were sophisticated investors "taking a flyer" on a risky project in hopes of a high rate of return. Furthermore, the risks of project failure had been disclosed, or at least flagged, in the POS, and were further spelled out in underlying documents. Given their expertise and the availability of information, the investors alleged ignorance of material facts was the result of failure to do their homework, not any negligence of Brent Bailey. Wilde called witnesses to counter the plaintiffs' evidence, including a Houston securities lawyer and a law professor, both of whom testified that Bailey had exercised due diligence.

Judge Lake instructed the jury at length (some 10,000 words) and, after closing arguments by counsel, sent them to consider and decide forty-nine separate questions. Following five days of deliberation, the jury returned verdicts against Keck, Mahin & Cate and the other defendants, finding that they had violated the Texas Securities Act and federal securities laws, and that they had committed common-law fraud. (The plaintiffs had abandoned their malpractice claim.) They awarded $34 million in compensatory damages to the plaintiff funds.

The jury also found that the defendants had committed unlawful acts with "actual malice" and "conscious indifference." As a result, a separate hearing was held to determine whether, and in what amount, punitive—in addition to compensatory—damages should be awarded. Attempting to stave off punitive damages, Wilde told the jury: "The reputation of this law firm has been destroyed. You have given them the kind of death blow that is immeasurable." Wilde failed to mention that Keck, Mahin, like most large law firms, was carrying a $100 million liability insurance policy. When Wilde went on to imply that his client would be unable to pay the $34 million in compensatory damages, he opened the door for plaintiffs' lawyer Patrick to reveal the liability policy. The jury returned punitive damage awards against Keck, Mahin for $2 million, and for a total of $12 million against the Graham brothers and N-Group Securities.

# Post Scripts

Brent Bailey made partner at Keck, Mahin in January 1990 but resigned in December 1991, shortly before Delta Municipal Fund and the other bondholders sued him and the firm. He was associated for a time with Of Counsel, Inc, which specializes in placing lawyers and paralegals in temporary jobs. He later took a house-counsel position with a Houston company. Keck, Mahin & Cate experienced a series of reverses during the 1990s in addition to the prison bond malpractice judgment, including other large malpractice cases and attendant bad publicity. In August 1997, the firm was sued for $1.3 million in office rent; by that time most of its lawyers had defected to other firms. Thereafter, Keck, Mahin & Cate was dissolved. Pat Graham moved on to bigger things. Toward the end of the trial, he appeared on CNN television to announce his offer to purchase the Minnesota Timberwolves National Basketball Association team for $152 million.

* * *

# Comments and Questions

1. Legal ethics are usually associated with higher standards of conduct than those the law minimally requires. There are situations, however, in which the legal standard is higher than a related rule of legal ethics. "The Gatekeeper" chapter provides an illustration. The jury found Keck, Mahin & Cate in violation of the anti-fraud provisions of the federal securities laws which require, not only that representations in securities offering statements be true, but, furthermore, that they be "not misleading." The drafter of such a statement must exercise "due diligence" to find and fully disclose information relevant to an investment decision.

The Model Rules set the ethical bar several notches lower for similar conduct. Under subpart (d) of Rule 1.2, "Scope of Representation": "A lawyer shall not counsel...or assist a client in conduct that the lawyer knows is criminal or fraudulent...." Rule 4.1, "Truthfulness in Statements to Others," requires the lawyer to disclose material facts, but only when necessary to avoid assisting a criminal or fraudulent act, and then only if disclosure is not prohibited by Rule 1.6, "Confidentiality of Information." Similarly, common-law fraud requires knowledge of falsity and intent to deceive, neither of which are elements of a claim under the federal securities laws.

The lower standard in the ethics rule regarding lawyer involvement in wrongdoing reflects a conscious choice by the drafters of the Model Rules. They incorporated the higher federal securities law standard in Rule 7.1(a) concerning lawyer advertising which defines a communication as "false or misleading" if it "omits a fact necessary to make the statement considered as a whole not materially misleading." Is actual knowledge that a client is engaged in criminal or fraudulent conduct the appropriate standard under Rule 1.2(d)? If not, what standard should apply? How about the objective standard of "reasonable belief" instead of actual knowledge?

Common-law rules of fiduciary duty were applied to lawyers long before the development of modern codes of legal ethics. The codes do not supercede fiduciary obligations but exist independent of them—primarily as a framework for lawyer discipline, not as a basis for a civil claim. In some circumstances, however, and depending on the jurisdiction's case law, the common law of fiduciaries may support a claim against a lawyer even though her conduct was fully consistent with ethics rules. Specialized practice standards, such as the National Association of Bond Lawyers standards referred to by Professor Hazard, are being cited increasingly in common-law liability cases and sometimes impose obligations more stringent that those embodied in state ethics rules. In addition, lawyers in some practice areas, such as securities and bankruptcy, sometimes develop specific understandings among themselves about what is required. Such understandings may never be formally adopted, but they are generally accepted and followed. For example, Ray Hutchison, an experienced Dallas bond lawyer, speaking of the amount of money that would be considered significant enough to require disclosure in securities offering documents, stated that: "Some in the industry would suggest that a materiality factor is reached at five percent." Such understandings would be admitted in malpractice cases to show the standard of care and whether the defendant acted reasonably. Because of their specificity, they may be more significant in litigation than generally-worded rules of ethics.

2. The plaintiffs' complaint included a claim for legal malpractice against Keck, Mahin & Cate. The later abandonment of that claim, without explanation, may have occurred because there was no lawyer-client relationship between the plaintiffs and Keck, Mahin. Traditionally, a lawyer-client relationship has been a required element of a legal malpractice claim. Under the rubric of "third party liability," however, lawyers may be held liable to "non-clients" in a growing number of situations in which reliance on the lawyer is deemed reasonable. Several such situations are spelled out in Section 73, "Duty of Care to Non-Clients" of Tentative Draft No. 8 of the American Law Institute's Restatement of the Law Governing Lawyers. The anti-fraud provisions of the federal securities laws are an example of statutory third-party liability that may be imposed on lawyers who draft offering statements that mislead members of the general public into buying securities. The lawyer may be held liable if he or she reasonably should have realized the need to independently verify the client's representations. *See, e.g., FDIC v. Clark*, 978 F.2d 1541 (C.A. 10 1992). The issue then is what kinds of warning signs ("red flags") are enough to put the lawyer on notice that investigation is necessary.

3. The importance of supervision of junior lawyers by senior lawyers has been increasingly recognized, both in the law of malpractice and in the Model Rules of Professional Conduct. Model Rules 5.1 and 5.2,

governing responsibilities of supervisory and subordinate lawyers, respectively, have no counterparts in the Model Code of Professional Responsibility, the American Bar Association's predecessor ethics rules. In
addition to "The Gatekeeper" chapter, lack of adequate supervision
played a major role in Chapter 5, "Two Scorpions in a Bottle" ($24.9
million verdict for actions of loose-cannon associate) and Chapter 3,
"Breaking Up Is Hard To Do" (senior associate liable notwithstanding
he followed partner's orders). Kai Nebel, the supervising partner in the
Chicago office, did not work closely with Brent Bailey in drafting the official statement for the prison bonds. It became apparent that Nebel had
not focused on what would become the major points of dispute in the
lawsuit—notably the hidden fee amount and the "maximum security"
description of the jails. Given that Nebel was in Chicago and that Bailey
had some experience in securities work, was Nebel's level of involvement appropriate under the circumstances? Viewing the situation from
Bailey's perspective, would he have felt that Nebel gave him adequate
support? Under Model Rule 5.1, a lawyer with supervisory authority
over another lawyer "shall make reasonable efforts to ensure that the
other lawyer conforms to the Rules of Professional Conduct." Although
the litigation record makes no reference to ethics rules, would the conduct of Bailey or Nebel have involved violations of the Model Rules?

The need for supervision of senior associates, despite their experience, may become more acute as the time approaches for their consideration to become partners. The candidate will want to look good during a
period of increased scrutiny. There was additional pressure on Brent Bailey in the prison bond deal: the firm would not be paid unless the deal
closed. There were indications that Bailey wanted very badly for the deal
to go through. Recall his eleventh-hour telephone calls to Texas counties
in an effort to convince the Texas Attorney General that a market existed
for the jails.

Claims involving inadequate supervision have mushroomed in recent years. One can speculate that this is linked to increasing competition for clients, and growing reliance of firms on business generation as
a critical factor in partnership compensation. Partners have to hustle
harder for business because they must count less on long-term client relationships. Every hour spent by a partner supervising an associate is an
hour she or he is not spending on business generation or billable matters. Under these circumstances, it is not surprising that associates feel
they are not getting the guidance they need.

4. Professor Hazard's "gatekeeper" is a striking metaphor, but is it a fair and realistic standard for testing a lawyer's due diligence in a complex securities transaction? Brent Bailey took the information others gave him and put it in the offering statement. Was he correct in saying that he was under no duty to probe his sources, that he was "entitled to assume that everybody in the transaction is acting ethically unless he got information that would lead him to believe otherwise?" Should he have found out that Pat Graham, the principal promoter, was a sleaze with a fraud judgment in his background? Should he have anticipated that H.A. Lott, a reputable construction contractor, would pay a kickback to Graham in exchange for the jail contract? Without the wisdom of hindsight, if you had been in Bailey's place would you have approached the drafting of the offering statement more skeptically?

The jury's attitude toward Bailey and Keck, Mahin, had to have been colored by these and other things for which, arguably, the law firm was not responsible, yet the firm was found to have committed fraud with "actual malice" — the predicate for punitive damages. Was that finding justified?

# Chapter 7

# Hot Seat

"You have to get up every morning ready to bite the ass off a bear."
— John Gutfreund, CEO of Salomon Brothers, Inc., to trainees;
quoted in *The Wall Street Journal,* December 12, 1992.

On August 9, 1991, Salomon Brothers — once crowned "King of Wall Street" by *Business Week* and acknowledged in *The Wall Street Journal* as "the dominant player in the U.S. Treasury bond market" — issued a press release stating that it had "uncovered irregularities and rule violations in connection with its submissions of bids in certain auctions of Treasury securities." The release described several of the violations, involving false bids for billions of dollars in Treasury notes, and stated that two managing directors on its government trading desk had been suspended. That same day, John Gutfreund, Chairman and CEO of Salomon, disclosed to federal officials for the first time that he and other senior officers of the firm had known of a false bid in a Treasury auction since late April.

Salomon's false bid disclosures mushroomed into the worst scandal in the firm's eighty-one year history. In the days immediately following, *The Wall Street Journal* headlined: "Top Salomon Officials Knew About Illegal Bid" and "Sullied Solly." *The New York Times* ran "Salomon Punished by Treasury" and "Such Is War for Salomon" stories on the front page, above the fold. On hearing of the false bids, William Simon, Secretary of the Treasury in the Nixon and Ford Administrations and a former head of Salomon's government and municipal bond departments, said: "I'll be damned. Good God. That can be my only reaction."

As the storm swirled around him, Gutfreund first tried to ride it out. Bloody, but unbowed and defiant, he was "not apologizing to anybody. Apologies don't mean [expletive]. What happened, happened." Gutfreund told Salomon executives: "A lot of people are upset, the stock's down big, but we'll work our way our of this." Two days later, however, following irate phone calls from the President of the Federal Reserve Bank of New York demanding immediate action, Gutfreund, Salomon President Thomas Strauss, and John Meriwether, Vice President in charge of fixed-income trading activities, offered resignations which were quickly accepted by Salomon's board. Donald Feuerstein, the head of Salomon's legal department, held onto his job for another week as accounts of critics inside and outside of Salomon appeared in the press faulting him for failing to take charge of the matter by reporting it to the government himself. Warren Buffett, the legendary investor from Omaha who owned sixteen percent of Salomon, agreed to step in as interim chairman and CEO, seeking to protect his stake in the firm. On August 23, Buffett requested and received Feuerstein's resignation. A thirty-year veteran lawyer at Salomon, Feuerstein found himself on the street at age fifty-four.

In the wake of Salomon's disclosures, the Department of Justice and the Securities and Exchange Commission launched investigations, followed by a civil action against Salomon in federal district court in Manhattan alleging numerous violations of federal securities laws. Salomon consented to the entry of an injunction barring future violations, to civil penalties of $190 million, and agreed to establish a $100 million fund to pay civil claims. The Commission also instituted an administrative proceeding which, in December 1992, culminated in an order making findings, imposing remedial sanctions, and reporting the results of its investigation. Without admitting or denying the Commission's findings, Gutfreund, Strauss and Meriwether consented to their entry and to the imposition of sanctions against them which were the result of negotiated settlements.

Donald Feuerstein was not a formal respondent in the administrative proceeding, but he consented to issuance of the SEC's report, without admitting or denying its accuracy. The SEC took the occasion to present its views on the responsibilities of a lawyer in Feuerstein's position to investigate, prevent, and report misconduct to regulatory authorities. This chapter will focus on Feuerstein's actions in response to learning of the false bid and on the Commission's retrospective evaluation of them.

The Treasury Department sells notes from time to time in billion-dollar auctions in order to finance government spending and the national debt. The auctions are limited to major securities dealers like Salomon who, in turn, sell to their customers and to other dealers, representing a $2 trillion market. In order to promote more equitable distribution of its notes and prevent price manipulation, a Treasury regulation prohibits individual dealers from buying more than thirty-five percent of the notes offered at a single auction. Salomon's false bids enabled it to buy substantially more than the thirty-five percent limit, putting it in a position to manipulate the market price. *The Wall Street Journal* described the fallout from one of Salomon's false bids: "Bond dealers who were shut out of the auction but needed two-year notes were forced to buy them from Salomon at much higher prices. But the biggest losers were speculators and traders who had taken short positions ahead of the auction. That strategy backfired and they lost huge sums when they had to buy from Salomon. Several traders lost their jobs."

Salomon's false bids were the work of Paul Mozer, the head of Salomon's government trading desk. An intense, hard-driving, thirty-six-year old, Mozer was one of Salomon's highest-paid employees, earning some $10 million in 1990. On February 21, 1991, the Treasury Department auctioned $9 billion of its five-year notes. Salomon submitted a bid in its own name for $3.15 billion at a yield of 7.51%, representing thirty-five percent of the amount at auction, the maximum allowable bid under the Treasury regulation. In the same auction, Salomon submitted two additional $3.15 billion bids at the same yield in the names of Mercury Asset Management and another customer, without the knowledge of either. The SEC later found that: "Both bids were in fact false bids intended to secure additional securities for Salomon." The three bids from Salomon were prorated with other bids at the same yield and Salomon received $5.1 billion of the notes—fifty-seven percent of the total sold at that auction, and twenty-two percent more than the maximum amount to which they were entitled under the regulation. Overriding normal procedures, Mozer directed clerks to manipulate the records generated by the unauthorized customer bids to conceal the true purpose of those transactions. He also directed that confirmations for the fictitious purchases not be sent to Mercury Asset and the other customer.

Salomon's false bids in the February 21 auction might have gone undetected but for the fact that the bid in the name of Mercury Asset raised questions at the Treasury Department when it was noticed that another subsidiary of Mercury Asset's parent company had submitted a $100 million bid in the same auction. Having no reason to believe otherwise, Treasury officials assumed that the Mercury Asset bid had been duly authorized. They decided to take no action with respect to the February 21 auction, but that future bids from Mercury Asset and the other subsidiary would be aggregated for purposes of the thirty-five percent regulation. That decision was conveyed to Mercury Asset by a letter of

April 17 to its Senior Director in London. That was the first that Mercury Asset knew about Salomon's unauthorized bid in its name.

A copy of the April 17 Treasury letter had been sent to Mozer. Seeing his scheme unravel and turning to damage control, Mozer telephoned the Senior Director of Mercury Asset in London. As the SEC described their conversation: "Moser told the Senior Director that the submission of the $3.15 billion bid was an 'error' by a clerk who had incorrectly placed the name of Mercury Asset on the tender form. Mozer told the Senior Director that he was embarrassed by the 'error' which had been corrected internally, and he asked him to keep the matter confidential to avoid 'problems.' The Senior Director indicated that such a course of action would be acceptable."

Mozer then went to the office of John Meriwether, his immediate supervisor, and handed him a copy of the Treasury letter to Mercury Asset. He informed Meriwether that the Mercury bid referred to in the letter had not been authorized and was in fact a bid for Salomon. Meriwether expressed shock, told him his action was "career threatening," and demanded an explanation. Mozer replied that he had submitted the false customer bids to meet demand at his government trading desk and the government arbitrage desk. He denied having submitted false bids either before or since the February 21 auction. (Subsequent investigation would show that Mozer had submitted false bids, both before *and* after the February 21 auction.) Mozer also told Meriwether about his conversation with the Senior Director of Mercury Asset. Meriwether said that he would have to take the matter to his supervisor, Thomas Strauss, President of Salomon.

Meriwether met with Strauss and Donald Feuerstein, head of Salomon's legal department, the following morning and related to them Mozer's disclosures about the false bid, the Treasury letter, and the phone conversation with the director of Mercury Asset. Feuerstein asked for and was given a copy of the Treasury letter. He said that Mozer's conduct was "a serious matter and that it should be reported to the government." Strauss said he wanted to talk with Gutfreund, who was then out of town.

John Gutfreund, then in his thirty-eighth year at Salomon, had started as a $45-a-week trainee, spent ten years as a bond trader, had held management positions, and became CEO in 1983. Arrogant and gruff, he was credited with creating the "macho" culture at Salomon described in *Liar's Poker*, the best-selling memoir by a former Salomon trainee which relates questionable, sometimes outrageous, behavior of some employees. One of Mozer's false bids had been intended as a practical joke on a retiring employee. Gutfreund himself was said to have bet $1 million in a game of liar's poker.

During the last week of April, Gutfreund, Strauss, Meriwether, and Feuerstein met for further discussion of the matter. Following Meriwether's summary of Mozer's actions, in the SEC's words: "Feuerstein told the group that he believed that the submission of the false bid was a criminal act. He indicated that, while there probably was not a legal duty to report the false bid, he believed they had no choice but to report the matter to the government." Discussion turned to whether a report should be made to the Treasury Department or to the Federal Reserve Bank of New York, its regulator in the area of Treasury securities. Because of animosity between Mozer and some Treasury officials growing out of adoption of the thirty-five percent regulation, the Federal Reserve Bank was considered preferable.

When the meeting ended, each of the four participants thought that a decision had been made to report the false bid. Each, however, had a different understanding of just how and by whom that decision would be implemented. Meriwether thought Strauss would visit and report to the president of the Federal Reserve Bank. Strauss thought that he and Gutfreund would visit the bank president, but that Gutfreund wanted to give the matter further thought. Gutfreund thought that he or Strauss, separately or together, would visit the bank president. For his part, Feuerstein thought the Gutfreund wanted to think further about how the bid should be reported. (The SEC decision does not comment on how these sophisticated businessmen could have thought it sufficient to report a multi-billion dollar false bid orally—the CEO of Salomon to the bank president—instead of in writing and through regular channels.)

The meeting of Strauss, Meriwether, and Feuerstein and their later meeting with Gutfreund were noteworthy for what was *not* discussed in them. There was no discussion of investigating what Mozer had done, of possible discipline, of placing restrictions on his activities, or of determining what had been done with the securities obtained by the false bid. Each of the four participants in those meetings would later place responsibility for inquiring into those matters on someone else. Feuerstein, as head of the legal department, also had oversight of the firm's compliance department. He took the position that, once the false bid was reported to regulatory authorities, they would tell Salomon how to investigate the matter. In the meantime, Feuerstein was waiting for Gutfreund to make up his mind about how to report the false bid. Contradicting an earlier statement that he intended to report personally to the Federal Reserve Bank president, Gutfreund said he thought that "other executives would take whatever steps were necessary to properly handle the matter."

When nothing had been done by mid-May to report the false bid of February 21 to the Federal Reserve Bank, Feuerstein met with Gutfreund and Strauss and urged them to report "as soon as possible." They told him they still intended to report to the bank. In late May and again in early June, Feuerstein separately urged Strauss and Gutfreund to report, but they took no action. At that point, Gutfreund was looking upon the false bid as a "minor aberration" and "not a matter of high priority."

Unbeknownst to the three senior officers and Feuerstein, Mozer continued to submit false bids in Treasury auctions, using the names of customers without their authority and manipulating records so that the notes ended up in Salomon's trading accounts. In a $12 billion auction of two-year Treasury notes on May 22, a false bid resulted in Salomon and two of its customers receiving eighty-six percent of the notes. Rumors then appeared in the press about a market "squeeze" which aroused interest at the Treasury Department and the SEC. Under those circumstances, Gutfreund, Strauss, and Meriwether met and decided to delay reporting the February 21 false bid until more was known about the May 22 auction. Feuerstein had not been informed of that meeting and was not advised of the decision to delay the report.

In early July, Feuerstein retained the New York law firm of Wachtell, Lipton, Rosen & Katz, its usual counsel, to conduct an internal investigation of Salomon's role in the two-year note auction of May 22. The outside lawyers were not initially informed of the false bid in the February 21 auction. When it became apparent that they were likely to find out about that bid, Feuerstein told them about it and it was agreed to widen the scope of the investigation to include a review of all Treasury bond and note auctions since July 1990, when the regulation limiting a single buyer to thirty-five percent of the auction amount had been adopted. By early August, the outside lawyers had discovered four false bids in three auctions and irregularities in two others. The results of their investigation were reported to Gutfreund, Strauss, Meriwether, and Feuerstein, the press releases followed, and all four would be forced to resign later that month. The SEC's subsequent investigation uncovered further wrongdoing. In its civil action filed in May 1992, the Commission alleged that Salomon had submitted ten false bids totaling $15.5 billion in nine separate

Treasury auctions between August of 1989 and May of 1991, resulting in illegal purchases of $9.5 billion in securities.

Section 15(b)(4)(E) of the Securities Exchange Act of 1934 authorizes the SEC to impose sanctions against responsible officials of a broker-dealer like Salomon if they have "failed reasonably to supervise, with a view toward preventing violations [of the federal securities laws], another person who commits such a violation, if such person is subject to [their] supervision." In its decision imposing sanctions on Gutfreund, Strauss, and Meriwether, the SEC quoted from an earlier decision: "In large organizations it is especially imperative that those in authority exercise particular vigilance when indications of irregularity reach their attention." When they were informed of Mozer's false bid of February 21 and having direct supervisory authority over him, they had a duty, "at a minimum... to investigate what had occurred and whether there had been other instances of unreported misconduct." Pending investigation, they were required "to increase supervision of Mozer and to place appropriate limits on his activities." Gutfreund, as CEO, was singled out for criticism for his failure to make a timely report of the false bid to the government.

The SEC's lengthy decision dealt, in conclusion, with Donald Feuerstein. The Commission began by observing that a lawyer in Feuerstein's position—chief legal officer of a securities dealer—does not become a "supervisor" within the meaning of section 15(b)(4)(3) solely by virtue of that position. The test is whether the lawyer has sufficient responsibility and authority to affect the conduct of the employee whose actions are in question. Applying that test to the circumstances of this case—particularly Feuerstein's involvement with senior management in their repeated failures to deal with the situation—he was found to meet that test and to be deemed responsible as a "supervisor."

The SEC summarized the regulatory responsibilities of a lawyer clothed with supervisory responsibilities over an employee's misconduct: "It is not sufficient for one in such a position to be a mere bystander to the events that occurred. Once a person in Feuerstein's position becomes involved in formulating management's response to the problem, he or she is obligated to take affirmative steps to ensure that appropriate action is taken to address the misconduct. For example, such a person could direct or monitor an investigation,...make appropriate recommendations for limiting the activities of the employee or for the institution of appropriate procedures designed to prevent and detect future misconduct, and verify that his or her recommendations...are implemented. If management [then] fails to act and that person knows, or has reason to know, of that failure, he or she should consider what additional steps are appropriate to address the matter. These steps may include disclosure of the matter to the entity's board of directors, resignation from the firm, or disclosure to regulatory authorities." In a footnote to the last quoted sentence, the Commission acknowledged that: "Of course, in the case of an attorney, the applicable Code of Professional Responsibility and the Canons of Ethics may bear upon what course of conduct that individual may properly pursue."

Salomon Brothers' profits from the illegal bids were estimated to range from $3.6 to $4.6 million—some twenty times more than the $190,000 civil fine imposed by the SEC. However, a profit calculated on that basis probably would have been erased by the fees of the outside lawyers called in to investigate the false bids and to defend the firm against the SEC, not to mention the business losses caused by the sandal. After the multiple false bids were uncovered, Paul Mozer and his deputy were fired and were later charged with criminal offenses.

The three executives had negotiated settlements with the SEC. Gutfreund agreed not to associate in the future, as chairman or CEO, with any securities firm subject to SEC jurisdiction, and to pay a civil penalty of $100,000. Strauss and Meriwether agreed to suspensions of six and three months, and to civil penalties of $75,000 and $50,000, respectively. (The New York Times observed that for former top executives of Salomon, such fines were "equivalent to a parking ticket to most people.") Gutfreund went into semi-retirement as an occasional investment adviser. In an interview with The Wall Street Journal, he reported two bright spots in his life after Salomon: his golf game had improved and "I don't have to be nice and listen to egomaniacs every day."

Donald Feuerstein was not directly disciplined by the SEC. However, a footnote to its opinion stated: "We note that Feuerstein has represented that he does not intend to be employed in the securities industry in the future."

\* \* \*

# Comments and Questions

1. According to an article in The American Lawyer (Orey, Salomon's Hot Seat, March 1993): "The key issue raised by the Salomon affair in-

volves how in-house lawyers respond when they learn of possible (or, in Solomon's case) definite corporate wrongdoing. For the more trouble a lawyer has in choosing a course of action, the more he or she feels that his or her independent judgment must defer to executive fiat, the more likely that real trouble for the company as a whole [i.e., the client] is brewing." Generally speaking, how would a house counsel position like Feuerstein's differ from that of a partner in an outside law firm like Wachtell, Lipton, Rosen & Katz in terms of the lawyer's independence and ability to give objective advice? Bear in mind that Feuerstein had only one client and, after the false bid fiasco, he had none. Assume further that the CEO of the company is a gruff and tough, Type-A personality, not a people person like John Gutfreund.

2. Donald Feuerstein was counsel to an "organization" or "entity" within the meaning of Model Rule Section 1.13, "Organization as Client." Under the rule, he represented Salomon Brothers "through its constituents"—the board of directors, the CEO, and other officers and employees. He did not represent those constituents personally (although in the real world it may often have seemed that way). Subsection (b) of the rule spells out a series of progressive, alternative actions the in-house lawyer may take when an officer or employee "is engaged in action" which is a violation of law and which "is likely to result in substantial injury to the organization." In the Salomon situation, action by Feuerstein might have been triggered when he first learned of Mozer's false bid—a criminal act that, if later discovered by the government, would have caused "substantial injury" to Salomon. However, Mozer's confession to Meriwether was of past misconduct which he denied having committed before or since. Feuerstein only discovered months later through the Wachtell, Lipton report that Mozer's false bids were an ongoing course of misconduct. Arguably, the "is engaged" language in the rule refers only to ongoing or future misconduct (cf. Model Rule 1.2(d)) which, if appropriate action is taken, may be prevented.

Alternatively, the rule might have triggered action by Feuerstein when CEO Gutfreund "refuse[d] to act in a matter...that is a violation of a legal obligation to the organization." Although there was no clear-cut duty under any statute or rule to report Mozer's false bid the to government, Gutfreund had a legal duty to act in the best interests of Salomon. Despite his "minor aberration" comment, he must have known that the matter was serious because he had contemplated a personal visit to the President of the Federal Reserve Bank to report it. Do you agree with either or both of these readings of the "trigger" language of subsection (b) of Rule 1.13?

Assume that one or both readings apply to Feuerstein's situation. The *American Lawyer* article suggests that once Feuerstein had advised the senior executives that the false bid was a criminal act and that it should be reported, as a practical matter there was nothing further he could have done. It points out that CEO Gutfreund was also chairman of the board of directors so that it would have been futile to take his failure to report to the board. Short of resigning and blowing the whistle (see below), should Feuerstein have taken any other action? If so, what?

3. The Salomon case raises difficult questions for an in-house lawyer who discovers corporate misconduct which, contrary to his advice, company managers refuse to report. Should he blow the whistle by telling the government? Under Model Rule 1.6, the answer is "no." The information about the false bid "relates to the representation" and does not fall within the exceptions in subsection (b). Proponents of the present version of the rule argued successfully that the need of corporate executives for good advice required complete candor which, in turn, depended on confidentiality, and that a lawyer's *threat* to resign should be sufficient to cause the company to report. However, the seemingly unequivocal language of the rule has been undercut to some extent by comment [16] following its text. That comment has become the basis for a "noisy withdrawal" concept which permits the lawyer to "give notice of the fact of withdrawal, and the lawyer may also withdraw or disaffirm any opinion, document, affirmation, or the like." Was Feuerstein in a position to make a noisy withdrawal? What could he have disclosed and how effective would it have been in alerting the government to the false bid?

"A Fine Kettle of Fish (and Arsenic)" by Professor Stephen Gillers, another article in the March 1993 issue of *The American Lawyer*, poses a hypothetical somewhat similar to Feuerstein's situation at Salomon. Five lawyers with expertise and varying perspectives on such problems were asked to respond to the hypothetical house counsel's request for advice. Not surprisingly, their responses differed markedly.

The exceptions to Rule 1.6 have been expanded in several respects in the versions of the Model Rules adopted in many states. In New York where the Salomon false bids occurred, there is an exception permitting a lawyer to report an "intention" to commit a criminal fraud which presumably would have applied to this situation if Feuerstein had learned of Mozer's intention to continue submitting false bids in time to prevent it. Section 124-101(c)(3). Moreover, the lawyer *must* report a client's ongoing crime or fraud. However, under the New York rule prior crimes of criminal fraud may only be reported if the lawyer's services were used in committing it.

4. In stating its views on the responsibilities of in-house lawyers for securities firms whose management rejects their advice to report misconduct, the SEC took the position that the lawyer "may" make "disclosure to regulatory authorities" — *i.e.*, blow the whistle. That position is contrary to the New York ethics rules which, as we have seen, prohibit whistleblowing except in exceptional circumstances not presented in the Salomon situation. The SEC then muddied the water by adding that applicable State ethics rules "may bear upon what course of conduct [the lawyer] may properly pursue." So what is a New York lawyer in Feuerstein's position to do? The SEC's position is based on federal statutes that, by virtue of Article VI of the Constitution, override conflicting state laws, including ethics rules. If Feuerstein had blown the whistle to the SEC about the false bids and if New York authorities had then initiated disciplinary proceedings against him for violating New York's version of Rule 1.6, would the SEC position on whistleblowing be a defense? Consider the experiences of Attorneys General Richard Thornburgh and Janet Reno who took the position that, in certain circumstances, federal lawyers are not bound by State ethics rules prohibiting contacts with defendants without the consent of their counsel. That controversial position, commonly known as the "Thornburgh Memorandum," caused a minor furor and was later nullified by statute.

# Chapter 8

# Ambulance Chasing Redux

"My friend and client is accused of being a greedy ambulance chaser when in fact he is a fine lawyer and an honorable man."
— Opening statement of counsel for John O'Quinn
in *Commission for Lawyer Discipline v. O'Quinn.*

On July 2, 1994, USAir Flight 1016 left Columbia, South Carolina for the short hop to Charlotte, North Carolina with fifty passengers and a crew of five. As the DC-9 approached for a landing, a thunderstorm broke over the Charlotte/Douglas International Airport. The pilot executed a "missed approach" and was climbing to regain altitude when the plane crashed in a wooded area, hit a house, and burst into flames. NBC news interviewed a woman who said she had witnessed the crash and had seen people "with their bones sticking out. There was blood everywhere." Thirty-seven passengers were killed. Survivors were dragged from the flaming wreckage by passing motorists who stopped to help.

All of the survivors were injured, none more seriously than Dorian Doucette, an Army private from Baytown, Texas. Following emergency treatment for third-degree burns over much of his body, Doucette was taken to the hospital at Ft. Sam Houston in San Antonio where he hovered near death for several weeks. He somehow survived but, in addition to disfiguring scars, he suffered brain damage and his left leg was amputated—a tragedy for young Dorian but a personal injury lawyer's dream. Doucette's Houston lawyers would later settle his case for $18.5 million. This chapter tells how the lawyers got themselves hired by Doucette's parents and by the families of others who died on Flight 1016. The story was played out before a jury in a disciplinary action brought against the lawyers by the Texas Commission for Lawyer Discipline.

The Commission's complaint charged lawyers John O'Quinn, Benton and Charles Musslewhite, and Carl Shaw with violating the Texas barratry statute which provides:

139

"Barratry occurs when a lawyer —

1. solicits employment, either in person or by telephone, for himself or for another; or
2. pays a person money to solicit employment; or
3. pays money to a prospective client to obtain legal representation; or
4. engages in a conspiracy to be employed by commission of any of the foregoing acts; or
5. knowingly invests funds that the lawyer knows or believes are intended to further the commission of any of the foregoing acts; or
6. knowingly accepts employment resulting from commission of any of the foregoing acts."

As will be seen, there was evidence that all six of these prohibitions were violated by one or more of the defendants. Barratry was classified as a misdemeanor when the alleged violations growing out of the crash of Flight 1016 occurred, but has since been made a felony, punishable by imprisonment for a minimum term of two years and a maximum of ten.

Barratry—usually called "solicitation"—is prohibited in every state and by the American Bar Association's Model Rules of Professional Conduct. The comments to Rule 7.3 point to the "potential for abuse inherent in direct, in-person contact with prospective clients. The situation is fraught with the possibility of undue influence, intimidation, and overreaching." Those possibilities are magnified when the potential client is hospitalized or grieving the death of a loved one when the lawyer knocks on the door uninvited. The original purpose of solicitation laws, like laws prohibiting lawyer advertising, was anti-competitive; they were later invoked to curb old-fashioned ambulance chasing. Today, their impact is felt, perhaps most, by lawyers who specialize in representing victims of catastrophic accidents.

Union Carbide's accidental release of a deadly gas from its plant near Bhopal, India in 1984 killed over 4,000. A swarm of American lawyers, retainer agreements in hand, flew to India. Since Bhopal, man-made disasters—the kind for which a solvent company can be blamed —have attracted growing numbers of lawyers who sometimes sign up clients before the victims are in the ground. With a cautious eye toward bar disciplinary authorities, some lawyers seek to distance themselves from a solicitation charge by sending non-lawyers—colloquially known as "runners"—to sign up clients at the scene. Solicitation laws are drafted (or interpreted) to reach lawyers who hire runners. Otherwise, the law could be easily circumvented.

Betty Edward first ran cases as an unpaid volunteer for Benton Musslewhite, a Houston personal injury lawyer, in the wake of an Exxon toxic chemical spill near Houston. As she recalled, "Mr. Musslewhite had us sign up everyone in the community." A middle-aged mother of three, Edward is a high school graduate. When hired by Musslewhite in the wake of the Flight 1016 crash, Edward was unemployed and living on Social Security disability benefits. She had no training in law or as an investigator, but she had another qualification for the job: like most of the passengers on Flight 1016, she is black. Edward later testified: "I was assigned to contact all the black families on the [passenger] list." Two others subsequently hired as runners, George Dillard and Carlos Williams, are also black.

Benton Musslewhite is a Texas native with undergraduate and law degrees from Southern Methodist University. He practiced in Texas for a time, moved to Washington, D.C. as an aide to Senator Ralph Yarbrough, and moved back to Texas in 1971 to develop a personal injury practice. When in Washington, he had been appointed by President Kennedy to advisory positions on the National Council on Physical Fitness and the Area Redevelopment Administration—appointments which probably had not come to the President's personal attention, but which would nevertheless impress some potential clients.

Benton Musslewhite had long-standing professional and personal relationships with John O'Quinn, one of the most successful personal injury lawyers in the country. When O'Quinn agreed to work a case with Musslewhite, it was O'Quinn who put up the money, called the shots, and received most of the fee. The two had been sued by bar discipline authorities in 1987 for using runners. O'Quinn got off with a reprimand, but Musslewhite was suspended for three years. Over time, Musslewhite borrowed heavily from O'Quinn until he owed some $10 million at a fifteen percent interest rate, a debt which eventually forced Musslewhite's bankruptcy.

Betty Edward was visiting her mother in Louisiana on July 2, 1994 when she heard a report about Flight 1016 on the evening news. About the same time, Benton Musselwhite learned about Dorian Doucette's injuries and began to visualize him as a case—a big case—against USAir. The day after the crash, Musselwhite phoned Edward and asked her to find out where Doucette was hospitalized. After she reported back that he was in the army hospital in San Antonio, Edward—still in Louisiana—called George Dillard, a part-time runner in Houston, and arranged for him to take O'Quinn's promotional brochure to San Antonio, though Doucette could not have been in any condition to read it at the time. Following her return to Houston on July 11, Edward drove to Baytown, Texas, the home of Dorian Doucette's parents, to set up an appointment for Musslewhite and his son Charles.

Charles Musslewhite is a 1983 graduate of the University of Texas School of Law. He practiced for several years with a prominent Houston firm before becoming a sole practitioner. Father and son often worked cases together, but the two maintained separate practices. After Benton, Charles, O'Quinn and Carl Shaw were formally charged with barratry by the Texas Commission for Lawyer Discipline, Charles entered into a plea agreement whereby he would plead guilty and, in return for truthful testimony against the other defendants, he would receive a Commission recommendation to the judge for leniency. The case against Charles was severed for later disposition, leaving three defendants.

Charles said of his father: "Benton and I have a love/hate relationship. We yell and scream at each other and then hug each other. My father comes across as very believable. A lot of times, though, the truth with him is a moveable object." Throughout the trial, the defense lawyers harped on the theme of betrayal—the son against the father—"against your daddy." Asked on the stand how he felt about being a witness, Charles replied: "I would rather be anywhere on the planet right now."

There had been indications that Charles might end up paying a financial as well as a personal price for cutting a deal with the Commission. Before the trial, he had encountered a lawyer in the O'Quinn firm's kitchen who said to him: "You're at a fork in the road. If you go down one path, everything is going to be fine with you and John. If you go down another path, you'll never work in this town again." Charles had responded: "I'm not going to lie." Shortly after Charles told his story to bar authorities, the O'Quinn firm stopped hiring him and deferred reimbursement of expenses he had incurred to the conclusion of pending cases.

When the Musslewhites arrived at the Doucette home in the evening of July 11, Betty Edward was waiting in the front yard with Floyd Doucette. It was doubtful at that point whether Dorian's parents would themselves have any claim against USAir. If Dorian survived—an outcome then very much in doubt—only he would have a claim; if Dorian were to die, his claim might pass entirely to his young son, Dante Doucette, born out of wedlock, partly to Dante's mother, or perhaps to the parents. In any case, there was a psychological advantage in getting the parents to sign up because the son probably would follow suit if he recovered. The question became moot when Dorian recovered sufficiently to sign up with Musslewhite and O'Quinn.

Following pleasantries in the front yard, the Musslewhites were invited inside where Benton made a pitch to Floyd Doucette to sign an agreement retaining him and O'Quinn as co-counsel. Dorian Doucette's truck was parked near the house. Betty Edward recalled that Benton offered "to pay the note on the truck if he was having problems with that." The talk continued for two hours until Floyd Doucette signed an agreement retaining Benton and O'Quinn. The following morning, Floyd Doucette accompanied his wife to O'Quinn's office where she co-signed the retainer agreement. Floyd joined O'Quinn to film a promotional video in which he expressed his satisfaction with O'Quinn's services, even though, less than twenty-four hours after he had signed up, no services had yet been rendered. Shortly thereafter, Charles Musslewhite returned to Baytown and secured the signature of little Dante's mother on a retainer.

O'Quinn and the Musslewhites met several times in the next several days to apportion shares of the expected fee from the Doucette case, and to make plans for signing up more victims from the crash of Flight 1016. Their agreement with the Doucettes provided that they would receive forty percent of all amounts recovered from USAir (or its insurance company). Among themselves, fees were to be split sixty-seven percent for O'Quinn, thirty percent for Benton, and three percent for Charles. O'Quinn would pay all expenses and would try the case if it were not first settled. As it turned out, O'Quinn did settle the case without going to trial.

Benton Mussslewhite was nominally in charge of pre-trial investigation, but O'Quinn hired the Information Bank of Texas to do the only real investigating. The Information Bank interviewed witnesses to the crash, obtained helicopter photographs of the site, and compiled lists of survivors and relatives of the deceased, including addresses, telephone numbers, and race identification. Most of the other work was undertaken by Charles Musslewhite at hourly rates of $115 to $125. Once the retainer agreement was signed, Charles hit the ground running, billing O'Quinn $12,812.50 for expenses and services performed in the latter part of July, largely attributable to his efforts in soliciting additional cases in South Carolina.

Carl Shaw, O'Quinn's associate, provided what might be called technical support for the solicitation efforts in the Carolinas. Shaw made the arrangements for videotaping O'Quinn and Floyd Doucette in

Houston and later when O'Quinn flew to Columbia, South Carolina for a press conference. Shaw also oversaw the drafting, editing, and mailing of so-called "*Shapero* letters" to all of the survivors and families of those killed on Flight 1016.

Lawyer advertising has been accorded limited First Amendment protection as "commercial" speech since the United States Supreme Court's 1977 decision in *Bates v. State Bar of Arizona*. In *Shapero v. Kentucky Bar Association*, the Court was confronted with another clash between a state's efforts to curb lawyer advertising and the First Amendment. Free speech prevailed. Briefly, lawyer Shapero had applied to Kentucky authorities for approval of a solicitation letter he proposed to send only to persons facing foreclosure suits, cases he specialized in defending. Advertising directed to the general public—yellow page ads, TV spots, billboards—are protected by the First Amendment. Kentucky authorities did not find the letter false or misleading but nevertheless disapproved it on the dubious theory that such a targeted letter was not constitutionally protected. The Kentucky Supreme Court affirmed. Dividing six to three, the Supreme Court reversed, holding that Shapero's letter was protected speech. It was not deceptive and would have been protected if sent to a wider audience; it would be ironic, the majority reasoned, if a letter targeted to those who might actually need the lawyer's services were not protected. Perhaps more important, the court majority observed that a letter would not have the immediate impact of an in-person sales pitch. The American Bar Association responded to the *Shapero* decision by amending its solicitation rule to make *Shapero* letters look like junk mail; the words "advertising material" must appear on the outside envelope.

A typical *Shapero* letter extols the lawyer's skills and track record, suggests the prospect of a large verdict, encloses a brochure and perhaps a promotional video, and offers a contingent fee contract with no out-of-pocket cost to the client. The recipient is urged to phone the lawyer's 800 number or to sign and return an enclosed form that includes an invitation to visit. *Shapero* letters apparently have become standard procedure among personal injury law firms specializing in catastrophic accidents. The record in the *O'Quinn* case included references to letters from Cleveland and Washington, D.C. law firms. *Shapero* letters have the social utility of informing victims about lawyers who specialize in catastrophic accidents, who can provide more effective service, and who, generally speaking, can obtain bigger recoveries than local lawyers to whom accident victims might otherwise turn from help. Whatever one may think of O'Quinn's promotional methods, his $18 million settlement for Dorian Doucette was almost certainly more then he would have gotten through a Baytown, Texas general practitioner.

Benton Musslewhite, with O'Quinn's concurrence, assembled a team of his son Charles, Betty Edward and George Dillard to go to the Carolinas to sign up more victims of Flight 1016. Benton would later insist that he had instructed the three to "cross the t's and dot the i's" and that there had been no talk of solicitation. Charles' recollections of their instructions were different. Benton and O'Quinn had spoken of t's and i's because "they wanted to make sure they could come into court and say that." Benton "talked in code." If, for example, he were asked about paying Betty Edward for running cases, he would say: "I paid her for her time."

The team left Houston on July 15 for Charlotte, North Carolina, their first stop, with a supply of brochures, videos, and retainer agreements. Charles recalled: "We talked about a cover story, about how we were going to go over there and perform an investigation as a pretext to be able to go and knock on somebody's door to see if they wanted to hire us. I knew it was wrong. But I thought that our excuse—or our pretext, ruse, whatever you want to call it—would be enough to keep us out of trouble. The reason I felt like it was okay was because John [O'Quinn] had said grace over it."

Betty Edward and George Dillard agreed to work for $375 per day, plus expenses. In addition, according to Edward she was to "receive $25,000 up front as a bonus [for each case she signed up], plus up to $100,000, depending on the value of the case." O'Quinn would fund the trip, spending $50,000 to cover expenses in July and August.

Betty Edward understood the purpose of their trip as Charles Musslewhite had. "Get out there and scout and see what you can find on the ground. When we get to families' homes, tell them that we are investigating the crash but that was only to get us inside the door." Edward described what typically happened once they got inside: "When we gave the spiel and showed the video of Mr. O'Quinn, they could see all these million-dollar verdicts and Mr. O'Quinn's plush office. And they knew their small Columbia lawyers didn't have it. [We would] find out if they are happy with their lawyer. If not, we were instructed on how to fire their lawyer and hire Mr. O'Quinn." Edward did not recall meeting any accident victims who were happy with their lawyer.

Rodney Willingham had been a passenger on Flight 1016 and was recovering from his injuries in a Charlotte hospital. Edward and Dillard went to the hospital uninvited, slipped in a side door after visiting hours, and found Willingham in his room visiting with a cousin. Edward described their meeting: "We delivered Mr. O'Quinn's packet to Mr. Willingham after we had did our spiel to him in the hospital room. He was very antagonistic, very insultive, and asked us to leave." Dillard pressured the visiting cousin to tell Willingham, when he felt like talking, to "give us a call and the first chance at the case." Edward then departed for Columbia, South Carolina; Dillard stayed in Charlotte to make unproductive pitches to Willingham's father, aunt, and sister.

Most of the victims of Flight 1016 and their families lived in South Carolina. The soliciting team checked into the Adams Mark Hotel in Columbia on July 15, renting the top suite of two bedrooms and a "war room"—so named, Betty Edward said, "because it was hell"—in which results of the previous day were reported and assignments given for the next. Charles Musslewhite acted as supervisor, except when he returned briefly to Houston. In his absence, Darlene Hopper, a nurse employed by O'Quinn's firm, took over supervision.

George Dillard had met an elderly minister on his flight from Charlotte to Columbia and had told him about their problems in finding families of victims. A few days later, the minister brought his son, Charles ("Carlos") Williams, minister of the Free Gospel Word and Worship Center in Columbia and a part-time insurance agent, to the Adams Mark and introduced him to Charles Musslewhite. Charles promptly hired Williams and fired Dillard for his surreptitious entry to the hospital in Charlotte and for making unwanted advances toward Betty Edward. Williams asked for $1,000 per day salary. Charles agreed, subject to O'Quinn's approval of that amount and of increasing Edward's salary correspondingly, from $375 to $1,000 per day. Williams, like Edward, had no training for investigating airplane crashes.

Four-year-old Ryan Price lost both his parents in the wreckage of Flight 1016. Betty Edward, Darlene Hopper, Carlos Williams, and Carl Shaw made strenuous efforts to get young Ryan as an O'Quinn client for a wrongful death suit against USAir. When those efforts failed, O'Quinn used his representation of Ryan's paternal grandparents against his maternal grandparents in a contested custody case as leverage to obtain a share of the legal fees that a suit against USAir would generate. The Commission for Lawyer Discipline viewed O'Quinn's intrusion into the custody dispute as "a very central part" of its case.

Pursuit of the Ryan Price case began two days after the team arrived in Columbia. Betty Edward and Darlene Hopper went uninvited to the home of Thelma and Lindberg Price, Ryan's paternal grandparents, in nearby Hartsville. One of Ryan's uncles was acting as family spokesman and he signed a retainer agreement although he had no legal standing to represent his nephew. Edward reported the signing to Charles Musslewhite who instructed her to return to the Price home and have Thelma Price sign as Ryan's "next friend." For that designation to ripen into custody, it would have to be formalized by a court but, at the time, it was the best a runner could do.

Sally and Charles Stephenson, Ryan's maternal grandparents, live a block from the Prices. Edward and Hopper knocked on their door uninvited, a "cold call" as Edward described it. They learned that by mutual agreement with the Prices, their grandson was staying with the Stephensons — an indication that custody would be awarded eventually to the Stephenson side of the family, as it was. At that point, as Edward recalled: "We spoke with the Price family and the Stephenson family and we had it set up where the Stephensons would have him for a few days and the Prices would have him for a few days until we could get the custody hearing." A few days later, seeking to solidify their position Betty Edward and Carlos Williams went to the Stephenson home armed with brochures, a video, a *Shapero* letter and a retainer agreement. Sally Stephenson declined to sign up.

The next day, Carl Shaw came to Columbia, primarily to arrange a press conference for John O'Quinn. Getting the Stephensons signed up, however, was viewed as a priority, so Shaw went to the Stephenson home with Edward and Williams for another attempt. According to Edward, the Stephensons declined to sign, saying that their son Charles would speak for them. Shaw went outside to make a cell phone call. After a few minutes, Edward went outside to see what was taking Shaw so long. Shaw told her "he was calling [a Columbia custody lawyer] and he was going to make sure that bitch didn't ever see Ryan any more."

Sally Stephenson is a retired garment inspector whose four children were college educated. She was flown to Texas from South Carolina to testify for the Commission for Lawyer Discipline. What stood out in her recollection was the importance Betty Edward repeatedly placed on hiring O'Quinn for the USAir claim in order to get custody of Ryan. "If I would hire Mr. O'Quinn, because the Price family already had hired him, I could get custody of Ryan." Stephenson wanted to sign "because

I wanted to have my grandson. And so I called [my son] Charlie, and Charlie called Jamie, our attorney, and he told us not to sign anything." Edward and Williams left and returned later with Carl Shaw who— Stephenson was led to believe—was "the custody lawyer." Stephenson recalled that Shaw had gone outside to make a phone call and, upon returning, had told her, in effect: "Unless I sign up with O'Quinn, I would never see my grandbaby again." Torn, but feeling bound by her son's advice, Stephenson did not sign.

Charlie Stephenson, Sally Stephenson's son, is a graduate of the University of South Carolina. He lives in Columbia and is employed as a manager for United Parcel Service. He is married and has two young sons. Betty Edward and Carlos Williams went to his home after being unsuccessful in persuading his mother to sign up with O'Quinn for the USAir case. As part of their pitch, they stated that Stephenson could get custody of Ryan, as he recalled, "because they felt like our home was the best home" —a direct conflict of interest since they had already committed O'Quinn to represent the Price family, the Stephensons' competition for custody. That same evening, Stephenson received a follow-up phone call from Carl Shaw who also urged him to sign with O'Quinn. Stephenson replied to the effect that he "wasn't interested in Mr. O'Quinn," that he and his family "would do everything we needed to do to make sure we got custody of the child, and that we were not going to be strong-armed by any attorneys." Charlie Stephenson had received *Shapero* letters from other lawyers, including a Jamie Lebovitz of Cleveland, whom he later hired.

Desa Ballard is a lawyer who practices in Columbia, South Carolina. Referred by Jamie Lebovitz, she was retained by the Stephenson family to be local counsel in the case against USAir. When a dispute arouse over custody of Ryan Price, she arranged for Charlie Stephenson and his wife to retain a local family court specialist. Ballard became involved in both the custody and accident cases and in probate proceedings for settlement of the deceased parents' estates.

An associate from O'Quinn's firm negotiated the custody case for the Price family. Ballard testified that during a mediation session O'Quinn's associate stated the firm's position: "The O'Quinn folks would give up the fight for custody on behalf of Thelma [Price] if we, on behalf of the Stephenson family, would agree to pay Mr. O'Quinn a portion of the attorneys' fees earned in the USAir litigation." There was nothing in writing to evidence acceptance of that condition, but events unfolded along those lines. Charlie Stephenson and his wife got uncontested custody of Ryan, with visitation rights for the Prices. From that point on, to Ballard's knowledge, the O'Quinn firm did nothing in the custody case or in the case against USAir, other than to furnish copies of documents.

John O'Quinn was questioned about his firm's participation and fee in the case against USAir. He denied Ballard's statement about his firm's trading off the custody dispute (and with it the Price's interests) in return for part of the fee from that case, but did not specify any services his firm had rendered. After the USAir case was settled by the Lebovitz firm for $1.5 million, Ballard sent a "referral fee" of $75,612.93 to the O'Quinn firm. Assuming that Lebovitz received about $500,000 — one-third of the USAir settlement — as his fee, O'Quinn apparently received about fifteen percent of that fee for doing very little.

Recruiting proceeded slowly during the team's first week in South Carolina. Charles Musslewhite called O'Quinn and said: "We need some press. Why don't you come over here and meet with the Prices and have a press conference." John O'Quinn flew to Columbia in a private jet on July 25, stopping on the way in Charlotte to pick up Rita Crosby, a correspondent for CBS news who had been the on-air reporter in a television story about the crash of Flight 1016 which O'Quinn had incorporated in his promotional video. Crosby participated in a filmed press conference featuring O'Quinn, Thelma Price, little Ryan Price and other members of the family. Portions of the press conference aired the next day.

Carl Shaw was asked if the purpose of O'Quinn's press conference in Columbia was "to facilitate the acquisition of legal business." He responded: "No. The primary purpose was to answer the request of a regional CBS correspondent who wanted to do a documentary about this military officer, the most severely injured person still alive." Shaw was referring to Private Dorian Doucette who was then in a hospital burn unit in San Antonio. Asked if he thought a press conference with the Prices in South Carolina had helped Doucette's case in some way, Shaw responded: "I think it was helpful for Dorian's case." He did not elaborate.

Betty Edward recalled the occasion of the press conference in Columbia as the only time she met O'Quinn personally. It was in the "war room" at the Adams Mark. "He shook my hand and told me to keep the good works up."

Charles Musslewhite thought another way to "get the word out that there were lawyers in town that could help you on the USAir case, [was to] tell them we had a psychiatrist that they could go get a free interview with." O'Quinn had agreed that some of the USAir families "might want to have some therapy." Steven Kramer, a Houston psychiatrist, had worked with O'Quinn on other cases. Carl Shaw arranged for Kramer to come to Columbia at the time of the press conference. A press release about Dr. Kramer's availability was picked up by a Columbia newspaper. As Musslewhite viewed the psychiatrist's contribution, Kramer met with families to talk about "the grief they were going through so that he could testify about that later." Kramer's main purpose, however, was "to help us get business."

Insurance adjusters, unlike lawyers, are free to knock on the doors of the injured—or the survivors of the dead—offering quick, cheap settlements which may appear generous to the unsophisticated. The adjuster's offer has the additional attraction of cutting out the lawyer's contingent fee—usually one-third of the recovery, sometimes more. Under the circumstances, it can be important for the lawyers to get to prospective claimants ahead of the insurance adjusters. Charles Musslewhite testified about one such case in a colloquy with counsel:

> Counsel: You weren't in any kind of race with the airline to see who could get these things taken care of first?
>
> Musslewhite: Sure was. We wanted to be hired before the airline got to them. There were a couple of kids who lost their parents, Timmy and Tammy Fisher. They worked at the Fat Boy Drive-In in Columbia.
>
> Counsel: And you sent Betty Edward and Carlos Williams to talk to them?
>
> Musslewhite: Initially, yeah, but I went out and talked to them myself. Then Betty and Carlos went to Ohio to meet their brother. He was supposedly the decision-maker. The kids didn't know what to do. [We discovered that] the airline had offered $40,000 for the loss of both parents which I felt was outrageous, but the kids had accepted it.

As a door opener, runners sometimes prefer an introduction from a friend to a cold call. Betty Edward described how she and Carlos Williams "got information on contacting [two families] from a family friend of Mr. Carlos Williams' mother. We paid her a thousand dollars for the introduction to the Plowden family." Following the family friend's intervention, Edward, Williams, and Darlene Hopper were invited to the Plowden home. Edward described the scene: "We did our spiel, the introduction and the video. Mrs. Plowden was in so much grief that she couldn't watch the video. Darlene Hopper was persistent on showing her the video and wanted to know everything about Mr. Nathaniel Plowden, Jr., the son that was killed. He was going to Charlotte to be ordained as a minister." According to Edward, Hopper did not "go over well because she had on a very short skirt, a low-neck blouse, and she was very insensitive to the family. And this is a minister's home." Mrs. Plowden left the room distraught, but the runners stayed for another hour trying to persuade Reverend Plowden to sign up. He refused to sign that day but, during the group's fourth visit, he gave in.

Bertha Cantey and her nephew were victims of Flight 1016. The $1,000 paid to the family friend for an introduction to the Plowdens also bought an introduction to the Canteys. An additional $250 was paid to family friend who accompanied Edward and Williams on the first visit. They were chagrined to learn that the Canteys had already hired a lawyer. On a subsequent visit, the team arrived in force: Benton and Charles Musslewhite, Betty Edward, Carlos Williams, the paid friend, and Dr. Steven Kramer, the psychiatrist. During the second visit, according to Edward: "We had [a family spokesman] write a letter firing their attorney."

While in Columbia, Charles reported periodically to O'Quinn by phone. He testified that O'Quinn "wasn't happy with how much money was being spent as compared with how many people were hiring us." In early September, O'Quinn told Charles: "It's time to shut down."

As the most knowledgeable source about what had happened in the field, Betty Edward was expected to be the Commission's star witness. But her credibility was severely damaged on cross-examination. The defense lawyers went on the attack over Edward's name. She admitted that Edward had never been her legal name. She had once lived with a Felix Edward and had agreed to pose as his wife in a lawsuit. When running cases arising from Flight 1016, she "'worked under" the name Betty Edward, but her legal name then was Betty St. Marie. She had since divorced and married again; her present name was Betty St. Marie Register. Edward was asked when she had last filed a federal income tax return—a question calculated to inflame a jury of taxpayers. Edward replied that she "didn't remember," and that she had been told the lawyers would pay her taxes on the amounts she received for running cases.

Edward dug herself into a deeper hole with her conflicting accounts of what she had been promised for her work. In a deposition she had claimed she was owed $7,500,000, which included $25,000 per case, plus bonuses based on her estimate of case values. On the witness stand, she first claimed $300,000 for her cases in South Carolina, a figure she later revised upward to $475,000. Edward counted as a "case" every family member she had signed up for a single case; for example, by her reckoning, she was entitled to $125,000 for the Doucette case, plus bonuses. Benton Musslewhite confirmed paying Edward $39,000, plus expenses.

In July 1995, Edward sent O'Quinn a bill for her services for $469,000, threatening to "spill the beans" if she weren't paid. She wasn't, and she hired a lawyer to make collection efforts that proved unsuccessful. Her complaints to the Texas Commission for Lawyer Discipline went unanswered. Frustrated, Edward took her case to the media; the result was a January 1996 *Wall Street Journal* article about O'Quinn, headlined "Master of Disaster," which reflected Edwards' version of events in South Carolina. Apparently spurred by the *Journal* article, the Texas Commission undertook an investigation, found that barratry had occurred, and sued O'Quinn, the Musslewhites, and Shaw, seeking to have them disbarred.

The Commission called Benton Musslewhite as an adverse witness. He was asked why he had hired Betty Edward to work on the USAir case. "I was impressed with her personality, her presentation, and the way she handled herself in the [Exxon toxic spill case]." Musslewhite stuck to the story that his son Charles, Betty Edward, George Dillard, and Carlos Williams had been in South Carolina for almost two months "on behalf of the three lawyers that represented the Doucettes, as part of the investigation, information-gathering process. We needed persons meeting with people, finding out what was going on in South Carolina, finding out who had lawyers and who didn't, whether they had been contacted by USAir." Upon her return to Houston, however, Edward did not bring back written statements, photographs, or any other information relevant to the Doucette case she was supposedly investigating. As Charles Musslewhite had testified, the investigation of negligence in an airplane crash case is done by the National Transportation Safety Board. Personal injury lawyers largely rely on the Board's report for proof of fault and on the victims' doctors and medical records to prove damages. There was nothing for a team of runners to investigate in South Carolina.

The Commission called Darlene Hopper as its last witness, over the objections of defense counsel. Hopper, it will be recalled, is the nurse employed by O'Quinn who sometimes accompanied Betty Edward and Carlos Williams on house calls. The lawyers on both sides knew in advance that Hopper would refuse to testify. The Commission's lawyers undoubtedly thought it would help them with the jury if a person intimately involved in the doings in South Carolina were to decline to answer questions for fear of self-incrimination. For their part, the defense lawyers must have wanted to keep Hopper off the stand, even if she would not provide any damaging information. The court allowed Hopper to be called and she gave her name in answer to the first question. The second question was: "How are you employed?" Hopper responded: "On the advice of counsel, I am relying upon my Fifth Amendment right to decline to answer all questions regarding this case." After giving the same response to five more questions, she was allowed to step down. The Commission then closed its case.

The three defendants, O'Quinn, Benton Musslewhite, and Carl Shaw, had separate lawyers but their interests were essentially similar and, for the most part, they put on a common defense. April Krieger, a former personal assistant to O'Quinn and the lead defense witness, was asked why Darlene Hopper had gone to South Carolina. She stated: "She had the medical expertise that was needed. Dorian Doucette had suffered horrendous injuries. She could speak medical language, talk to the ambulance drivers, and so she was critical for the investigation of the case." Dorian Doucette was being treated in Texas while Darlene Hopper was making cold calls on other victims of Flight 1016 in South Carolina. On cross-examination, Krieger admitted that she had not talked to Hopper about what she had done.

Floyd Doucette, Dorian's father and a retired foreman for Armco Steel, testified that O'Quinn had paid Dorian's considerable medical expenses and that O'Quinn and Musslewhite had accepted a reduced fee, one third of the $18.5 million settlement, instead of the forty percent called for in their retainer agreement. Asked how he felt about Mr. Musslewhite's representation, Doucette replied: "I feel very good about him."

John O'Quinn took the stand as the last witness. The son of a Houston automobile mechanic, O'Quinn was first in his law school class while working part time for his father, writing for the law review, and participating on the debate team. He was the first graduate of his school to be hired by the prestigious Houston firm of Baker & Botts. O'Quinn recalled: "The University of Houston was looked down on in those days. They took a chance on me." Twelve years later, O'Quinn founded his own firm that would grow to twenty lawyers and one hundred forty employees, specializing in representing victims of catastrophic accidents. O'Quinn and a partner had been pictured on the cover of *Fortune* magazine under the headline "Lawyers from Hell." *Forbes* magazine has estimated that O'Quinn made $40 million in 1993, a figure he denied.

O'Quinn concentrated on putting distance between himself and the case-running operation in the Carolinas, claiming that everything he had done had been for Dorian Doucette's case. (The defense contended that the Doucette case had not been obtained by illegal solicitation because Benton Musslewhite had a "prior professional relationship" with the Doucette family; he claimed to have represented them in the Exxon spill case.) During much of the summer of 1994, O'Quinn had been "totally consumed by getting ready for the Dow Chemical [breast implant] trial which was going to affect the rights of 2,000 women." Putting up money for the Doucette investigation was his responsibility, but he had not had time to supervise Charles Musslewhite and had no idea what was going on in South Carolina. He had not sent his employee, Darlene Hooper, to South Carolina, she "just went." In an oblique reference to cold-call solicitations, O'Quinn was asked what he would have done had he known what was going on. He replied: "There would have been some rear ends chewed out and there would have been some people sent home. There would be a whole different set of people investigating."

Concerning the *Shapero* letters he had sent to the victims, O'Quinn claimed: "I was looking for allies. In all likelihood, Dorian's case would end up being tried in South Carolina so he would be a stranger. I would be a stranger. And if I could network with South Carolina lawyers and South Carolina victims, it would help Dorian's case immensely." He had held the press conference in South Carolina with the Price family because "it could help Dorian's case for people to see me on television, to hear me tell the message about this plane crash."

O'Quinn, the Musslewhites, and Carl Shaw had been charged with criminal offenses in South Carolina arising out of the Flight 1016 crash. O'Quinn, Benton Musslewhite, and Shaw entered into agreements under which they had pled guilty to unauthorized practice of law, a misdemeanor, and the soliciting charges were dismissed, subject to several conditions. The Commission's lawyer extracted those conditions from a reluctant O'Quinn. He had paid a modest fine of $2,500. In addition, however, he had agreed to fund a seminar on legal ethics for three years, including a speaker and written materials; he had agreed to fund another three-year program through the South Carolina Attorney General's Office to prosecute cases of unauthorized practice of law. Finally, he had agreed to reimburse South Carolina authorities $5,000 for the expenses of their investigation. O'Quinn demurred to the suggestion that those obligations would end up costing him about $500,000. Asked how much he had been required to put in escrow, O'Quinn replied: "I don't know."

O'Quinn denied any knowledge whether Charles Musslewhite, Betty Edward, Carlos Williams, or George Dillard had done any investigating or prepared any reports in return for the $50,000 he had spent, ostensibly for those services. It had been his intention, he claimed, that the recipients of the *Shapero* letters would not be contacted unless they first responded to the letter. But he never told Charles' team *not* to contact them. Instead: "I told them to do what was lawful." Concluding, the Commission's lawyer pulled out all the stops: "You say you told them to leave no stone unturned. You never got an investigation report. You never got a photograph. You never got a statement. You never got a video. And you knew all along they were out there soliciting cases, didn't you?" O'Quinn shot back: "False, false, false!"

Following closing arguments, the judge instructed the jury on the law and they retired to deliberate. After a nine-day trial that generated over one hundred exhibits and a transcript of some 2,000 pages, the jury returned in less than an hour with a unanimous verdict for the defendants.

In addition to the statutory prohibition of barratry, the Texas Rules of Disciplinary Conduct cover similar conduct as "soliciting." Following seven days of administrative hearings the year before, the Commission on Lawyer Discipline had found that O'Quinn, the Musslewhites, and Shaw had not only committed barratry, but had also violated the Commission's rule prohibiting personal solicitation of potential clients. The defendants were entitled to a jury trial on the charge of barratry, a criminal offense, but Commission findings of solicitation, a disciplinary violation, are heard by the court. Although the jury had found in favor of the defendant lawyers on the barratry charge, the Judge ruled that they had violated the anti-soliciting rule for doing essentially the same thing.

Following a hearing on the appropriateness of sanctions, the judge ruled that "no sanctions shall be assessed" against O'Quinn, Benton Musslewhite, or Shaw.

Charles Musslewhite, the lawyer who blew the whistle, was stuck with the plea bargain he had made before the trial. In accordance with its terms, he was found, like the others, to have violated the soliciting rule. In addition, he was suspended from the practice of law for thirty days, and to perform 300 hours of community service work of a menial nature by volunteering at the hospice facility of the Texas Medical Center in Houston.

## Post Script

Sensing that a jury might be sympathetic to the defendants, the Commission for Lawyer Discipline had offered to waive a jury before the trial began. The defendants and their counsel, veteran trial lawyers all, had demanded a jury. The day after the jury verdict, John O'Quinn wrote letters to the Chairman and trial counsel for the Commission which read: "May God grant you and your family peace and happiness this Christmas, as He has mine. We say we believe in the jury system. Let our deeds show that we truly believe what we say."

\* \* \*

## Comments and Questions

1. In *Ohralik v. Ohio State Bar Association*, 436 U.S. 447 (1978), a unanimous Supreme Court upheld Ohio's anti-solicitation rule—similar to Model Rule 7.3—prohibiting in-person solicitation against a claim that it violated the First Amendment. Ohralick's conduct in pursuing two teenage victims of a car accident was sleazy—including a hospital visit and a concealed tape recorder—and might have resulted in a narrow ruling based on egregious facts. Instead, the Court upheld the rule on its face, rejecting Ohralik's argument that the Bar Association had the burden of proving that "his conduct constituted actual overreaching or inflicted some specific injury. The rules prohibiting solicitation are prophylactic measures whose objective is the prevention of harm before it occurs."

The Court adopted a critical view of solicitation:

Unlike a public advertisement, which simply provides information
and leaves the recipient free to act upon it or not, in-person solicitation may exert pressure and often demands an immediate response,
without providing an opportunity for comparison and reflection....
The substantive evils of solicitation have been stated over the years
in sweeping terms: stirring up litigation, assertion of fraudulent
claims, debasing the legal profession and potential harm to the
solicited client in the form of overreaching, overcharging, under-
representation, and misrepresentation. 436 U.S. at 461.

The Court did not acknowledge that solicitation might also serve worth-
while ends—such as giving potential clients access to experienced
lawyers, and protecting them from insurance adjusters who are not subject to solicitation rules (see paragraphs 2 and 3, below).

Fifteen years later, the Court distinguished *Ohralik,* holding unconstitutional a Florida statute which prohibited in-person solicitation by
accountants. *Edenfield v. Fane,* 507 U.S. 761 (1993). Accountant Fane
obtained some of his clients "through direct, personal, uninvited solicitation." The Court reasoned, in part:

Unlike a lawyer, a CPA is not a professional trained in persuasion.
A CPA's training emphasizes independence and objectivity, not
advocacy. The typical client of a CPA is far less susceptible to
manipulation than the young accident victims in *Ohralik.*

What is left of *Ohralik* after *Edenfield*? Does *Edenfield* mean that tax
lawyers can solicit?

2. There is no necessary relationship between in-person soliciting and
the quality of legal representation. Although some old-fashioned ambulance chasers probably are marginal performers, some undoubtedly are
not, and firms like John O'Quinn's which specialize in mass torts can
provide quality representation and secure top-dollar settlements or verdicts. The defenders of anti-solicitation rules typically invoke the mantra
of "consumer protection." However, anti-solicitation rules can have the
effect of steering accident victims to local general practitioners or other
lawyers who have no experience in complex accident litigation. How
does that promote consumer protection?

John Coale, a successful personal-injury lawyer from Washington,
D.C., has been the subject of solicitation complaints arising from nu-

merous major accidents. Coale has also been known to take cases for contingent fees as low as fifteen percent, a practice which has aroused animosity among other mass-tort lawyers. For a profile of this controversial lawyer, *see* MacLachlan, "Warning: Hot Coale," *The National Law Journal*, June 7, 1993, p. 1.

3. Charles Musselwhite described how he and his runners were in a race with USAir's insurance adjusters who were in the field almost immediately after the accident attempting to settle claims. There is nothing to prevent insurance adjusters from soliciting cheap settlements. How, except by lawyers, can consumers be protected from overreaching by insurance adjusters?

4. *Shapero v. Kentucky Bar Association*, 486 U.S. 466 (1988) and the targeted mailing technique it held protected by the First Amendment are described in the story. Relying on *Shapero*, John O'Quinn and other accident and disaster lawyers send out promotional letters, resumes, videos, and invitations to telephone them collect to victims and their families promptly after the event. Given in-person solicitation's potential for abuse, why shouldn't a *Shapero* letter be a sufficient means for mass tort lawyers to make their services available?

A few states have reacted to *Shapero* by prohibiting written solicitations in personal injury and wrongful death cases during the thirty-day period following the event. The constitutionality of the Florida statute was upheld against First Amendment claims in *Florida Bar v. Went For It* (1995). In 1996, the United States Congress imposed a ban on contacts with victims of airline accidents or their families for a thirty-day period. 49 U.S.C. 1136(g)(2). Are these "cooling-off period" approaches reasonable?

5. As the author read the trial record, there was no doubt that Benton Musselwhite, John O'Quinn, and Carl Shaw were guilty of barratry. Yet after a nine-day trial, it took a lay jury less than an hour to find in their favor. Among a populace becoming inured to telemarketing, what might this say about its attitude toward solicitation by lawyers?

6. One violation of a rule of ethics tends to breed others—perhaps most commonly, the obligation under Model Rule 8.3 (the "ratfink" rule) to report another lawyer's misconduct. We saw this phenomenon of proliferating violations in Chapter 5, "Two Scorpions in a Bottle." In this chapter, consider the statement to Charles Musselwhite by the lawyer in O'Quinn's firm to the effect that Musselwhite's career would be in jeop-

ardy if he "went down the wrong path." Obstruction of justice and witness tampering are federal offenses. 18 U.S.C. 1512. Under Model Rule 8.4, "Misconduct," it is "professional misconduct" for a lawyer to "commit a criminal act that reflects adversely on the lawyer's honesty, trustworthiness, or fitness as a lawyer in other respects, or engage in conduct that is prejudicial to the administration of justice." Was the lawyer's threatening statement to Charles Musslewhite an obstruction of justice and/or professional misconduct? Are the same issues raised by Betty Edwards' testimony that the runners—on instructions from the lawyers—convinced some accident victims to fire lawyers they had previously retained, presumably knowing nothing about the other lawyers?

7. In the popular film, *Erin Brockovich*, Julia Roberts plays a runner for an aging, low-energy, personal-injury lawyer. Brockovich is a caring and conscientious runner who signs up over 600 claimants injured by a toxic spill from a nearby power plant. Feeling outgunned, the lawyer joins forces with a firm of specialists and, following arbitration, they recover $333 million from Pacific Gas & Electric Co., of which forty percent ($133 million) represents their fee. (The audience gets the impression that the claimants are happy to get the other $200 million.) As the film ends, the lawyer's firm has moved to classy new digs, Erin gets a $2 million bonus and is hard at work running several new cases. The film makes no reference to the fact that California (and every other State) prohibits solicitation by lawyers, and that Erin's employer could have been disciplined, perhaps even disbarred, for what she was doing on his behalf. Apart from its entertainment value, does *Erin Brockovich* present a convincing argument in favor of solicitation? Should solicitation rules contain an exception for caring, conscientious, drop-dead gorgeous runners? Only in California?

# Chapter 9

# Spectator Sport

"It's the only death penalty case you can find in the State of Georgia where not one objection was made during the entire trial. There was absolutely no adversary process here."
— Opening statement of Stephen Bright, habeas corpus counsel for the petitioner in *Fugate v. Thomas, Warden.*

Wallace ("Buck") Fugate stood motionless in the downstairs game room when he heard the front door open. He knew he wasn't supposed to be there—in the lakeside house he had built himself—after his ex-wife Pattie had obtained a court order keeping him off the property without her written consent, which, given the hostility between them, she wasn't about to grant. Buck was carrying a .38 caliber Taurus revolver he had taken with him when his car broke down on the highway earlier that day. Hearing footsteps upstairs, he stepped into the adjoining bathroom, hoping Pattie and their teenage son Mark were only stopping by. Moments later, Mark came down the basement stairs carrying his .22 rifle. He turned on the game room light and called out: "I know you're in there. Come out. I've got a gun." Buck came out, saying: "Don't shoot son. I'm not here to hurt anybody." Mark aimed the rifle at his father and pulled the trigger, but it failed to fire.

Pattie had been complaining to the sheriff that, despite the court order, Buck had been harassing her; she wanted him jailed. Buck had complaints of his own; he had been making child support payments but Patty wouldn't let him see his son. Now that he was caught in violation of the order, Buck thought he might as well turn himself in. He went upstairs to ask Pattie to drive him to the sheriff.

Pattie and Mark had known when they arrived at the house that Buck, a skilled mechanic, was somewhere about. Buck's 1956 Mustang—to be Mark's when he turned eighteen—had been left in the garage, out of commission. Now it was halfway out of the garage with the hood up. Pattie and Mark had gone in the house and she tried to call the police, but the line was busy. She called her sister Vicky and was speaking with her when Buck came into the room. A heated argument ensued, escalating to a physical struggle—first in the house, then in the yard, and finally in Vicky's van, where it ended with a pistol shot and Pattie dead on the ground.

Buck drove away in Pattie's van, leaving Mark in the front yard with his mother's body. Several hours later, Buck turned himself in. Joe Briley, District Attorney of the Ocmulgee Judicial Circuit, presented the case to a grand jury which indicted Buck for murder, burglary, kidnapping with bodily injury, theft by taking, and two counts of aggravated assault. District Attorney Briley had a track record of death penalties in homicide cases. He filed notice of his intention to seek the death penalty for Buck Fugate.

*State of Georgia v. Wallace M. Fugate, III*, Case No. 91 CR-129-7 in the Superior Court for Putnam County, Georgia, was assigned to Judge William A. Prior, Jr. Judge Prior telephoned Reginald ("Reg") Bellury to inform him of his appointment as counsel for Buck Fugate. The Judge granted Bellury's request that his office mate, Leo Browne, be appointed co-counsel.

Reg Bellury had been practicing law in and around Putnam County, Georgia for twenty years when he entered the *Fugate* case as lead defense counsel. Early in his career, he had served as an assistant district attorney for three years, prosecuting criminal cases under the supervision of Joe Briley, the long-time District Attorney who was now his opponent. A bottom feeder in private practice, Bellury depended heavily on court appointments to represent indigents in criminal cases.

Reg Bellury had limited experience as defense counsel in death penalty cases. Most of the homicide cases he had handled in the past, whether as prosecutor or defense counsel, involved one spouse killing another or a relative—usually considered "crimes of passion" and therefore less serious than killing a clerk, execution-style, at a convenience store. Defendants in such cases were usually allowed to plead guilty to voluntary manslaughter, thus avoiding the possibility of a life sentence or, in aggravated cases, the death penalty. In return for saving the State of Georgia the expense of a trial, defendants typically received a twenty-year sentence with the possibility of parole in about five years. Reg Bellury viewed Buck Fugate's case as a "domestic relations homicide"—a tragic event, but understandable in human terms. But Bellury made no attempt to plea bargain with District Attorney Briley to reduce the murder charge to manslaughter, or at least to take the death penalty off the table.

Judge Prior had first appointed another lawyer, Martin Fierman, to represent Buck Fugate, but Fierman had been removed at Buck's request. Fierman had filed pretrial motions which were pending when Reg Bellury was appointed, including motions for an independent analysis of the State's physical evidence; for funding to retain an investigator and expert witnesses; for an independent psychological examination; for a specification of facts underlying the death penalty request and to strike that request. Bellury withdrew all of those motions at the first prehearing conference.

Buck Fugate, a forty-two-year-old contractor from Eatonton, Georgia, piney-woods country 60 miles southeast of Atlanta, went on trial for his life on April 27, 1992. The first day and the following morning were spent selecting a jury. During the afternoon of the second day, the prosecution called fifteen witnesses in rapid succession and rested its case. The State established largely undisputed facts about the whereabouts of Buck and Pattie that day and introduced into evidence a signed statement Buck had made to a sheriff's deputy and the .38 Taurus revolver. The State called three expert witnesses: a forensic serologist who testified about blood samples; a criminalist who testified about the pistol; and the forensic pathologist who had performed an autopsy on Pattie's body. The State's key witness was sixteen-year-old Mark Fugate, Buck's son and the only other person at the scene.

Mark testified on direct examination about what happened the day his mother was killed. They had both worked until 4 p.m. at Hallman's Wood Products. After work, they drove to Rabbit Skip Road to feed their horses, taking longer than usual because the tail of Mark's horse had to be amputated. Patti's boyfriend Steve, a construction worker in South Carolina, had called her at Hallman's and invited them for a weekend of horseback riding. They had planned to drive to South Carolina after stopping by the house to pick up clothes.

Pattie and Mark arrived at the house about 5:30, Mark recalled, saw the Mustang, and went inside expecting to find Buck. After Mark confronted him in the game room and his rifle failed to fire, Buck went upstairs to Pattie's bedroom. Mark testified that he followed his father and came upon him hitting Pattie with the butt of his pistol. Mark hit his father with his rifle stock. Pattie was wearing her long dark hair in a ponytail and Buck "grabbed her by the hair and started dragging her out of the house." He proceeded to get her into the driver's side of the van, but she wouldn't go, so he kept beating her and beating her, to get her into the van." After repeated unsuccessful attempts to force Pattie into the van, "I saw him grab her. Holding her by her hair, he tilted her head back, put the gun in her face, and pulled the trigger." Pattie's body went limp and fell forward to the ground. Buck moved one of Pattie's legs "because it was under the tire, got in the van, and left."

Mark recalled that after his mother was shot: "I screamed for awhile and then I checked her pulse. There was no pulse." He went in the house to find a bullet for his rifle. "I didn't want to live because I didn't want to be without her." But he changed his mind about killing himself "because I knew they'd need a witness to put him away." Then he called the police.

That Buck Fugate shot his wife was undisputed. His defense was that his revolver had discharged by accident during their struggle. It was critical to Buck's defense that Mark's testimony be discredited. Reg Bellury conducted a rambling and often pointless cross-examination. He seemed intent on underlining the most damaging part of Mark's story — that he had seen the fatal shot. Bellury initiated the following exchange with Mark Fugate:

At the time the fatal shot was fired, did you witness that?

Yes, sir.

Or were you on the other side of the van?

I was on the same side that Buck was, about six feet away from him.

So your testimony is that you actually saw it ?

I did not see the bullet hit her face, because I blinked my eyes at that moment when he pulled the trigger. But I watched him let go of her hair and drop her, and I watched him tilt her back when he shot her.

How far away was the gun from her head?

Approximately a foot.

About an hour after the shooting, Mark Fugate had given the police a signed statement about what had occurred. A copy was provided to the defense before trial. Mark's description of what he had been able to see when the shot was fired differed significantly from his trial testimony:

"I ran to the back of the van. I peeked around, I heard a shot. I saw my mother's head hit the ground. *I could not tell if he held her head back, or not. He had his back to me.* He was holding her by the head of the hair" (italics supplied).

If Mark had been unable to see whether Buck "held her head back" — his contemporaneous written version of events — then, contrary to his trial testimony, he could not have "watched him tilt her head back" when he shot her. In addition, in his opening argument the Assistant District Attorney said that Mark was "behind the van" when the fatal shot was fired and that "when he looks back around the edge of the van his mother is dead on the ground." This indicates that when Mark was talking with the prosecutors before trial — Mark refused to talk to the defense — his account of what he had seen was even more favorable to Buck's accident defense because his view had been blocked, not by his father's back, but by the van. Bellury did not ask Mark to explain these conspicuous and critical inconsistencies. He did not call as a witness the police officer who had taken Mark's statement. Nor did Bellury focus on Mark's hatred of his father as a source of bias. Mark admitted on the witness stand wanting to kill his father and he had attempted to do just that during their initial confrontation in the game room.

Buck Fugate took the witness stand to gave his account of what happened that Saturday. He left home that morning intending to visit a friend and to talk to the sheriff about what he might do to satisfy Pattie's complaints. Buck's car overheated on the highway. "I thought I had blowed a head gasket. So I parked it because it's an antique 1957 Ford, the one that was used in *Driving Miss Daisy*. I pushed it off the side of the road so nobody would accidentally hit it. I had a pistol in there I had bought for [my girlfriend] Connie. I didn't want to leave it in the car, afraid somebody would break in and steal it." Buck set off on foot, thinking he might get a tow from a friend who lived nearby. Unfortunately, the friend wasn't home.

Pattie's house was also located nearby and Buck "got to thinking about what my son had said, about wanting me to fix the Mustang." The previous Wednesday, Buck had found a note from Pattie in his mailbox telling him that she and Mark planned to spend the weekend in South Carolina with her boyfriend Steve. The note was one of several Buck had received from Pattie, who avoided speaking to him. With Pattie gone for the weekend, Buck thought he could go on the property and work on the Mustang without the risk of being caught in violation of the court order.

"The first thing I wanted to do was make sure she was in South Carolina." Pattie's note had included the phone and room number of a Day's Inn where she would be staying. Buck phoned the motel but there was no response in the room. He waited, called twice more, and a male voice answered. Buck hung up, satisfied that Pattie was with Steve, and turned his attention to the Mustang. He discovered a missing gasket that had caused hot exhaust gas to disable the starter. He took the starter off and fixed it, installed a battery, and the car was running again. Buck went back in the house and was going through a stack of mail Pattie had failed to forward to him when he heard the van pull into the driveway. He retreated to the game room in the basement.

Buck described his encounter with Pattie. "I walked in the bedroom and she was talking on the phone to somebody. I mashed the receiver on the telephone and said: 'Would you take me to the Sheriff? You know, you could have me locked up.' I had the pistol in my hand, but I didn't have it pointed at nobody. I told her, 'Don't worry, I ain't here to hurt anybody. I'll put this thing away.' And I took the pistol and was shoving it in my pocket. At that moment, without saying anything, she jumped off the bed and butted me with her head and the pistol flew out of my hand." Pattie tried to grab the pistol but Buck recovered it. Mark appeared with his rifle and Pattie yelled "Shoot him." Buck grabbed Pattie "and spun her around and put my arm across her chest to where I could keep her from hitting me. She again told Mark to shoot me and I said: 'Mark, you ain't going to shoot me with your mama standing here.'" The struggle continued—with Pattie trying to scratch Buck and Buck trying to restrain Pattie—in the yard and then near Pattie's van. Still wanting Pattie to take him to the Sheriff, Buck picked her up (according to the medical examiner's report, Pattie weighed one hundred pounds) and placed her in the driver's seat of the van.

At that point, Buck noticed a spot of blood on Pattie's hair. He said to her: "'Your head is bleeding. Let me see what happened to it.' Because, it wasn't like I hated this woman. I still cared a lot for her. I leaned in the van. I had the pistol in my hand, on top of the driver's seat. She just laid back and she drawed her legs up and kicked me right square in the chest as hard as she could, which caught me off guard. I throwed my hands up to keep myself from falling and the pistol hit the top of the door frame of the van and it discharged. For a few minutes I held her in my arms and I tried to get her to talk to me. There wasn't no pulse. She wasn't breathing. And I sat down on the ground and I was holding her and I just lost my head after that. I got up, picked up my pistol, and I jumped in the van and left."

District Attorney Briley conducted a devastating, sometimes abusive, cross-examination of Buck Fugate, an ordeal for which Bellury had not prepared him. Briley repeatedly accused Buck of lying. At one point, the cross-examination degenerated into an argument between the two. Later, during the habeas corpus hearing, the judge asked Bellury: "Was any objection made by you or [co-counsel] Browne about badgering the witness or any instruction given by the court to defuse that atmosphere?" Bellury responded: "No, we didn't. I just didn't know what to do then. I never experienced anything quite like that." Neither then nor at any other point in the trial did Bellury or Browne interpose an objection.

The low point came when Buck asked Briley for permission to show the jury how he had been holding the pistol while he and Pattie struggled. Briley was surprised by Buck's request and willingly handed Buck the pistol. Briley asked Buck to "squeeze the trigger and make the hammer come back and go down." Defense counsel Bellury did not object and Buck complied. Briley then asked Buck to show how he had been holding the pistol when Pattie was shot. Demonstrating with the pistol, Buck testified that he had his finger off the trigger but when she kicked him "my finger came back on the trigger. That's the only way I can explain it." Briley responded sarcastically: "You could sell the Golden [Gate] Bridge."

After District Attorney Briley completed his cross-examination, Reg Bellury had no questions for redirect, apparently believing he could not rehabilitate his client. Bellury rested his case after calling his client as the only defense witness. Once the jury was selected, the presentation of evidence by *both* sides took less than one day, extraordinary for a capital case.

The defense—such as it was—left questions unanswered. Why hadn't an expert witness been called to testify about the pistol's design? Could it easily discharge by accident? The .38 caliber Taurus had been manufactured in several models, indicating the possibility of design flaws. Buck's claim of accident might have been given technical support.

Had Buck gone armed to Pattie's house intending to kill her, or had he honestly believed she was away for the weekend? The note with the South Carolina phone number which Buck claimed to have received from Pattie earlier that week might have answered that question. Prosecutor Briley accused Buck of lying, that there wasn't any note. He asserted—without any support in the record—that Buck had gotten the number from a pad by the phone in Pattie's house. Buck testified that he had left the note in Pattie's van in the pocket of the plaid shirt he was wearing that day. Briley contended that there had been no plaid shirt, that it had been too hot for a plaid shirt that day. The van had been sold before the trial, but a police photograph clearly showed a plaid shirt draped over the driver's seat. Bellury failed to bring the photograph to the jury's attention. The police had confiscated Buck's clothing and personal effects, but the plaid shirt was somehow lost—the note, if any, along with it.

The last trial day began with closing arguments. Bellury and Browne divided that responsibility. Bellury went first and presented a workmanlike, if uninspired, review of the evidence, asking the jury to find Buck not guilty. He avoided saying anything critical about Pattie who, as the victim, probably was a sympathetic figure in the jury's eyes. District Attorney Briley followed Bellury and portrayed Buck as a liar and cold-blooded killer.

Leo Browne made the final statement to the jury. He began with a lengthy monologue about his experiences as a lawyer, his feelings about working with Reg Bellury, his age and the state of his health—a series of irrelevancies immediately after his opponent had shredded and trashed his client. When Browne began getting to the point, he was interrupted repeatedly by objections, which the judge sustained, for expressing personal opinions and asserting facts not supported by the record. Browne blundered badly when, without consulting with co-counsel Bellury, he attacked Pattie Fugate. He recalled Mark's testimony that Pattie had cried out: "Shoot him." According to Browne, that cry showed that "Mark Fugate had been programmed already to kill his own father." Attempting to negate the kidnapping charge and level the playing field in the fatal struggle, Browne stated: "You don't go kidnapping a Bengal Tiger. That's what he had on his hands with Pattie Fugate. She fought him like a tiger. He was trying to protect himself." Attempting to convince the jury that Pattie "did not fear Wallace Fugate," Browne went on to compare her to a grizzly bear.

After lunch Judge Prior charged the jury, sending them off to deliberate at 2:48 p.m. They returned with their verdict at 3:45 p.m., slightly less than an hour later. The jury foreman intoned the verdict: "Count One, murder, we the jury find the defendant guilty." The foreman's litany continued until Buck Fugate was found guilty on all counts— burglary, kidnapping, two counts of aggravated assault, and theft of Pattie's van.

The United States Supreme Court's 1972 decision in *Furman v. Georgia* fundamentally altered the structure of capital cases to require a separate penalty phase following a finding of guilt, taking into account aggravating and mitigating circumstances of the crime and the defendant's background. Subsequent decisions have established that those convicted of capital offenses have wide latitude in attempting to avoid the death penalty.

Bellury and Browne threw together a brief and perfunctory case in opposition to the death penalty. Buck had given them a list of twenty-seven people he knew who might speak well of him. The two lawyers made telephone calls to a few of those on the list, coming up with four witnesses, including Buck's mother. Mary Fugate told the jury that her son had been "a real good boy. He's never been in no trouble. He's always worked, ever since he was small—farming, construction, just about anything you can name, he done it. He was a good father. He never whipped Mark in his life, as far as I know." Bellury and Browne made no attempt to obtain records of Buck's life history. His military service record might have been particularly helpful before the rural Georgia jury. They even failed to bring out that Buck had no prior criminal record.

The prosecution did not offer any evidence during the penalty phase, apparently assuming—correctly, as it turned out—that evidence from them would not be necessary. Unlike the federal system, Georgia does not require preparation of a pre-sentence report about the defendant's background, even in a capital case.

The jury retired to deliberate at 5:12 p.m. and returned with their unanimous verdict at 6:55 p.m. At Judge Prior's request, District Attorney Briley read the verdict: "We, the jury, having found the defendant guilty of murder and finding statutory aggravating circumstances, to wit, kidnapping with bodily injury and burglary, hereby recommend that the defendant's punishment be death." Whereupon, the judge pronounced sentence: "William Marvin Fugate, III, I now order that you be taken from the Bar of this Court to the common jail of Putnam County, Georgia until you shall be removed therefrom and delivered to the Director of Corrections for the State of Georgia at such penal institution as may be designated by the said Director. In such institution, you shall be submitted to the penalty of death by electrocution between the hours of 10 a.m. and 6 p.m. on the first day of July, 1992. May God have mercy on your soul."

Judge Prior informed Buck that because he had received the death penalty, his case would be appealed automatically to the Georgia Supreme Court and that an attorney would be appointed to represent him. Buck's execution date was stayed pending the outcome of his appeal. Reg Bellury did not wish to continue as Buck's counsel, and the feeling was mutual. Judge Prior appointed another local lawyer to represent Buck on appeal. The judge subsequently awarded Bellury $7,500 for his representation of Buck Fugate, more than double what he had earned in the past in any death penalty case, but far less than a criminal defense lawyer would charge a private client for defending a capital case.

On June 21, 1993, a unanimous Georgia Supreme Court decided *Fugate v. State*, affirming Buck's conviction and death sentence. The court's recitation of the facts depicted a brutal, cold-blooded murder. Given defense counsel's performance at trial, that view of the facts was not surprising, and it probably helped to override the technical points raised on appeal, which focused largely on alleged errors in the court's instructions. Several other points, including alleged prosecutorial misconduct, were deemed waived for failure to raise them at trial. The court concluded that "the sentence of death is neither excessive not disproportionate to penalties imposed in similar cases." Buck was on death row when he got the news that his appeal had been rejected; a new execution date was set.

Stephen Bright, Director of the Southern Center for Human Rights in Atlanta, agreed to represent Buck Fugate in a habeas corpus proceeding alleging ineffectiveness of counsel at his trial. Bright filed a petition for habeas corpus—the ancient writ designed to test the legality of detention—in the Superior Court for Butts County, Georgia, the county where Buck was incarcerated. Assistant Attorney General Susan Boleyn represented the State, defending the conviction and death penalty. Judge John R. Harvey heard evidence on the issue of Bellury's ineffectiveness for three days in January 1996—almost five years after Pattie Fugate was killed.

Buck was led into the courtroom in handcuffs and leg irons by two Department of Corrections guards. As an additional security measure, an electrical device connected to a 50,000-volt power source and remotely controlled by a guard was rigged to deliver a disabling shock to Buck's kidneys should he make a false move. Bright's objection to the shock device as unnecessary and inhumane and to the handcuffs as an impairment of Buck's ability to participate were overruled, except that the judge allowed one uncuffed hand so that Buck could take notes.

Bright contended that Bellury had been ineffective for multiple reasons, the cumulative effect of which had deprived Buck Fugate his due process right to a fair trial. Bellury failed to make a single objection throughout the trial, thereby allowing inadmissible evidence and improper argument to be heard by the jury. He failed to impeach Mark Fugate's testimony with prior inconsistent statements about what he had seen of the shooting. He failed to present expert evidence of a design defect in the pistol making it susceptible to accidental discharge. He failed to present a consistent theory of defense. He failed to represent Buck at the penalty phase, only going through the motions of his case for leniency.

Bright, an experienced defense lawyer in capital cases and a leading scholar on the death penalty, was an aggressive and articulate advocate. "Counsel that represented Wallace Fugate at this trial were not loyal to Wallace Fugate. They were loyal to a system in which, in order to get appointments, they had to go along with the program and basically serve as spectators at trial. They came, they watched, they gave some closing arguments, that was basically it."

Reg Bellury, Bright's first witness, spent almost a full day on the stand. To a reader of the cold record, Bellury appears to answer Bright's questions candidly, that is, when he was able to recall what he had done five years before. Often, however, his memory failed him. Bellury could have refreshed his recollection by reading the trial transcript. He claimed, however, that he "had not had an opportunity to look at the transcript since [the trial]," suggesting that he took the habeas corpus hearing no more seriously than he had taken the trial itself. For his part, Bright knew the record cold.

Bright led Bellury through a lengthy recital of things he had admittedly failed to do. He never looked at the victim's clothes. He never listened to the tape of an interview Buck had given to the police; when the tape turned up missing, he did no research on inferences to be drawn when the State loses evidence. He did not object to the sale of the van before trial; the van could have been helpful to the defense—for the location of bloodstains, to show how Pattie could have been injured in falling against a sharp edge, to recover Pattie's note from Buck's plaid shirt last seen in the van. The note would have been objective evidence of Buck's belief that Pattie was out of town for the weekend, that he had not gone to the house intending to kill her. But Bellury did not think the note would have been significant evidence. He did not investigate design features of the .38 Taurus. He had seen no need to hire a blood spatter expert; at the trial, the State's blood expert was unable to "offer an opinion [about blood spatter] because I've only been to one class in that." Bellury claimed he had done legal research in preparation for the trial, but he was unable to respond to questions about leading United States Supreme Court death penalty cases. Concerning his failure to make any objections during the trial, Bellury explained: "Every time we asked for something or raised an issue, we got what we asked for, or Mr. Briley essentially went along with whatever we contended."

Reg Bellury's gravest dereliction was his failure to prepare his client for testifying in his own defense. Bright asked Bellury: "Did you go through any direct examination just before you actually went in the courtroom and [gave] it? Bellury replied: "Just before? No." Bright: At any time?" Bellury: "Well, not in the sense of what I would ask him as if he were on the witness stand and I were the attorney, no." As a result, Buck's testimony rambled in a loose, often redundant, narrative. He did not control himself under aggressive questioning by prosecutor Briley — arguing instead of answering questions directly. Buck should have been told not to touch the pistol in front of the jury unless the prosecutor insisted on a physical demonstration of what had happened. Not knowing any better, Buck himself asked to hold the pistol, and when the prosecutor asked him to squeeze the trigger, Buck complied. The sight of Buck squeezing the trigger was only calculated to inflame the jury. Briley had already established through an expert witness how the pistol functioned and how much finger pressure was required to fire it. Bright asked Bellury: "Was it a surprise to you when Buck asked to hold the weapon?" Bellury replied: "Oh, absolutely, yes. I did not specifically tell him not to hold the weapon. It never occurred to me that he would, so that never came up."

Leo Browne, Bellury's co-counsel, had acted as second chair during the trial, only getting to his feet for his part of the closing argument. Bright asked if he remembered his argument and Browne replied: "Oh, Lord no. I never have recalled one and I've never prepared one. I tried one time. I thought I had made a particularly good one, and I tried to get a copy of it. And the girl who transcribed it quit that day, or got fired or something, and I never did get a transcript." Bright continued: "Your practice would be just to get up in front of the jury and make an argument, right?" Browne responded: "That's exactly right. After having devoted perhaps four or five hours on a river bank thinking about what I might say. No notes, no prepared argument."

Bright asked about the analogies Browne had drawn to wild animals: "Do you remember your argument about Pattie being a Bengal Tiger?" Browne replied: "Did I say that?" Browne did recall that there had been a history of violence between Buck and Pattie and he wanted to show that the fault for that had been shared. Bright asked: "So your goal was to show that Pattie Fugate had a propensity to violence?" Browne replied: "Right." His co-counsel Reg Bellury had taken the opposite tack only minutes before, avoiding harsh words about Pattie, saying that "there was still some feeling, some caring, between the two of them." Bellury testified that Browne had not told him he intended to use wild animal analogies.

Like his co-counsel Bellury, Browne was not familiar with United States Supreme Court death penalty decisions, such as *Furman v. Georgia*. Beyond that, Bright asked Browne: "Can you tell me what criminal law decisions from any court you're familiar with?" Browne replied: "Well, off the top of my head I can't tell you any cases I'm familiar with." Bright: "Not even one?" Browne: "None. Not even one."

Bright sought to show that systemic failures had contributed to depriving Buck Fugate of his right to counsel. He called the Acting Director of the Georgia Indigent Defense Council to describe one source of assistance for death penalty defense lawyers. The Defense Council provides financial assistance and training programs for indigent defense in Georgia counties. A three-member county committee submits an annual application for assistance. That committee is responsible for ensuring that the program is operated in compliance with Council guidelines. As the program is designed, failure to comply should result in corrective action from the Council. Unfortunately, the system broke down in Putnam County when Buck Fugate was charged with murder.

Bright's co-counsel called Charles Howell, a contractor from Putnam County who had served as a member and as chairman of the Local Governing Committee for the Indigent Defense Counsel of Putnam County for several years and during 1991. This colloquy followed:

Did that committee ever hold any meetings?

No, not to my recollection.

Do you know what kind of indigent defense system Putnam County operated?

No. I don't. When I was asked to serve on this committee I was informed that it was only for paperwork, for the purpose of getting the grant that come from the State.

To your knowledge, did that committee ever make any decisions at all about the indigent defense system in Putnam County?

To my knowledge the committee never existed, no more than on paper.

Did you have any official duties?

No, I had no official duty. The only thing—a check for $1,100 came and I took it down to the Commissioners and turned it in.

Lawyers appointed to defend death penalty cases in Georgia can draw on other resources for advice and assistance in trial tactics, finding and paying for experts and investigators, and in drafting motions and briefs. Bright offered Michael Mears as an expert witness on those resources and, given their availability, on the standards applicable to Georgia defense lawyers in capital cases. Active as a defense lawyer in death penalty cases since 1984, Mears had impressive qualifications. He was Director of the Multi-County Public Defender's Office, a death penalty defense resource center established by the legislature. Mears regularly consulted with and conducted seminars for defense lawyers in capital cases. He had qualified as an expert in death penalty cases in State courts and in federal habeas corpus proceedings.

The State's attorney objected to Mears as an expert, citing Georgia Supreme Court cases holding that a lawyer witness is not permitted to give opinions about the quality of a criminal defense lawyer's representation. She argued: "You can't have a battle of experts. Your Honor is charged only with determining whether, in the context of this case, at that time, with the materials they had, and whomever they consulted, whether they were effective. Even if there is some standard out there—which we submit there isn't—it's irrelevant to the determination you have to make." In response, Bright compared this case with medical malpractice cases in which experts routinely testify about the standard of care for doctors. Reaching for a distinction from hostile precedents, Bright said he would not ask Mears for opinions about Bellury's performance, only about relevant standards, leaving it to the court to form the opinions. Judge Harvey appeared troubled by the issue. He thought Mear's testimony could be relevant to show "what the available resources were. How can the court [determine ineffectiveness] unless it's got some [standards] to go by. I mean the court's got to weigh it...." The court reserved ruling on the State's objection pending further study, and allowed Bright to proceed with an offer of proof.

Mears described the assistance available through his Public Defenders Office. The office maintains a current checklist of things for the defense lawyer to do. The Office keeps defense lawyers apprized of decisions affecting their cases. There are two file drawers of resumes from experts in such areas as fingerprints, ballistics, and blood spattering. Experts can be helpful, not only for their testimony but also in formulating cross-examination of the prosecution's experts.

Mears testified that motions are critically important in death penalty cases. Early and aggressive motions practice can sometimes induce the prosecution to plea bargain. "We maintain what we call a motions bank, an outline including pre-trial motions, jury motions, ex parte motions for experts, and suppression motions. There are probably 175 to 180 motions that the attorneys are asked to consider." After an attorney reviews the outline, there is a sit-down discussion to go over the facts of the case and decide which motions are appropriate. Mears' Office maintains updated forms of motions and assists attorneys in adapting them to their cases. Bellury had filed three boilerplate motions on Buck's behalf.

Mears described necessary preparation for the penalty phase of a capital case. "You've got to paint a picture of the person's life. Very basically, you get all the school records, employment records, hospital records, then you use them to develop possible mitigation witnesses. You go out and you interview all these individuals face to face. You need to do an evaluation of how that witness if going to present themselves. Sometimes it takes a selling job and you can't do that over the phone. You have to walk these witnesses through in some detail as to what their purpose is and what their proposed testimony would be." Buck Fugate's defense lawyers did none of those things.

At the conclusion of Mears' testimony, Bright asked two questions:

Have you ever seen a death penalty case where prior to trial the defense lawyer withdrew all but one of the pending motions?

I have never seen a case where motions were withdrawn like that.

Have you ever seen a death penalty case where there was not a single objection made during the entire trial?

I just can't fathom that happening.

Both the trial and the habeas corpus hearing included subtle, and not-so-subtle, indications of a closed, self-protective, system of which prosecutors, defense lawyers, judges, and the law itself were members. After the trial evidence was closed, Judge Prior asked Briley and Bellury whether either wished to put anything in the record about conduct of counsel. Briley responded: "Yes, sir. Counsel has been exemplary for the defendant in this case." Bellury returned the compliment: "I'd have to say the same." Judge Prior added: "Well, I note for the record that both counsel have been well prepared." On the witness stand in the habeas hearing with a colleague's professional reputation on the line, District Attorney Briley bent over backwards to bolster Bellury's credentials as a defense lawyer. Referring to an earlier case, Briley recalled: "He beat the socks off me. He got an acquittal, the only one I've ever had happen to me in a death penalty case." When Briley's testimony was completed, Judge Harvey said: "Thank you, Joe. You're excused and it's good to see you." On October 5, 1996, Judge Harvey denied habeas corpus relief. His ninety-two page "Findings of Fact and Conclusions of Law" tracked the State's trial brief. The system is protected by Georgia appellate decisions that make it difficult to challenge a defense lawyer's effectiveness with expert opinions.

The Georgia Supreme Court, dividing four to three, denied Buck Fugate's petition for a finding of probable cause to appeal. In December 1997, the Putnam County Superior Court rescheduled his execution date for December 12, 1997. On December 10, 1997, Bright filed a petition for habeas corpus in the United States District Court for the Middle District of Georgia. A federal judge granted a stay of execution but denied the petition in June 1998. Bright thereupon filed an appeal to the United States Court of Appeals for the Eleventh Circuit, more than eight years after Buck Fugate was incarcerated following his wife's death. Had he been allowed to plead guilty to voluntary manslaughter, in all probability he would have been released on parole and back in Eatonton by then.

The appeal was argued in August 1999 and finally decided by the Eleventh Circuit in August 2001, two years later. The court rejected Fugate's claim that he had been denied his constitutional right to an effective counsel. The court adopted a narrow scope of review which it considered to be required by the Supreme Court's decision in *Strickland v. Washington*, and by recent amendments to federal habeas corpus statutes. As the Eleventh Circuit viewed it: "The court must indulge a strong presumption that counsel's conduct falls within the wide range of reasonable professional assistance." Further, a petitioner "must establish that no competent counsel would have taken the action that his counsel did take." The court proceeded to consider separately, and to rationalize away, each of the actions and inactions by Bellury and Brown that Fugate had cited as ineffective. Fugate's claim for habeas relief depended importantly on the aggregate effect of those actions and inactions, on his trial counsels' overall abysmal performance, a perspective the court of appeals declined to consider.

Following the court of appeals' decision, Stephen Bright, Fugate's habeas corpus counsel, filed a petition for certiorari in the United States Supreme Court. Like any such petition, however, its chances of being granted seemed slim. When this book went to press, the petition had not yet been acted on, and no new date for Buck Fugate's execution had been set.

\* \* \*

# Comments

1. " Spectator Sport" was included to illustrate just how bad the criminal justice system still is in some parts of the country, almost forty years after *Gideon v. Wainwright.* The performances of Reg Bellury and Leo Browne as defense counsel for Buck Fugate were abysmal by any standard, except possibly the ineffectiveness standard of *Strickland v. Washington,* 466 U.S. 668 (1984). Stephen Bright, Buck Fugate's habeas corpus counsel, contends that under *Strickland* "the courts cannot deliver on the promise of equal justice for rich and poor." Bright cites three capital cases tried in Houston, Texas in which defense lawyers slept during trial and claims of ineffectiveness of counsel were rejected on appeal. In one case, the judge had called a recess to arouse the sleeping defense lawyer. The lawyer explained: "It's boring." The trial continued and the defendant was convicted. The trial judge took the position that "the Constitution doesn't say the lawyer has to be awake." Rejecting an ineffectiveness argument, the Texas Court of Criminal Appeals affirmed. *McFarland v. Texas,* 928 S.W.2d 482 (1996).

2. Viewing the performances of Bellury and Bright from a legal ethics

perspective, Model Rule 1.1, "Competence," requires a lawyer to "provide competent representation to a client," bringing to it "the legal knowledge, skill, thoroughness, and preparation necessary for the representation." Lead counsel Bellury did have some experience in criminal defense cases, including capital cases. Apart from that, it would be hard to imagine a less skillful, less thorough, less prepared performance by a defense counsel. In the habeas corpus hearing, Browne, the second chair, was unable to name a single court decision on criminal law.

3. The statements of prosecutor Briley and Judge Prior that the defense had been "exemplary" apparently were included in the record to counter any claim of ineffectiveness of counsel in the automatic appeal which follows imposition of the death penalty in Georgia. Given the performances of Bellury and Browne, these statements suggest that the prosecutor and the judge were virtually conspiring with the defense lawyers to see that Buck Fugate's conviction would be upheld. The American Bar Association's "Standards Relating to the Administration of Criminal Justice" state the traditional view that "the duty of the prosecutor is to seek justice, not merely to convict." The ABA's "Model Code of Judicial Conduct" enjoins judges to "uphold the integrity and independence of the judiciary" (Canon 1) and "to perform judicial duties without bias or prejudice (Canon 3)." The criminal justice system in Putnam County, Georgia hasn't always worked that way.

4. In addition to his work as Director of the Southern Center for Human Rights, Stephen Bright has written and lectured extensively on criminal justice issues. The following excerpts from "Neither Equal Nor Just: The Rationing and Denial of Legal Services to the Poor When Life and Liberty Are at Stake," *New York University School of Law, Annual Survey of American Law*, 1997 Vol., Issue 4, raise troubling concerns about legal representation in the present system, not only in capital cases, and not only in the South where most executions take place.

> The rations of legal services for the poor person accused of crime have been remarkably thin in most of the United States.... Many states have yet to provide capable lawyers to represent the accused and the resources necessary to conduct investigations and present a defense. The poor person who is wrongfully convicted may face years in prison or even execution without any legal assistance to pursue avenues of post-conviction review.

Governments are increasingly awarding contracts to provide representation to indigent defendants to the lawyer who submits the lowest bid. Many states pay lawyers appointed to represent the poor such low rates that lawyers may make less than the minimum wage in some cases. Many jurisdictions have been unwilling to establish public defender programs or have established programs but so underfunded them that caseloads are staggering.

What has been the response of the vast majority of the legal profession — the silk stocking lawyers with six- or seven-figure incomes at the prosperous law firms — to the sleeping lawyers in Houston, to the defiance of Gideon v. Wainwright, and the denial of access to courts for those most in need? A small number have been concerned about these shocking injustices. But most lawyers simply ask, "Did we have a good year? "What's my draw? The plight of the poor is out of sight and out of mind.

Law schools and law students must be involved in responding to the lack of legal services for those accused of crime. The law schools must send their graduates out with the skills necessary to represent criminal defendants in the places where there is the greatest need. For the most part, law schools are not doing this.

Does the individual lawyer have an ethical duty to respond to the need for representation of the poor? Under the Model Rules of Professional Responsibility, the answer is "yes and no." Comment [1] to Model Rule 6.1 states: "Every lawyer, regardless of professional prominence or professional workload, has a responsibility to provide legal services to those unable to pay." However, the rule itself takes away what the comment seems to grant; it states that "a lawyer should *aspire* to render at least (50) hours of pro bono publico legal services per year." The key word is "aspire." Under the rule, there is no enforceable ethical duty to do any pro bono work, and many, perhaps most, lawyers don't. Men and women graduating from the law schools have to answer the question of duty for themselves.

# Afterword

"There are occasions and causes why and wherefore in all things."
— William Shakespeare, *Henry V*, Act V, scene 1.

It's hard to quarrel with Shakespeare, but the whys and wherefores of lawyer misconduct are not always easy to identify. Why does a partner in a flourishing law firm systematically overbill his biggest client? To make more money is the short answer. The bottom line drives law firms today as never before. The big firms are amassing profits and partner shares undreamed of thirty years ago. Some firms pay signing bonuses to top law graduates, like quarterbacks and point guards. Directly or indirectly, greed is a root cause of much of the trouble lawyers get into. Money undoubtedly was a motivating factor in several of the stories in this book—why Michael Abbell crossed lines for the Cali cartel, why Deanne Siemer failed to acknowledge an obvious conflict of interest, and why John O'Quinn sent runners after the victims of the Flight 1016. As these examples suggest, however, greed underlies many different types of misconduct. Explaining too much, it explains little that is useful in promoting the ethical level of the profession.

The Model Rules of Professional Conduct recognize that a law firm's culture has a critical influence on the conduct of its lawyers, especially young associates who look to the partners for guidance. If the partners are people of integrity and sensitive to issues of ethics, if sound procedures for addressing those issues exist and are followed, and if debatable issues are sometimes resolved contrary to financial interest, the firm will have a good ethics record, in fact and by reputation. On the other hand, if a firm's senior members are insensitive to questions of ethics, addressing them perfunctorily, if at all, and more-or-less consistently resolving them in their own financial interest, the entire firm may eventually be corrupted, even destroyed. "Two Scorpions in a Bottle" provides anecdotal evidence of that dynamic.

The reader will recall how Stanford Hess, a senior partner and member of the executive committee of Baltimore's Weinberg & Green,

181

systematically overbilled Malcolm Berman's bank to the tune of $475,000. We can understand—perhaps even sympathize with—Hess's anger and frustration at Berman's chiseling and procrastination and with Hess's emotional need to get even, for himself and his firm. The reasons for lawyer misconduct at the individual level are complex, more the province of psychiatry than law. From a regulatory perspective, however, we can't condone stealing from a client, no matter how sympathetic the offender, or how severe the provocation.

Had Hess acted alone and had he been expelled from the firm upon discovery of his scheme, the incident might not have reflected unfavorably on the firm. But that didn't happen. Several senior partners knew of the overbilling—including the managing partner and the finance committee chairman—but they took no action, and for many months withheld the information even from other members of the firm. There was evidence that associates had been drawn into the scheme, one of whom filed a false fee petition in court knowing that Hess had inflated the billable hours it claimed. Hess continued as a partner in Weinberg & Green for seven years after the scheme came to light. The firm did not report the overbilling to Maryland's Attorney Grievance Committee.

Malcolm Berman's malpractice case against Weinberg & Green, decided in August 1995, spread the sordid details of the overbilling scheme on the public record. A year later, in an unrelated malpractice case, the jury returned a $25 million verdict against the firm. About the same time, James Carbiner, head of the firm's litigation department and the partner who had pressed for an internal investigation of the overbilling, left the firm. After that, most of the associates began to bail out and, by 1998, only a handful was still there. The following year, Weinberg & Green, an institution in the Baltimore legal community since 1917, merged to survive as the last names in Saul, Ewing, Weinberg & Green.

Pepper, Hamilton & Scheetz lived on after the *Maritrans* case, but its ethical lapses, revealed on the witness stand, may have been largely responsible for the injunction entered against it. In "Chinese Walls and Comfort Zones" Judge Gafni found that the "absence of candor" in Peter Hearn's testimony would have failed to "inspire confidence in Maritrans as to Pepper's good faith." The judge was also influenced by the "absence of sensitivity" exhibited by Pepper lawyers D'Angelo and Haller. The *Maritrans* case is not a sufficient basis for comment about the Pepper firm's culture at that time, but it does show how insensitivity to ethics can have a profound effect on a judge's perspective and can even change the outcome of a case.

It's not surprising that a firm culture of insensitivity to ethics can lead to patterns of ethics violations. Why that culture develops in the first place is another question. Without unduly romanticizing the law firms of the past, they did enjoy greater stability than firms enjoy today, both in terms of lawyer's careers with the same firm and long-term client loyalties. That stability—the law firm as brotherhood—was an atmosphere in which a culture of legal ethics could take root and grow. Many successful lawyers today identify themselves more as individuals with a portfolio, less as members of a firm. And there is intense competition for clients who tend to shop around. Some law firms are loose confederations, held together by profits and vulnerable to loss of their rainmakers to greater profits across the street, or across the country. The proliferation of big-firm branch offices contributes to a sense of anomie. We have come a long way from the law firm as brotherhood.

The stories illustrate some generic problems which are subsets of a firm's culture. In "Breaking Up Is Hard to Do," Keith Mendelson, a senior associate up for partner at Pillsbury, Madison & Sutro, was in a dilemma. He was uncomfortable about helping Admiral Murphy dismantle Murphy & Demory, a client of the firm. But Deanne Siemer, the partner in charge of the matter, kept telling him that working for the Admiral did not involve a conflict of interest. Mendelson raised the conflicts issue with a member of the firm's ethics committee and also telephoned his usual supervisor, then in Sweden, with his concerns; both deferred to Siemer. In the subsequent malpractice suit, the court found that "Pillsbury, Madison & Sutro's internal mechanisms for resolution of ethical issues are seriously deficient. The partner in charge of the client relationship who is least likely to be objective is the ultimate arbiter of whether the firm has a conflict of interest."

According to the author of the article, "Firms Take Divergent Paths in Responding to Associates Ethics Concerns," in the *Of Counsel* issue of August 15, 1994: "The real issue is one of recourse. Where do associates go if they're trapped in an ethical cul-de-sac? Can associates really blow the whistle on partners without ruining their careers." The article continued: "*Of Counsel* has found a number of firms with only looselydefined policies. Others describe more formal and apparently efficacious policies. Some won't even talk about it."

Shortly after Pillsbury lost the malpractice case, the chairman of its professional responsibility committee issued a memorandum specifying procedures to be followed in similar situations in the future, including permission to raise ethics concerns with the committee anonymously. *Of Counsel* quoted ethics scholar Charles Wolfram of Cornell Law School estimating that "one-third to one-half of firms have systems in place that afford associates meaningful recourse when they have ethical dilemmas." Model Rule 5.1 concerning responsibilities of supervisory lawyers does not address the problem directly, and the comments following refer to it only in general terms. Marvin Frankel, former federal judge and a member of the Kutak Committee has questioned whether this complex problem is amenable to fair and effective solution. Review of recent experience might confirm Frankel's view, but it may also point the way to more specific guidance in the Model Rules.

"The Gatekeeper" underlines the need for supervision of associates who, without it, get in over their heads. Brent Bailey might have been saved a lot of grief if his putative supervisor had taken a more active role in the jail bond offering. Weinberg & Green's associate Mark Tomiano, a freewheeling associate in "Two Scorpions in a Bottle," was allowed to handle a complex corporate transaction without meaningful supervision. The result was a $25 million malpractice verdict against the firm. Francisco Laguna ("The Case of the Frozen Broccoli") was in his first job out of law school when he asked his supervisor, Michael Abbell: "What is our responsibility about presenting a false affidavit to somebody for their signature?" According to Laguna, Abbell "told me that our job as attorneys was not to worry about the content of the affidavit." One would hope that a law school graduate would not have to ask that question.

The comments following "Two Scorpions in a Bottle" looked at the widespread practice among law firms of requiring associates to meet specified billable-hour targets, say, 2,000 hours per year. These requirements put pressure on associates to inflate billable hours on their time sheets, a form of billing fraud. Commentators have suggested that the single most significant reform in billing practices would be to do away with annual billable-hour requirements. The firms could to this voluntarily, or such requirements could be prohibited by a phophylactic rule designed to prevent billing fraud.

Personalities played a role in several of the stories. Elihu Root, a former Secretary of State and Wall Street lawyer, once observed: "About half the practice of a decent lawyer is telling would-be clients that they are damned fools and should stop." When the client is strong-willed, wealthy, and ruthless, the lawyer may have an especially hard time saying "no." Michael Abbell couldn't refuse Miguel Rodriguez-Orejuela. Stanford Hess deferred to Malcolm Berman to his face and overbilled him behind his back. Lawyers who choose to enter into such relationships need more spine; rules of ethics aren't much help.

The pressures on in-house lawyers are similar when the CEO is strong-willed and demanding. Arguably, Donald Feuerstein, house counsel for Salomon Brothers in "Hot Seat," did the best that could have been expected of him. He faced up to the problem and gave sound advice. The only thing he didn't do was report the false bid himself, an action that may have violated New York's version of Model Rule 1.13. He was fired anyway, losing his only client. The vulnerability of in-house lawyers—to pressure for the desired answer, or to being fired—seems to be inherent in the job.

Patterns which emerge from "Ambulance Chasing" suggest the need for less regulation, rather than more. The O'Quinn firm's soliciting in South Carolina is typical of what often happens after a catastrophic accident that can be blamed on a solvent corporation. For an especially gross example, *see* Hansen, "Nothing," *The American Lawyer*, January 1996 at p. 61, describing packs of lawyers descending on the scene of a sulphuric acid release in Richmond, California to solicit clients. Greed, it seems fair to say, is the cause of such conduct, but a socially-useful cause. The personal injury firms that specialize in mass torts and hasten to the scene are experienced in such cases and are likely to get better results than lawyers who are not. Equally important, the rapid arrival of insurance adjusters on victims' doorsteps to press for cheap settlements suggests the desirability of leveling the playing field. Model Rule 7.3 is prophylactic, prohibiting personal solicitations without proof of overreaching or invasions of privacy. That rule could be modified to cover only cases of actual abuse. In addition, or in the alternative, a thirty-day rule allowing soliciting after that time, similar to the Florida statute upheld in *Florida Bar v. Went For It*, 515 U.S. 618 (1995), might be considered.

The most pervasive pattern of ethics violations is lawyers' failure, or refusal, to report violations by other lawyers. We leave it to the clients to blow the whistle. This pattern was graphically illustrated in Chapter 5, "Two Scorpions in a Bottle." The ethical mandate is in place in Model Rule 8.3 and its state counterparts, yet disciplinary authorities rarely seek to enforce reporting rules. Should they choose to make an example of some violators in the future, it could have a healthy effect on compliance.

# Sources

The foregoing chapters are based on the records of the following cases, except as noted:

Chapter 1. *Breezevale Limited v. Dickinson, et al.*, Civil No. 10818-92, Superior Court for the District of Columbia, and on associated depositions; *reversed and remanded*, Court of Appeals for the District of Columbia, 759 A.2d 627 (2000), *rehearing denied*, slip opinion, October 18, 2001.

Chapter 2. *United States v. Abbell and Moran*, Case No. 93-0470, United States District Court, Southern District of Florida, *affirmed in part and reversed in part*, United States Court of Appeals for the Eleventh Circuit, *slip opinion*, No. 99-12058, November 7, 2001.

Chapter 3. *Murphy & Demory v. Admiral Daniel J. Murphy*, Chancery No. 128219, Circuit Court, Fairfax County, Virginia.

Chapter 4. *Maritrans G.P., Inc., et al. v. Pepper Hamilton & Scheetz and J. Anthony Messina, Jr.*, No. 238, February Term 1988, Court of Common Pleas of Philadelphia County, Pennsylvania, *reversed*, 572 A.2d 737 (Superior Court of Pennsylvania, 1990), *reversed*, 602 A.2d 1277 (Supreme Court of Pennsylvania, 1992).

Chapter 5. *Fairfax Savings, F.S.B. v. Weinberg & Green*, Circuit Court for Montgomery County, Maryland, *affirmed*, 112 Md. App. 587 (Md. Ct. Special Appeals, 1996).

Chapter 6. *[Delta] Municipal Fund, Inc., et al. v. N-Group Securities, Inc., et al.*, Civ. No. H-92-546, United States District Court, Southern District of Texas.

Chapter 7. *In the Matter of John H. Gutfreund, et al.*, Securities Exchange Act of 1934, Release No. 31551, December 3,
1993, Administrative Proceeding File No. 3-7930. This
chapter is based in part on information from stories in
*The Wall Street Journal* editions of August 12, 15, and
19, 1991 and December 4, 1992 and *The New York
Times* editions of August 19 and 24, 1991 and December 4, 1992.

Chapter 8. *Commission for Lawyer Discipline v. John M. O'Quinn,
et al.*, Cause No. 98-06290, District Court for Harris
County, Texas.

Chapter 9. *State v. Wallace M. Fugate, III*, Case No. 91CR-129-7,
Superior Court for Putnam County, Georgia, *affirmed*,
431 S.E.2d 104 (Supreme Court of Georgia); *Fugate v.
Thomas*, Civ. No. 94-V-195, Superior Court for Butts
County, Georgia (habeas corpus relief denied); *Fugate v.
Head, Warden*, 261 F.3d 1206 (United States Court of
Appeals, Eleventh Circuit, 2001).

# Index